A DICTIONARY

of

MUSICAL THEMES

REVISED EDITION

A DICTIONARY

of

MUSICAL THEMES

REVISED EDITION

by

HAROLD BARLOW and SAM MORGENSTERN

Introduction by
JOHN ERSKINE

CROWN PUBLISHERS, INC. NEW YORK

Library of Congress Cataloging in Publication Data

Barlow, Harold.
　　A dictionary of musical themes.

　　Includes indexes.
　　1.　Instrumental music—Thematic catalogs.
I.　Morgenstern, Sam, joint author.　II.　Title.
ML128.I65B3　　1975　　016.78　　75-15687
ISBN 0-517-52446-5

PRINTED IN THE UNITED STATES OF AMERICA

Original edition sixteen printings
Revised edition second printing

CONTENTS

* *Bach's Fugue in G Minor, Organ "The Little Fugue" appears on page xiv.*

Elgar's Symphony No. 2 in E flat (Op. 63) appears on page xiv.

Tschaikowsky Melodie, Op. 42, No. 3 from Souvenir D'Un Lieu Cher, Vn. & Pft. appears on page xiv.

ACKNOWLEDGEMENTS

The Publishers have to acknowledge the following copyright permissions:

Items A 29, E 49, F 124—7, F 214—5, G 185—201, H 723—91, K 90—118, M 396—400, P 66, P 78—84, P 100—7, R 123—4, R 155—6, R 162, S 1523—34, S 1534a—g, S 1535—40, S 1546—7, S 1599—1608, T 119—22c, T 301—2, T 315—20 by permission of Schott & Co. Ltd., London, for all countries with the exception of Germany (Where these works are controlled by B. Schott's Sohne, Mainz) and the U.S.A. (where these works are controlled by The Associated Music Publishers Inc., New York).

Items B 1728—37, C 584—8, D 269—94, D 300—38, D 350—425, D 434—69, S 145—61, S 166—71, S 1609—15 by permission of N. Simrock—Richard Shauer, London.

Items B 434—6, P 163—4, R 285—92 by permission of D. Rahter—Richard Shauer, London.
Permission is also acknowledged from Messrs. Alfred Lengnick & Co. Ltd. as publishers for the British Empire for the following:—
Items C 584, D 292—4, D 357—73, D 466—9.

Items S 812—5 by permission of Elkin & Co. Ltd., London. Permission is also acknowledged from Elkin & Co. Ltd., as publishers for the British Empire for the following:— M 18—20, M 23—26, M 37—45.

Items S 1094—5, S 1365—75, S 1376—92, S 1419—24, S 1425—30 S 1468—74, S 1475—9 by permission of the copyright owners, Peter Edition, London, Frankfurt and New York.

INTRODUCTION

By John Erskine

This dictionary of musical themes, by Harold Barlow and Sam Morgenstern, supplies an aid which students of music have long needed. When the authors showed me the plan of it a year ago, or somewhat earlier, I applauded at once, and agreed to write a word of preface. We should now have something in musical literature to parallel Bartlett's *Familiar Quotations*. Whenever a musical theme haunted us, but refused to identify itself no matter how much we scraped our memory, all we should have to do would be to look up the tune in Barlow and Morgenstern, where those ingenious dictionary-makers would assemble some ten thousand musical themes, with a notation-index or theme-finder, to locate the name of the composition from which the haunting fragment came, and the name of the composer.

After a brief but exciting conversation, Mr. Barlow and Mr. Morgenstern went off with my promise of a preface, as it were, in their pocket, leaving me very thoughtful — and inclined to become more thoughtful with each passing hour. I knew there had already been attempts to index music, and I was fairly familiar with the difficulties which had in the past tripped up bold experimenters. A dictionary such as Bartlett's can classify quotations according to the subject with which they deal, and can arrange them in the usual index method by the letter-order of the opening words. But no method has been hit on to index musical sounds, nor the variations in pitch by which a theme is articulated. No method, that is, which permits the musical material of a theme to remain strictly musical.

I understood what Mr. Barlow and Mr. Morgenstern would try to do; since letters can easily be indexed, and musical notes cannot be, they would try to translate the notes into letters. After much thought I feared this would prove a task far beyond even their enthusiasm, and the result might be less useful than they hoped. But they put an end to my doubts by bringing to my study one day a section of the theme index, and challenging me to give them a theme they couldn't speedily locate. My conversion was prompt. I am glad to record here my confidence in the theory of this book, and my admiration for the manner in which the theory has been worked out.

As the authors are more than ready to admit, the ten thousand themes, more or less, which can be identified quickly and easily with the help of this book, do not encompass the entire literature of music, but they do include practically all the themes which can be found in compositions that have been recorded. It is hardly likely that a music student will be haunted by a theme from a composition not yet considered worthy of recording.

The authors believe, and I agree with them, that their dictionary of musical themes will be useful to the trained musician, even to the professional performer, who is more likely than the beginner or the amateur to have a firm grasp of the musical material which has gone into well-known masterpieces.

The book is divided into two parts. The first part contains ten thousand or more musical themes arranged by composers. The second part is the notation-index or theme-finder. If we consult the dictionary in order to locate a theme, we shall begin with the second part of the book, and conclude with the passage in the first part which gives the answer we have been looking for. But there are many occasions when a musician needs to refresh his memory about the themes in a given composition. Though he knows the name of the composition and of the composer, he may need to remind himself of the theme in the first movement, or the second, or the third. Of course he can go to his music shelves and consult his copy of the complete work. That is, if his music shelves are large enough to contain the scores of ten thousand sonatas or symphonies. I suspect that the convenience of the Barlow-Morgenstern dictionary will soon be recognized by serious students of musical literature.

How enormous that body of literature is, and how rapidly it increases, we sometimes forget. It is well within the truth to say that no pianist, no violinist, and no singer, pretends to have in his repertoire all the important compositions for piano, violin, or voice. Each musician has probably read over hundreds of pieces he would gladly include in his repertoire if life were long enough. A pianist who keeps in his repertoire, and in condition for performance, a thousand pieces of respectable length and difficulty, is an unusual artist. If his repertoire were three times as large, he would still be something of a specialist; the piano repertory has long since grown beyond human capacity to master completely. If recital programs do not seem more repetitious than they sometimes are, it is because of the helpful capacity of audiences to forget music which they themselves do not play. Sometimes they wish to recall at least a theme or two of what they have forgotten. From now on they will probably consult the Barlow and Morgenstern dictionary of themes.

The present volume does not contain themes from vocal music. To cover vocal as well as instrumental compositions, another volume would be needed as large as this.*

I have been speaking of trained musicians as well as of the average music lover. Both can use this dictionary without difficulty. The theme index is ingenious and, as I now believe, simple. If a theme or a tune is running through your head, and if your musical ear is good enough, you will be able to play it in the key of C major or C minor. Then if you write down the letters by which the notes are named, and find the resulting letter sequence in the index, you will be directed at once to the name of the original work and the name of its composer.

It is this process of identifying the theme when it is played by ear that seemed to me at first complicated and likely to discourage those who consult the dictionary. But I am confident now that once we have tried the method for ourselves, we shall find it extraordinarily simple.

Like any other dictionary of quotations, this book will perhaps be most useful to the young. Music is now a well-established subject in American education. Though many children in our schools are fortunately taught to play and sing, all of them — and this is equally their good fortune — are put in the way of listening to recorded music, to great masterpieces performed by great artists of yesterday and today. Not so long ago school children

---

* A Dictionary of Opera and Song Themes.

used to go along the street humming a snatch of ragtime or jazz. Nowadays the youngsters are just as likely to hum a passage from Schubert or Tschaikovsky, or whoever was the composer who last spoke to them from the disc in the music class.

"What is that you are humming?"

Sometimes the children remember, but more often, like the elders, they forget. But when they have learned to consult this dictionary, they will place the passage at once.

I believe this book is destined to a wide and increasing usefulness, both to mature music lovers now and to the army of children whom our schools are training to be the music lovers of tomorrow.

PREFACE

WHEN we began the research for this book, we both felt like the Sorcerer's Apprentice, for each theme that we found seemed to loose a crowd of others waiting for us. It looked as if this one book might stretch into volumes. However, the limits we set ourselves made the completion of the work seem possible within a lifetime.

This work contains about 10,000 themes. They have been chosen primarily from recorded, instrumental pieces. No vocal works, excepting those which in instrumental arrangement have become better known than their originals, have been included. We feel that the book contains almost all the themes the average and even the more erudite listener might want to look up.

Certain works we omitted because the scores were unavailable in libraries, and publishers who were more than helpful could not supply them. A few other works we left out because we could not, after great effort, secure copyrights. Though the book does not exhaust the subject, by far, we feel that we have compiled a fairly complete index of themes, not only first themes, but every important theme, introduction, and salient rememberable phrase of the works included. In certain modern works where a number of varied phrases could be construed as thematic, we tried to present them all. Naturally, in the development of a work certain phrases occur which are as rememberable as the themes themselves. To include these would amount to reprinting the pieces in their entirety. A few ultra-modern works we left out. We felt that anyone likely to remember their themes, or more aptly their combinations of notes, would in all probability know their source. Consequently, these works would hardly fit into the scope of this volume.

Careful search through so many hundreds of works by different composers living in different eras in divers countries leads the research student to rather interesting generalizations. Permeating the work of many of the great and prolific composers we find certain combinations of notes, a certain "melos." This "melos" or melodic line seems to be a strong ingredient of their style. Schubert, Beethoven, Mozart, each has his ever-recurring theme song, but so disguised that it makes for artistic variety rather than monotony.

Many themes in compositions of the same period seem to possess similar melodic lines. In our notation key we had to carry some themes to seven or eight letters before their lines began to diverge. It is not that the composers were necessarily imitative. Melodic thinking of the period simply took on certain characteristics, rhythm and harmonic background giving these almost identical lines their variety.

Since the folk tune plays such an integral part in serious composition, one finds special national characteristics in the melodic lines of composers of various lands. Certain interval as well as rhythmic combinations make for Spanish, Russian, German, and French themes, and those of other countries too, of course. Identical motives are used again and again by composers, both consciously and unconsciously. The famous Mannheim motive (G C Eb G C Eb D C B C) as found in Beethoven's First Piano Sonata, Mozart's G Minor Symphony, and Mendelssohn's E Minor String Quartet, is probably the most obvious example of this. We found a rather wry footnote to the first page of one of Clementi's Bb Major Piano Sonatas, stating that when he played this piece for Kaiser Franz Joseph, Mozart was in the audience. The theme of the Sonata is identical with the overture of The Magic Flute, which appeared a few years later. Mozart was famous for his phenomenal memory.

Parody quotations of themes, such as the Tristan Prelude in Debussy's Golliwogg's Cake Walk, are both plentiful and amusing. The Lullaby in Strauss's Domestic Symphony is a steal from a Venetian Boat Song by Mendelssohn, and whether Prokofieff knows it or not, the last half of the second theme in the second movement of his Sixth Piano Sonata bears more than a sneaking resemblance to Mendelssohn's Spring Song.

And so the research student becomes a tone sleuth.

The book should prove useful not only to those who are bothered by a theme and can't remember its source, but also to those who know the source but can't remember the theme. We ourselves shall certainly use it in both capacities.

A book of these dimensions could never have appeared without the aid and encouragement of a great many interested people. We owe a debt of deep and sincere gratitude first to Miss Gladys Chamberlain, Director of the 58th St. Music Library of New York City, who turned over the entire resources of that splendid organization to us, and gave us unreservedly of her time and advice. We want to thank the members of her staff, Miss Mary Lee Daniels, Miss Eleanor Chasan, Miss Lilly Goldberg, Mrs. Hilda Stolov, Mrs. Leah Silton, Mrs. Elsa Hollister, who were more than helpful.

In the music division of the main library of New York City, we wish to thank Mr. Philip Miller, and two of his indefatigable pages, George Klinger and Noel Schwartz.

Our thanks for the special kindness of James Blish, Mrs. Rose Gandal, Alex. M. Kramer, Robert Lowndes, Ben Meiselman, Dr. Rudolf Nissim, Herbert Weinstock, and the many music publishers and copyright owners who gave us assistance. We are indebted to Robert Simon, of Crown Publishers, for his constant encouragement in the undertaking; and to Miss Elizabeth Galvin, his assistant, without whom this book would probably never have appeared.

S. M.

New York, N. Y.
April, 1948

Fugue in G Minor, Organ "The Little Fugue" Bach — B99a

Symphony No.2, Op. 63 Elgar
By permission of Novello & Co., Ltd., London

1st Movement 1st Theme, A — E73a

1st Movement 1st Theme, B — E73b

1st Movement 2nd Theme, A — E73c

1st Movement 2nd Theme B — E73d

2nd Movement Intro. — E73e

2nd Movement 1st Theme — E73f

2nd Movement 2nd Theme — E73g

3rd Movement 1st Theme — E73h

3rd Movement 2nd Theme — E73i

4th Movement 1st Theme — E73j

4th Movement 2nd Theme — E73k

Mélodie, Op. 42, No. 3 from Souvenir D'Un Lieu Cher. Vn. & Pft. Tschaikovsky — T153a

In a very few instances, copyright difficulties forced the use of blank staves. The reasons are given in the Introduction.

ADAM, Adolphe (1803-1856)

La Poupée de Nuremberg
(The Nuremberg Doll)
Overture — 1st Theme

Si J'Étais Roi
Overture

ALBÉNIZ, Isaac M. F. (1860-1909)

Suite Española, Pft.
Cadiz (Saeta)
By permission of Associated
Music Publishers, Inc.

Cuba

Seguidillas

Sevillanas

Iberia I, Pft.
Evocación
By permission of Associated
Music Publishers, Inc.
Fête Dieu à Seville

Iberia II, Pft.
Triana
By permission of Associated
Music Publishers, Inc.

2nd Theme — A19

Iberia III, Pft.
El Albaicin (El Polo)
By permission of Associated
Music Publishers, Inc.
— A20

Iberia IV, Pft.
Jerez
By permission of Associated
Music Publishers, Inc.
— A21

Malaga — A22

Cordoba (Nocturne), Pft.
By permission of Associated
Music Publishers, Inc.
1st Theme — A23

2nd Theme — A24

Pavana-Capricho, Op. 12, Pft.
By permission of Associated
Music Publishers, Inc.
1st Theme — A25

2nd Theme — A26

Sous Le Palmier, in E Flat (Tango Flamenco), Pft.
By permission of Associated
Music Publishers, Inc.
1st Theme — A27

2nd Theme — A28

Tango in D, Pft.
By permission of Associated
Music Publishers, Inc.
— A29

ALFVÉN, Hugo (1872-1960)

Midsommarvarka (Swedish Rhapsody), Op. 19, Orch.
By permission of Associated
Music Publishers, Inc.
1st Theme — A30

2nd Theme — A31

3rd Theme — A32

4th Theme — A33

ARENSKY, Anton (1861-1906)

Suite No. 1, Op. 15, 2 Pfts.
Copyright by the Oxford
University Press
Reproduced by permission.
I. Romance 1st Theme — A34

2nd Theme — A35

II. Valse 1st Theme — A36

2nd Theme — A37

**Trio in D Minor,
Op. 32, Vn., Pft., & Vcl.**
By permission of
International Music Co.

1st Movement / 1st Theme — A38

1st Movement / 2nd Theme — A39

2nd Movement / 1st Theme — A40

2nd Movement / 2nd Theme — A41

3rd Movement (Elégie) / 1st Theme — A42

3rd Movement / 2nd Theme — A43

4th Movement / 1st Theme — A44

4th Movement / 2nd Theme — A45

ATTERBERG, Kurt (1887-1974)

**Symphony No. 6,
in C, Op.31**
By permission of Associated
Music Publishers, Inc.

1st Movement / 1st Theme — A46

1st Movement / 2nd Theme — A47

1st Movement / 3rd Theme — A48

2nd Movement / 1st Theme — A49

2nd Movement / 2nd Theme — A50

3rd Movement / 1st Theme — A51

3rd Movement / 2nd Theme — A52

AUBER, Daniel François (1782-1871)

**Le Cheval de Bronze
Overture**

1st Theme — A53

2nd Theme — A54

Le Domino Noir Overture

3rd Theme — A55

1st Theme — A56

2nd Theme — A57

3rd Theme — A58

4th Theme — A59

Fra Diavolo Overture

1st Theme — A60

2nd Theme — A61

3rd Theme — A62

La Muette De Portici Overture

1st Theme — A63

2nd Theme — A64

AUBERT, Louis (1877-1968)

Habañera, Orch.
Permission for reprint granted by Durand & Cie, Paris. Elkan-Vogel Co.,Inc.Philadelphia, Copyright Owners

1st Theme — A65

2nd Theme — A66

Suite Breve, Op. 6, Orch.
I. Menuet
Permission for reprint granted by Durand & Cie, Paris. Elkan-Vogel Co.,Inc. Philadelphia,Copyright Owners,

1st Theme — A67

2nd Theme — A68

II. Berceuse — A69

III. Air de Ballet

1st Theme — A70

2nd Theme — A71

3rd Theme — A72

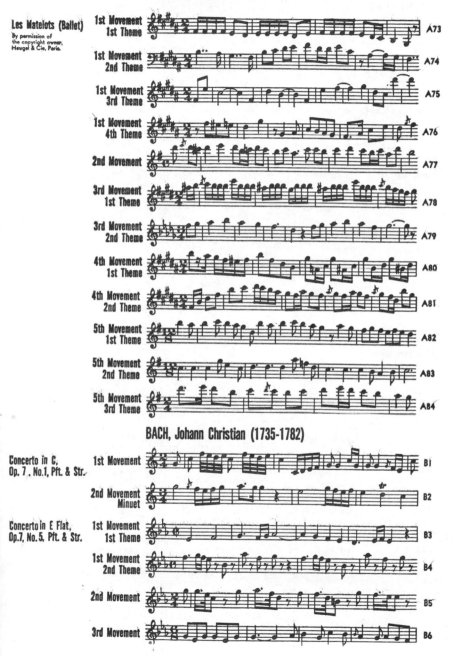

AURIC, Georges (1899-   )

Les Matelots (Ballet)
By permission of
the copyright owner,
Heugel & Cie, Paris.

- 1st Movement / 1st Theme — A73
- 1st Movement / 2nd Theme — A74
- 1st Movement / 3rd Theme — A75
- 1st Movement / 4th Theme — A76
- 2nd Movement — A77
- 3rd Movement / 1st Theme — A78
- 3rd Movement / 2nd Theme — A79
- 4th Movement / 1st Theme — A80
- 4th Movement / 2nd Theme — A81
- 5th Movement / 1st Theme — A82
- 5th Movement / 2nd Theme — A83
- 5th Movement / 3rd Theme — A84

BACH, Johann Christian (1735-1782)

Concerto in C,
Op. 7, No.1, Pft. & Str.
- 1st Movement — B1
- 2nd Movement / Minuet — B2

Concerto in E Flat,
Op.7, No.5, Pft. & Str.
- 1st Movement / 1st Theme — B3
- 1st Movement / 2nd Theme — B4
- 2nd Movement — B5
- 3rd Movement — B6

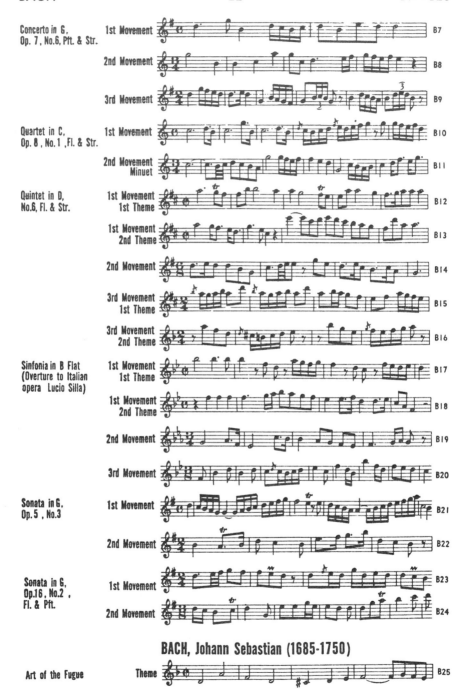

Concerto in G, Op. 7, No.6, Pft. & Str.	1st Movement	B7
	2nd Movement	B8
	3rd Movement	B9
Quartet in C, Op. 8, No.1 , Fl. & Str.	1st Movement	B10
	2nd Movement Minuet	B11
Quintet in D, No.6, Fl. & Str.	1st Movement 1st Theme	B12
	1st Movement 2nd Theme	B13
	2nd Movement	B14
	3rd Movement 1st Theme	B15
	3rd Movement 2nd Theme	B16
Sinfonia in B Flat (Overture to Italian opera Lucio Silla)	1st Movement 1st Theme	B17
	1st Movement 2nd Theme	B18
	2nd Movement	B19
	3rd Movement	B20
Sonata in G, Op. 5 , No.3	1st Movement	B21
	2nd Movement	B22
Sonata in G, Op.16 , No.2 , Fl. & Pft.	1st Movement	B23
	2nd Movement	B24

BACH, Johann Sebastian (1685-1750)

Art of the Fugue	Theme	B25

Christ Lag in Todesbunden
(Church Cantata, No. 4) — B26

Jesu, Joy of Man's
Desiring (from
Cantata 147) — 1st Movement 1st Theme — B27

1st Movement 2nd Theme — B28

Eine Feste Burg Ist Unser Gott — B29

Komm Süsser Tod
(Schemelli No. 42) — B29a

Wachet Auf
Organ Chorale — B29b

Brandenburg
Concerto No. 1,
in F, 2 Hns.,
3 Oboes, Fg., Vn.,
Str. & Cembalo — 1st Movement — B30

2nd Movement — B31

3rd Movement — B32

4th Movement Minuetto, 1st Theme — B33

4th Movement 2nd Theme Trio — B34

5th Movement — B35

Brandenburg
Concerto No. 2,
in F, Tpt., Vn.,
Fl., Ob., Str.
& Cembalo — 1st Movement 1st Theme — B36

1st Movement 2nd Theme — B37

2nd Movement — B38

3rd Movement — B39

Brandenburg
Concerto No. 3,
in G (2nd
Movement is
only a bridge) — 1st Movement — B40

3rd Movement — B41

Brandenburg
Concerto No. 4,
in G, 2 Fl., Vn.,
Str. & Cembalo — 1st Movement — B42

2nd Movement — B43

3rd Movement   B44

Brandenburg Concerto No. 5, in D, Fl., Vn., Str. & Cembalo   1st Movement   B45

2nd Movement   B46

3rd Movement   B47

Brandenburg Concerto No. 6, in B Flat, Viola Solos & Strings   1st Movement   B48

2nd Movement   B49

3rd Movement   B50

Concerto No. 8, in A Minor, Fl., Vn., Pft. & Orch.   1st Movement   B51

2nd Movement   B52

3rd Movement   B53

Concerto No. 1, in D Minor, Pft. & Orch.   1st Movement   B54

2nd Movement   B55

3rd Movement   B56

Concerto No. 2, in D, Pft. & Orch.   1st Movement   B57

2nd Movement   B58

3rd Movement   B59

Concerto No. 4, in A, Pft. & Orch.   1st Movement   B60

2nd Movement   B61

Concerto No. 5, in F Minor, Pft. & Orch.   1st Movement   B62

2nd Movement   B63

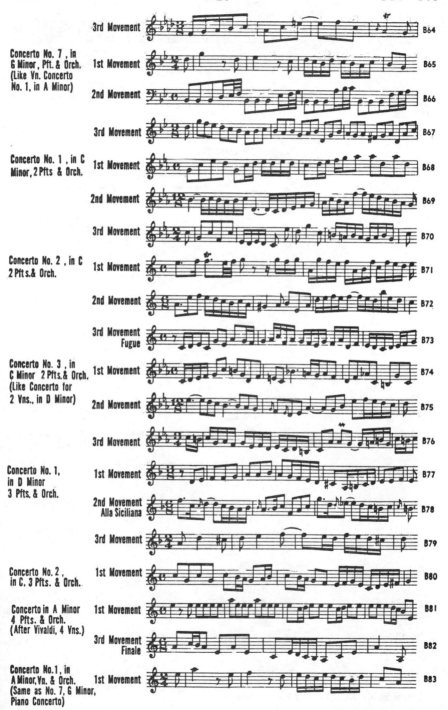

3rd Movement — B64

Concerto No. 7, in
G Minor, Pft. & Orch.
(Like Vn. Concerto
No. 1, in A Minor) — 1st Movement — B65

2nd Movement — B66

3rd Movement — B67

Concerto No. 1, in C
Minor, 2 Pfts & Orch. — 1st Movement — B68

2nd Movement — B69

3rd Movement — B70

Concerto No. 2, in C
2 Pfts.& Orch. — 1st Movement — B71

2nd Movement — B72

3rd Movement
Fugue — B73

Concerto No. 3, in
C Minor 2 Pfts.& Orch.
(Like Concerto for
2 Vns., in D Minor) — 1st Movement — B74

2nd Movement — B75

3rd Movement — B76

Concerto No. 1,
in D Minor
3 Pfts. & Orch. — 1st Movement — B77

2nd Movement
Alla Siciliana — B78

3rd Movement — B79

Concerto No. 2,
in C, 3 Pfts. & Orch. — 1st Movement — B80

Concerto in A Minor
4 Pfts. & Orch.
(After Vivaldi, 4 Vns.) — 1st Movement — B81

3rd Movement
Finale — B82

Concerto No.1, in
A Minor, Vn. & Orch.
(Same as No. 7, G Minor,
Piano Concerto) — 1st Movement — B83

2nd Movement — B84

3rd Movement — B85

Concerto No. 2
in E
Vn. & Orch.

1st Movement — B86

2nd Movement — B87

3rd Movement — B88

Concerto in D Minor,
2 Vns. & Orch.

1st Movement — B89

2nd Movement — B90

3rd Movement — B91

Chromatic Fantasie
& Fugue

Fugue Theme — B92

Prelude & Fugue,
in A Minor, Organ

Prelude — B93

Fugue — B94

Prelude & Fugue, in G
Minor, Organ

Prelude — B95

"Little Fugue" — B96

Organ Fugue, No. 9, in D Minor — B97

Organ Fugue, No. 12, in G Minor — B98

Fugue in D
Organ

*

— B99

Fugue in A Minor, Pft. — B100

Aria for Goldberg
Variations, Pft. — B101

Two-part Inventions
Pft.

No. 1, in C — B102

No. 2, in C Minor — B103

*For Fugue in G Minor, Organ, B99a, see page xiv.

No.13 , in A Minor   B124

Italian Concerto   1st Movement   B125

2nd Movement   B126

3rd Movement 1st Theme   B127

3rd Movement 2nd Theme   B128

Musikalische Opfer   Theme   B129

Sinfonia (from Easter Oratorio Kommt, Eilet)   B130

Partita, No. 1, in B Flat, Pft.   Prelude   B131

Sarabande   B132

Minuet I   B133

Minuet (Trio)   B134

Gigue   B135

Partita, No. 2, in C Minor, Pft.   Prelude (Sinfonia)   B136

Sarabande   B137

Rondeau   B138

Capriccio   B139

Partita, No. 3, in A Minor, Pft.   Fantasia   B140

Burlesca   B141

Scherzo   B142

Gigue   B143

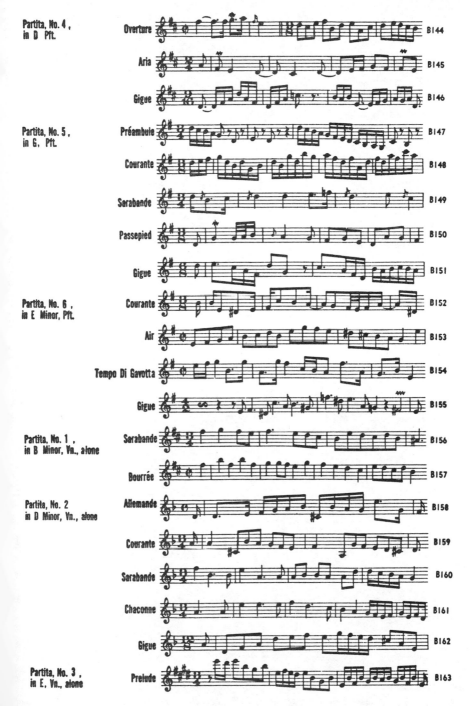

Partita, No. 4, in D Pft.	Overture		B144
	Aria		B145
	Gigue		B146
Partita, No. 5, in G, Pft.	Préambule		B147
	Courante		B148
	Sarabande		B149
	Passepied		B150
	Gigue		B151
Partita, No. 6, in E Minor, Pft.	Courante		B152
	Air		B153
	Tempo Di Gavotta		B154
	Gigue		B155
Partita, No. 1, in B Minor, Vn., alone	Sarabande		B156
	Bourrée		B157
Partita, No. 2 in D Minor, Vn., alone	Allemande		B158
	Courante		B159
	Sarabande		B160
	Chaconne		B161
	Gigue		B162
Partita, No. 3, in E, Vn., alone	Prelude		B163

Loure   B164

Gavotte En Rondeau
1st Theme   B165

2nd Theme   B166

Minuet   B167

Bourrée   B168

Gigue   B169

*Passacaglia, in
C Minor, Organ   B170

Sonata No. 1 in B
Minor, Fl. & Harpsi.   1st Movement   B171

2nd Movement   B172

3rd Movement   B173

Sonata No. 2 in E Flat,
Fl. & Harpsi.   Siciliana   B174

Sonata No. 1 in G
Minor, Vn., alone   1st Movement
Adagio   B175

Fugue   B176

Siciliana   B177

Finale
Presto   B178

Sonata No. 2, in A Minor,
Vn., alone   Grave   B178a

Fugue   B179

Andante   B180

Allegro   B180a

Sonata No. 3
in C, Vn., alone   Adagio   B181

*Bach borrowed the theme from André Raison, a Paris organist in the reign of Louis XIV (1638–1715).

Fugue — B182

Largo — B183

Allegro — B184

Sonata No. 1, in B Minor, Vn. & Pft. — 1st Movement — B185

2nd Movement — B186

4th Movement — B187

Sonata No. 2, in A Vn. & Pft. — 1st Movement — B188

2nd Movement — B189

3rd Movement — B190

4th Movement — B191

Sonata No. 3 in E Vn. & Pft. — 1st Movement — B192

2nd Movement — B193

3rd Movement — B194

4th Movement — B195

Sonata No. 4, in C Minor, Vn. & Pft. — 1st Movement Siciliana — B196

2nd Movement — B197

3rd Movement — B198

4th Movement — B199

Sonata No.5 in F Minor, Vn. & Pft. — 1st Movement — B200

2nd Movement — B201

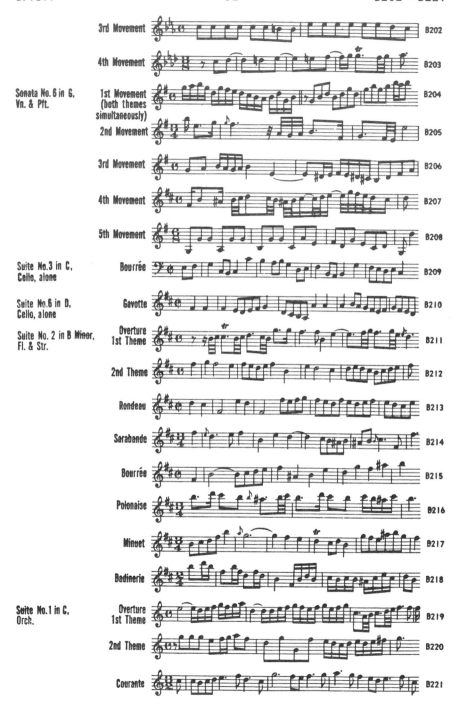

3rd Movement	B202
4th Movement	B203
Sonata No. 6 in G, Vn. & Pft. — 1st Movement (both themes simultaneously)	B204
2nd Movement	B205
3rd Movement	B206
4th Movement	B207
5th Movement	B208
Suite No. 3 in C, Cello, alone — Bourrée	B209
Suite No. 6 in D, Cello, alone — Gavotte	B210
Suite No. 2 in B Minor, Fl. & Str. — Overture 1st Theme	B211
2nd Theme	B212
Rondeau	B213
Sarabande	B214
Bourrée	B215
Polonaise	B216
Minuet	B217
Badinerie	B218
Suite No. 1 in C, Orch. — Overture 1st Theme	B219
2nd Theme	B220
Courante	B221

Bourrée I   B242

Bourrée II   B243

Gigue   B244

English Suite, No.3,   Prelude   B245
in G Minor, Pft.

Allemande   B246

Sarabande   B247

Gavotte   B248

Musette   B249

Gigue   B250

English Suite, No. 4   Prelude   B251
in F, Pft.

Sarabande   B252

Minuet I   B253

Minuet II   B254

Gigue   B255

English Suite, No. 5   Prelude   B256
in E Minor, Pft.

Courante   B257

Sarabande   B258

Passepied I   B259

Passepied II   B260

Gigue   B261

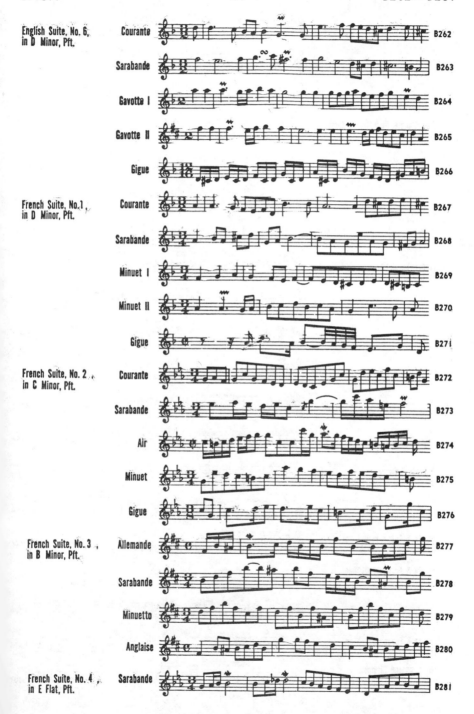

English Suite, No. 6, in D Minor, Pft. — Courante B262
Sarabande B263
Gavotte I B264
Gavotte II B265
Gigue B266

French Suite, No.1, in D Minor, Pft. — Courante B267
Sarabande B268
Minuet I B269
Minuet II B270
Gigue B271

French Suite, No. 2, in C Minor, Pft. — Courante B272
Sarabande B273
Air B274
Minuet B275
Gigue B276

French Suite, No. 3, in B Minor, Pft. — Allemande B277
Sarabande B278
Minuetto B279
Anglaise B280

French Suite, No. 4, in E Flat, Pft. — Sarabande B281

	Gavotte	B282
	Minuet	B283
	Gigue	B284
French Suite, No.5, in G, Pft.	Sarabande	B285
	Gavotte	B286
	Bourrée	B287
	Gigue	B288
French Suite, No. 6, in E, Pft.	Allemande	B289
	Gavotte	B290
	Polonaise	B291
	Bourrée	B292
	Minuet	B293
	Gigue	B294
Toccata & Fugue, in C, Organ	Toccata	B295
	Fugue	B296
Toccata & Fugue, in C Minor Pft.	Fugue	B297
Toccata & Fugue, in D Minor Organ	Toccata	B298
	Fugue	B299
Toccata & Fugue, in G Minor Organ	Fugue Theme	B300
Well-tempered Clavichord Book I	Prelude No. 1	B301

Fugue No. 1 — B302
Prelude No. 2 — B303
Fugue No. 2 — B304
Prelude No. 3 — B305
Fugue No. 3 — B306
Prelude No. 4 — B307
Fugue No. 4 — B308
Prelude No. 5 — B309
Fugue No. 5 — B310
Prelude No. 6 — B311
Fugue No. 6 — B312
Prelude No. 7 — B313
Fugue No. 7 — B314
Prelude No. 8 — B315
Fugue No. 8 — B316
Prelude No. 9 — B317
Fugue No. 9 — B318
Prelude No. 10 — B319
Fugue No. 10 — B320
Prelude No. 11 — B321

Fugue No.11 — B322
Prelude No. 12 — B323
Fugue No.12 — B324
Prelude No.13 — B325
Fugue No.13 — B326
Prelude No.14 — B327
Fugue No.14 — B328
Prelude No.15 — B329
Fugue No.15 — B330
Prelude No.16 — B331
Fugue No.16 — B332
Prelude No.17 — B333
Fugue No.17 — B334
Prelude No.18 — B335
Fugue No.18 — B336
Prelude No.19 — B337
Fugue No.19 — B338
Prelude No.20 — B339
Fugue No.20 — B340
Prelude No.21 — B341

Fugue No. 21 — B342
Prelude No. 22 — B343
Fugue No. 22 — B344
Prelude No. 23 — B345
Fugue No. 23 — B346
Prelude No. 24 — B347
Fugue No. 24 — B348

Well Tempered Clavichord
Book II

Prelude No. 1 — B349
Fugue No. 1 — B350
Prelude No. 2 — B351
Fugue No. 2 — B352
Prelude No. 3 A — B353
B — B354
Fugue No. 3 — B355
Prelude No. 4 — B356
Fugue No. 4 — B357
Prelude No. 5 — B358
Fugue No. 5 — B359
Prelude No. 6 — B360
Fugue No. 6 — B361

Prelude No.17	B382
Fugue No.17	B383
Prelude No.18	B384
Fugue No.18	B385
Prelude No.19	B386
Fugue No.19	B387
Prelude No. 20	B388
Fugue No.20	B389
Prelude No. 21	B390
Fugue No. 21	B391
Prelude No. 22	B392
Fugue No. 22	B393
Prelude No. 23	B394
Fugue No. 23	B395
Prelude No. 24	B396
Fugue No. 24	B397

BACH, Karl Philipp Emanuel (1714-1788)

Abschied Von Meinem Silbermannischen Klaviere, Pft.		B398
Concerto No. 3 , in A Cello & Str. Orch.	1st Movement	B399
	2nd Movement	B400

3rd Movement   B401

Solfeggio (Solfeggietto), Pft.   B402

Sonata No. 1 in
A Minor , Pft.   1st Movement   B403
(from Würtemberg Sonatas)

2nd Movement   B404

3rd Movement   B405

Sonata No. 4 in B Flat   1st Movement   B406
Pft.
(from Würtemberg Sonatas)

2nd Movement   B407

3rd Movement   B408

Sonata No. 1 in G,
Pft. (from Für Kenner   1st Movement   B409
und Liebhaber Collection
No. 2)

2nd Movement   B410

3rd Movement   B411

Sonata No. 3 in F Minor,
Pft. (from Für Kenner   1st Movement   B412
und Liebhaber Collection
No. 3)

2nd Movement   B413

3rd Movement   B414

Concerto in D, Orch.   1st Movement   B415

2nd Movement   B416

3rd Movement   B417

Symphony No.1   1st Movement   B418
in D,

2nd Movement   B419

3rd Movement   B420

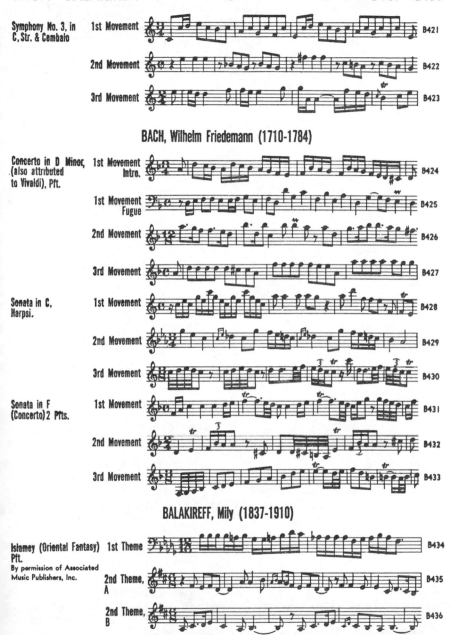

Symphony No. 3, in C, Str. & Cembalo — 1st Movement — B421

2nd Movement — B422

3rd Movement — B423

BACH, Wilhelm Friedemann (1710-1784)

Concerto in D Minor, (also attributed to Vivaldi), Pft. — 1st Movement Intro. — B424

1st Movement Fugue — B425

2nd Movement — B426

3rd Movement — B427

Sonata in C, Harpsi. — 1st Movement — B428

2nd Movement — B429

3rd Movement — B430

Sonata in F (Concerto) 2 Pfts. — 1st Movement — B431

2nd Movement — B432

3rd Movement — B433

BALAKIREFF, Mily (1837-1910)

Islamey (Oriental Fantasy) Pft. — 1st Theme — B434

By permission of Associated Music Publishers, Inc. — 2nd Theme, A — B435

2nd Theme, B — B436

Russia (symph. poem) — 1st Theme — B437

2nd Theme — B438

3rd Theme   B439

4th Theme   B440

Thamar (Tamara)
(symph. poem)
By permission of Associated
Music Publishers, Inc.

1st Theme   B441

2nd Theme   B442

3rd Theme   B443

4th Theme   B444

BALFE, Michael (1808-1870)

The Bohemian Girl
Overture

1st Theme   B445

2nd Theme   B446

3rd Theme   B447

4th Theme   B448

BANTOCK, Sir Granville (1868-1946)

The Pierrot of the Minute
Overture
By permission of Associated
Music Publishers, Inc.

1st Theme   B449

2nd Theme   B450

3rd Theme   B451

4th Theme   B45

BARBER, Samuel (1910-   )

Adagio for Strings, Op. 11
Copyright 1939 by
G. Schirmer, Inc.

  B452

Essay for Orchestra,
Op. 12
Copyright 1941 by
G. Schirmer, Inc.

1st Theme   B45

2nd Theme   B45

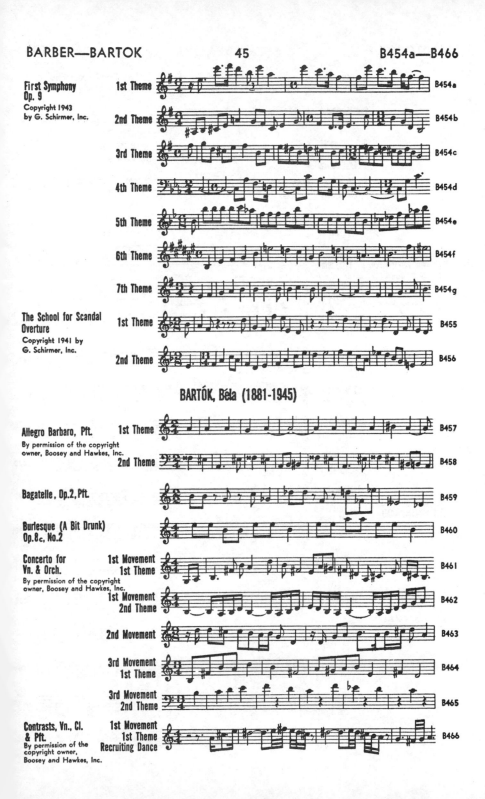

**First Symphony
Op. 9**
Copyright 1943
by G. Schirmer, Inc.

1st Theme — B454a

2nd Theme — B454b

3rd Theme — B454c

4th Theme — B454d

5th Theme — B454e

6th Theme — B454f

7th Theme — B454g

**The School for Scandal
Overture**
Copyright 1941 by
G. Schirmer, Inc.

1st Theme — B455

2nd Theme — B456

BARTÓK, Béla (1881-1945)

Allegro Barbaro, Pft.
By permission of the copyright
owner, Boosey and Hawkes, Inc.

1st Theme — B457

2nd Theme — B458

Bagatelle, Op.2, Pft. — B459

**Burlesque (A Bit Drunk)
Op.8c, No.2** — B460

**Concerto for
Vn. & Orch.**
By permission of the copyright
owner, Boosey and Hawkes, Inc.

1st Movement
1st Theme — B461

1st Movement
2nd Theme — B462

2nd Movement — B463

3rd Movement
1st Theme — B464

3rd Movement
2nd Theme — B465

**Contrasts, Vn., Cl.
& Pft.**
By permission of the
copyright owner,
Boosey and Hawkes, Inc.

1st Movement
1st Theme
Recruiting Dance — B466

1st Movement / 2nd Theme — B467

2nd Movement / Relaxation — B468

3rd Movement / 1st Theme / Fast Dance — B469

3rd Movement / 2nd Theme — B470

3rd Movement / 3rd Theme — B471

Hungarian Folk Songs / Ungarische Volksweisen / (Arranged by Szigeti), / Vn. & Pft. / By permission of the copyright owner, Boosey and Hawkes, Inc.

1st Movement / 1st Theme — B472

1st Movement / 2nd Theme — B473

1st Movement / 3rd Theme — B474

2nd Movement / 1st Theme — B475

2nd Movement / 2nd Theme — B476

3rd Movement / 1st Theme — B477

3rd Movement / 2nd Theme — B478

Hungarian Sketches, No. 1 / (Est a Szeklyeknel)

1st Movement / An Evening / in the Village / 1st Theme — B479

1st Movement / 2nd Theme — B480

2nd Movement / Bear Dance — B481

Quartet No. 1, / Op. 7, Str. / By permission of the copyright owner, Boosey and Hawkes, Inc.

1st Movement — B482

2nd Movement / Intro. — B483

2nd Movement / 1st Theme — B484

2nd Movement / 2nd Theme — B485

3rd Movement / Intro. — B486

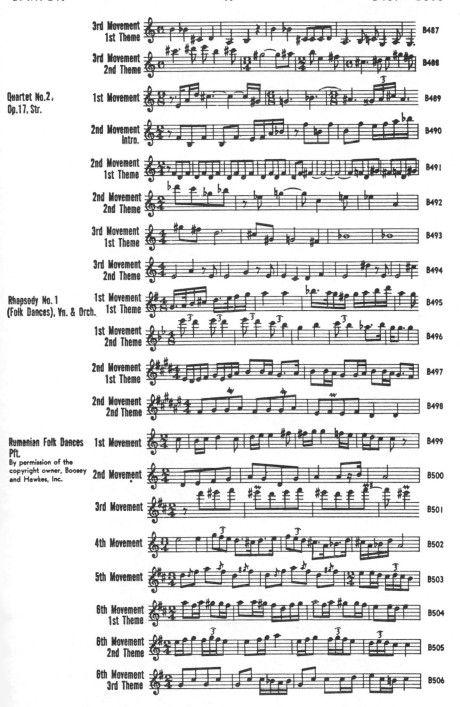

Quartet No.2,
Op.17, Str.

Rhapsody No.1
(Folk Dances), Vn. & Orch.

Rumanian Folk Dances
Pft.
By permission of the
copyright owner, Boosey
and Hawkes, Inc.

3rd Movement 1st Theme — B487
3rd Movement 2nd Theme — B488
1st Movement — B489
2nd Movement Intro. — B490
2nd Movement 1st Theme — B491
2nd Movement 2nd Theme — B492
3rd Movement 1st Theme — B493
3rd Movement 2nd Theme — B494
1st Movement 1st Theme — B495
1st Movement 2nd Theme — B496
2nd Movement 1st Theme — B497
2nd Movement 2nd Theme — B498
1st Movement — B499
2nd Movement — B500
3rd Movement — B501
4th Movement — B502
5th Movement — B503
6th Movement 1st Theme — B504
6th Movement 2nd Theme — B505
6th Movement 3rd Theme — B506

BAX, Sir Arnold Trevor (1883-1953)

Fantasy-Sonata,
Viola & Harp
Copyright 1922 Murdock,
Murdock & Co., London.
Carl Fischer, Inc., N. Y.,
Sole Agents for the U.S.A.

1st Movement
1st Theme — B507

1st Movement
2nd Theme — B508

2nd Movement — B509

3rd Movement — B510

4th Movement — B511

Mediterranean, Orch.
Copyright 1923 Murdock,
Murdock & Co., London.
Carl Fischer. Inc., N. Y.,
Sole Agents for the U.S.A. — B512

Overture to a Picaresque
Comedy
Copyright 1934 Murdock,
Murdock & Co., London.
Carl Fischer, Inc., N. Y.,
Sole Agents for the U.S.A.

1st Theme — B513

2nd Theme — B514

3rd Theme — B515

Sonata, Viola & Pft.
Copyright 1923 Murdock,
Murdock & Co., London.
Sole Agents for the U.S.A.

1st Movement
1st Theme — B516

1st Movement
2nd Theme — B517

2nd Movement
1st Theme — B518

2nd Movement
2nd Theme — B519

3rd Movement — B520

BEETHOVEN, Ludwig Van (1770-1827)

Andante Favori, F — B521

Concerto No. 1, in C
Op.15, Pft.

1st Movement
1st Theme — B522

1st Movement
2nd Theme — B523

2nd Movement
1st Theme — B524

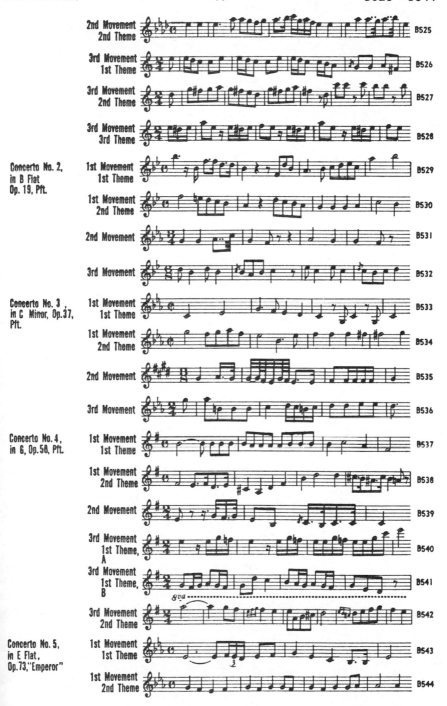

2nd Movement / 2nd Theme — B525

3rd Movement / 1st Theme — B526

3rd Movement / 2nd Theme — B527

3rd Movement / 3rd Theme — B528

Concerto No. 2, in B Flat Op. 19, Pft.

1st Movement / 1st Theme — B529

1st Movement / 2nd Theme — B530

2nd Movement — B531

3rd Movement — B532

Concerto No. 3, in C Minor, Op. 37, Pft.

1st Movement / 1st Theme — B533

1st Movement / 2nd Theme — B534

2nd Movement — B535

3rd Movement — B536

Concerto No. 4, in G, Op. 58, Pft.

1st Movement / 1st Theme — B537

1st Movement / 2nd Theme — B538

2nd Movement — B539

3rd Movement / 1st Theme, A — B540

3rd Movement / 1st Theme, B — B541

3rd Movement / 2nd Theme — B542

Concerto No. 5, in E Flat, Op. 73, "Emperor"

1st Movement / 1st Theme — B543

1st Movement / 2nd Theme — B544

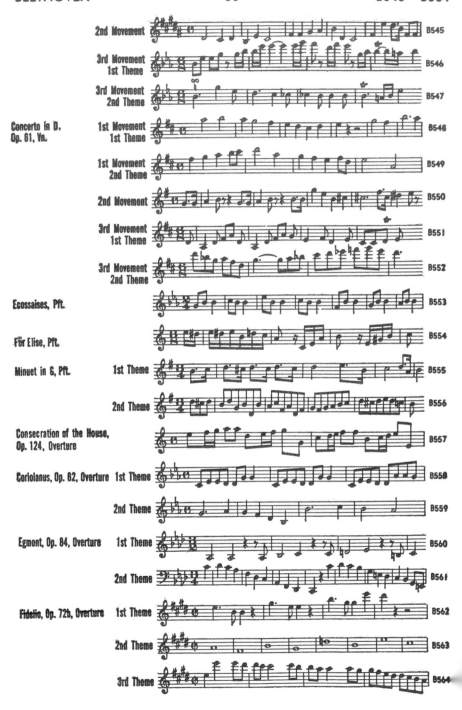

Leonore, No. 1, Op. 138, Overture 1st Theme B565

2nd Theme B566

3rd Theme B567

Leonore, Nos. 2 & 3, Op. 72a, Overtures 1st Theme B568

2nd Theme B569

3rd Theme B570

Prometheus, Op. 43, Overture 1st Theme B571

2nd Theme B572

3rd Theme B573

Quartet in F, Op. 18, No. 1 1st Movement 1st Theme B574

1st Movement 2nd Theme B575

2nd Movement B576

3rd Movement Scherzo B577

4th Movement B578

Quartet in G, Op. 18, No. 2 1st Movement 1st Theme B579

1st Movement 2nd Theme B580

2nd Movement 1st Theme B581

2nd Movement 2nd Theme B582

3rd Movement 1st Theme Scherzo B583

3rd Movement 2nd Theme Trio B584

Quartet in B Flat, Op.18, No.6 — 1st Movement 1st Theme — B604

1st Movement 2nd Theme — B605

2nd Movement — B606

3rd Movement — B607

4th Movement La Malinconia Intro. — B608

4th Movement Theme — B609

Quartet in F Op.59, No.1 "Rasoumowsky" — 1st Movement — B610

2nd Movement — B611

3rd Movement — B612

4th Movement — B613

Quartet in E Minor, Op.59, No.2 "Rasoumowsky" — 1st Movement — B614

2nd Movement 1st Theme — B615

2nd Movement 2nd Theme — B616

3rd Movement 1st Theme — B617

3rd Movement 2nd Theme — B618

4th Movement — B619

Quartet in C, Op.59, No.3, "Rasoumowsky" — 1st Movement — B620

2nd Movement — B621

3rd Movement — B622

4th Movement — B623

Quartet in E Flat, Op.74, "Harp" — 1st Movement Intro. — B624

1st Movement — B625

2nd Movement — B626

3rd Movement — B627

4th Movement — B628

Quartet in F Minor, Op.95, — 1st Movement — B629

2nd Movement 1st Theme — B630

2nd Movement 2nd Theme — B631

3rd Movement — B632

4th Movement Intro. — B633

4th Movement — B634

Quartet in E Flat, Op.127 — 1st Movement 1st Theme — B635

1st Movement 2nd Theme — B636

2nd Movement — B637

3rd Movement — B638

4th Movement 1st Theme — B639

4th Movement 2nd Theme — B640

Quartet in B Flat, Op.130 "Scherzoso" — 1st Movement Intro. — B641

1st Movement — B642

2nd Movement — B643

3rd Movement   B644

4th Movement / 1st Theme   B645

4th Movement / 2nd Theme   B646

4th Movement / Cavatina   B647

5th Movement   B648

Quartet in C Sharp Minor, Op.131   1st Movement   B649

2nd Movement   B650

3rd Movement   B650a

4th Movement   B651

5th Movement / 1st Theme   B652

5th Movement / 2nd Theme   B653

6th Movement   B654

7th Movement / 1st Theme   B655

7th Movement / 2nd Theme   B656

Quartet in A Minor, Op.132   1st Movement / Intro. & 1st Theme   B657

1st Movement / 2nd Theme   B658

2nd Movement / 1st Theme / Two Motives   B659

2nd Movement / 2nd Theme   B660

3rd Movement   B660a

4th Movement   B660b

5th Movement — B661

Quartet
Grosse Fuge in
B Flat, Op.133 — Theme — B662

Countersubject — B663

Quart. in F
Op. 135, Str. — 1st Movement 1st Theme — B663a

1st Movement 2nd Theme — B663b

2nd Movement — B664

3rd Movement — B665

Motives "Muss Es
Sein?"
"Es Muss Sein" — 4th Movement Intro. — B666

4th Movement — B667

Quintet, in E Flat
Op. 16 (Pft. Ob., Cl.,
Hn., & Fg.) — 1st Movement Intro. — B667a

1st Movement — B667b

2nd Movement — B667c

3rd Movement Rondo — B667d

Romance No. 1, in
G, Op. 40, Vn. & Orch. — B668

Romance No. 2, in
F, Op. 50, Vn. & Orch. — B669

Rondo in C,
Op. 51, No. 1, Pft. — B670

Rondo in G,
Op. 129 "Rage Over
the Lost Penny" — B671

Septet in E Flat,
Op. 20 (Vn., Viola, Cello,
Bass, Hn., Cl., Fg.) — 1st Movement 1st Theme — B672

1st Movement 2nd Theme — B673

2nd Movement — B674

3rd Movement · · · · · · · · · · B675

4th Movement · · · · · · · · · · B676

5th Movement · · · · · · · · · · B677

6th Movement · · · · · · · · · · B678

7th Movement · · · · · · · · · · B679

Serenade, Op. 8,
Vn., Viola & Cello · · · 1st Movement · · · · · · · · · · B679a

2nd Movement · · · · · · · · · · B679b

3rd Movement
Minuet · · · · · · · · · · B679c

4th Movement
1st Theme · · · · · · · · · · B679d

4th Movement
2nd Theme · · · · · · · · · · B679e

5th Movement
Alla Polacca · · · · · · · · · · B679f

6th Movement · · · · · · · · · · B679g

Sonata No. 2, in
G Minor, Op. 5, No. 2,
Cello & Pft. · · · 1st Movement
Intro. · · · · · · · · · · B679h

1st Movement · · · · · · · · · · B680

2nd Movement · · · · · · · · · · B680a

Sonata No. 3 in A,
Op. 69, Cello & Pft. · · · 1st Movement · · · · · · · · · · B681

2nd Movement
1st Theme · · · · · · · · · · B682

2nd Movement
2nd Theme · · · · · · · · · · B683

3rd Movement · · · · · · · · · · B684

Sonata No. 4, in C,
Op. 102, No. 1,
Cello & Pft. · · · 1st Movement
Intro. · · · · · · · · · · B685

1st Movement — B686
2nd Movement — B686a
3rd Movement — B686b
Sonata in F
Op. 17, Horn & Pft. 1st Movement — B687
2nd Movement — B688
3rd Movement — B688a
Sonata No. 1, in F Minor, 1st Movement, 1st Theme — B689
Op. 2, No. 1, Pft.
1st Movement 2nd Theme — B690
2nd Movement — B691
3rd Movement 1st Theme Minuet — B692
3rd Movement 2nd Theme — B693
4th Movement 1st Theme — B694
4th Movement 2nd Theme — B695
Sonata No. 2. in A 1st Movement 1st Theme — B696
Op. 2, No. 2, Pft.
1st Movement 2nd Theme — B697
2nd Movement — B698
3rd Movement 1st Theme — B699
3rd Movement 2nd Theme — B700
4th Movement 1st Theme — B701
4th Movement 2nd Theme — B702

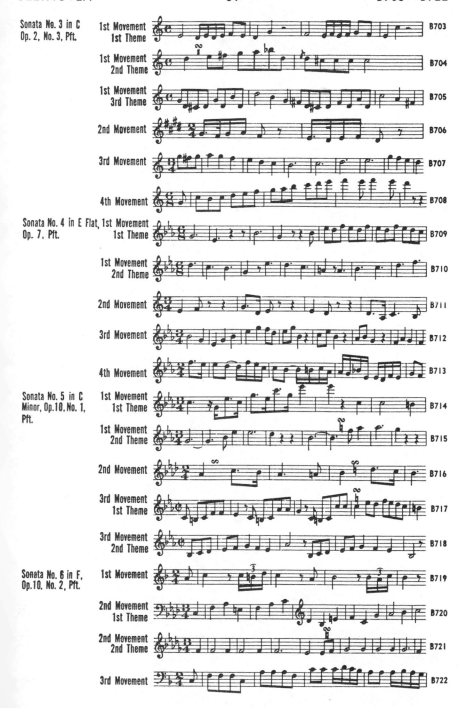

Sonata No. 3 in C
Op. 2, No. 3, Pft. — 1st Movement 1st Theme — B703

1st Movement 2nd Theme — B704

1st Movement 3rd Theme — B705

2nd Movement — B706

3rd Movement — B707

4th Movement — B708

Sonata No. 4 in E Flat, 1st Movement 1st Theme — B709
Op. 7, Pft.

1st Movement 2nd Theme — B710

2nd Movement — B711

3rd Movement — B712

4th Movement — B713

Sonata No. 5 in C Minor, Op.10, No. 1, Pft. — 1st Movement 1st Theme — B714

1st Movement 2nd Theme — B715

2nd Movement — B716

3rd Movement 1st Theme — B717

3rd Movement 2nd Theme — B718

Sonata No. 6 in F, Op.10, No. 2, Pft. — 1st Movement — B719

2nd Movement 1st Theme — B720

2nd Movement 2nd Theme — B721

3rd Movement — B722

Sonata No. 7 in D, Op. 10, No. 3, Pft. — 1st Movement 1st Theme — B723
1st Movement 2nd Theme — B724
2nd Movement — B725
3rd Movement Minuetto — B726
4th Movement — B727

Sonata No. 8, in C Minor, Op. 13, Pft. "Pathetique" — 1st Movement Intro — B728
1st Movement 1st Theme — B729
1st Movement 2nd Theme — B730
2nd Movement 1st Theme — B731
2nd Movement 2nd Theme — B732
3rd Movement 1st Theme — B733
3rd Movement 2nd Theme — B734
3rd Movement 3rd Theme — B735

Sonata No. 9, in E Op. 14, No. 1, Pft. — 1st Movement 1st Theme — B736
1st Movement 2nd Theme — B737
2nd Movement 1st Theme — B738
2nd Movement 2nd Theme — B739
3rd Movement — B740

Sonata No. 10, in G Op. 14, No. 2, Pft. — 1st Movement — B741
2nd Movement — B742

3rd Movement / 1st Theme — B743

3rd Movement / 2nd Theme — B744

Sonata No.11, in B Flat, Op.22, Pft. / 1st Movement / 1st Theme — B745

1st Movement / 2nd Theme — B746

1st Movement / 3rd Theme — B747

2nd Movement — B748

3rd Movement — B749

4th Movement — B750

Sonata No.12, in A Flat, Op.26, Pft. / 1st Movement — B751

2nd Movement / 1st Theme — B752

2nd Movement / 2nd Theme — B753

3rd Movement — B754

4th Movement — B755

Sonata No.13 in E Flat, Op.27, No.1 (Sonata Quasi Una Fantasia) / 1st Movement / 1st Theme — B756

1st Movement / 2nd Theme — B757

2nd Movement / 1st Theme — B758

2nd Movement / 2nd Theme — B759

3rd Movement — B760

4th Movement — B761

Sonata No.14 in C Sharp Minor, Op.27, No.2, Pft. (Sonata Quasi Una Fantasia) "Moonlight" / 1st Movement / Intro. — B762

1st Movement — B763

2nd Movement
1st Theme — B764

2nd Movement
2nd Theme — B765

3rd Movement
1st Theme — B766

3rd Movement
2nd Theme — B767

Sonata No.15 in D
Op.28. Pft.
"Pastoral"

1st Movement
1st Theme — B768

1st Movement
2nd Theme — B769

1st Movement
3rd Theme — B770

2nd Movement
1st Theme — B771

2nd Movement
2nd Theme — B772

3rd Movement
1st Theme — B773

3rd Movement
2nd Theme — B774

4th Movement — B775

Sonata No.16 in G
Op.31, No. 1, Pft.

1st Movement
1st Theme — B776

1st Movement
2nd Theme — B777

2nd Movement — B778

3rd Movement — B779

Sonata No.17 in D
Minor, Op. 31, No. 2,
Pft.,"Tempest"

1st Movement
1st Theme — B780

1st Movement
2nd Theme — B781

2nd Movement
1st Theme — B782

2nd Movement / 2nd Theme — B783
3rd Movement / 1st Theme — B784
3rd Movement / 2nd Theme — B785

Sonata No. 18 in E Flat Op.31, No. 3, Pft.
1st Movement / 1st Theme — B786
1st Movement / 2nd Theme — B787
2nd Movement — B788
3rd Movement / 1st Theme / Minuetto — B789
3rd Movement / 2nd Theme — B790
4th Movement / 1st Theme, A — B791
4th Movement / 1st Theme, B — B792

Sonata No. 19 in G Minor Op.49, No.1, Pft.
1st Movement / 1st Theme — B793
1st Movement / 2nd Theme — B794
2nd Movement / 1st Theme — B795
2nd Movement / 2nd Theme — B796

Sonata No.20 in G Op.49, No.2, Pft.
1st Movement / 1st Theme — B797
1st Movement / 2nd Theme — B798
2nd Movement — B799

Sonata No.21 in C Op.53, Pft. "Waldstein"
1st Movement / 1st Theme — B800
1st Movement / 2nd Theme — B801
2nd Movement / Intro. — B802

2nd Movement
Rondo — B803

Sonata No.22 in F
Op.54, Pft.
1st Movement
1st Theme — B804

1st Movement
2nd Theme — B805

2nd Movement — B806

Sonata No.23 in F Minor,
Op.57, Pft.
"Appassionata"
1st Movement
1st Theme — B807

1st Movement
2nd Theme — B808

1st Movement
3rd Theme — B809

2nd Movement — B810

3rd Movement
1st Theme — B811

3rd Movement
2nd Theme — B812

Sonata No.24 in
F Sharp, Op.78, Pft.
1st Movement
1st Theme — B813

1st Movement
2nd Theme — B814

2nd Movement — B815

Sonata No.25, in G
Op.79, Pft.
(Alla Tedesca)
1st Movement — B816

2nd Movement
1st Theme — B817

2nd Movement
2nd Theme — B818

3rd Movement — B819

Sonata No.26 in E
Flat, Op.81a, Pft.
Les Adieux
1st Movement
Intro. — B820

1st Movement
1st Theme,
A — B821

1st Movement
1st Theme,
B — B822

2nd Movement
l'absence — B823

3rd Movement
et le retour — B824

Sonata No. 27 in E
Minor, Op. 90, Pft.
1st Movement — B825

2nd Movement
Rondo — B826

Sonata No. 28,
in A, Op.101,
Pft.
1st Movement — B827

2nd Movement — B828

3rd Movement — B829

4th Movement — B830

Sonata No. 29,
in B Flat, Op.106, Pft.
"Hammerklavier"
1st Movement
1st Theme,
A — B831

1st Movement
1st Theme,
B — B832

1st Movement
2nd Theme — B833

2nd Movement
Scherzo — B834

3rd Movement
1st Theme — B835

3rd Movement
2nd Theme — B836

4th Movement
1st Theme — B837

4th Movement
2nd Theme — B838

Sonata No. 30 in E
Op.109, Pft.
1st Movement — B839

2nd Movement — B840

3rd Movement — B841

Sonata No. 31,
in A Flat, Op.110, Pft.
1st Movement
1st Theme,
A — B842

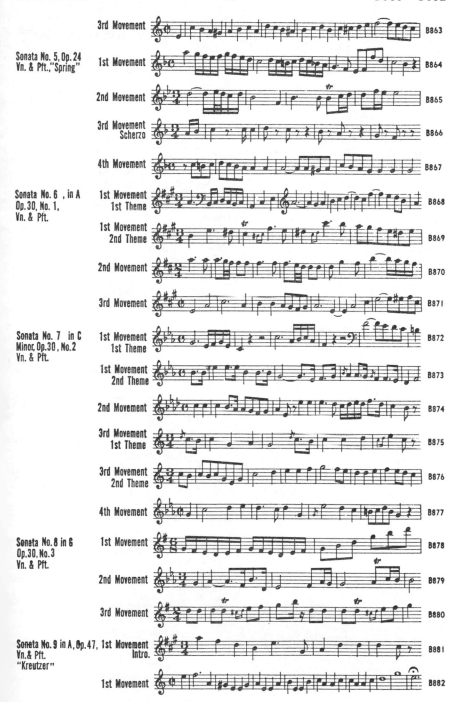

3rd Movement — B863

Sonata No. 5, Op. 24
Vn. & Pft., "Spring"   1st Movement — B864

2nd Movement — B865

3rd Movement
Scherzo — B866

4th Movement — B867

Sonata No. 6 , in A
Op. 30, No. 1,
Vn. & Pft.   1st Movement
1st Theme — B868

1st Movement
2nd Theme — B869

2nd Movement — B870

3rd Movement — B871

Sonata No. 7 in C
Minor, Op. 30, No. 2
Vn. & Pft.   1st Movement
1st Theme — B872

1st Movement
2nd Theme — B873

2nd Movement — B874

3rd Movement
1st Theme — B875

3rd Movement
2nd Theme — B876

4th Movement — B877

Sonata No. 8 in G
Op. 30, No. 3
Vn. & Pft.   1st Movement — B878

2nd Movement — B879

3rd Movement — B880

Sonata No. 9 in A, Op. 47,   1st Movement
Vn. & Pft.   Intro. — B881
"Kreutzer"

1st Movement — B882

Symphony No.2, in D
Op.36

Symphony No.3,
in E Flat, Op.55
"Eroica"

4th Movement 1st Theme — B903
4th Movement 2nd Theme — B904
1st Movement Intro. — B905
1st Movement 1st Theme — B906
1st Movement 2nd Theme — B907
2nd Movement 1st Theme, A — B908
2nd Movement 1st Theme, B — B909
2nd Movement 2nd Theme — B910
2nd Movement 3rd Theme — B911
2nd Movement 4th Theme — B912
3rd Movement 1st Theme — B913
3rd Movement 2nd Theme — B914
4th Movement 1st Theme — B915
4th Movement 2nd Theme — B916
4th Movement 3rd Theme — B917
1st Movement 1st Theme — B918
1st Movement 2nd Theme — B919
1st Movement 3rd Theme — B920
1st Movement 4th Theme — B921
1st Movement 5th Theme — B922

1st Movement / 6th Theme — B923

2nd Movement / 1st Theme — B924

2nd Movement / 2nd Theme — B925

2nd Movement / 3rd Theme — B926

2nd Movement / 4th Theme — B927

3rd Movement / 1st Theme, A — B928

3rd Movement / 1st Theme, B — B929

3rd Movement / 2nd Theme — B930

4th Movement / 1st Theme — B931

4th Movement / 2nd Theme — B932

4th Movement / 3rd Theme — B933

4th Movement / 4th Theme — B934

Symphony No. 4, in B Flat, Op. 60

1st Movement / Intro. — B935

1st Movement / 1st Theme — B936

1st Movement / 2nd Theme — B937

1st Movement / 3rd Theme — B938

1st Movement / 4th Theme — B939

2nd Movement / 1st Theme — B940

2nd Movement / 2nd Theme — B941

2nd Movement / 3rd Theme — B942

4th Movement
4th Theme — B963

4th Movement
5th Theme,
A — B964

4th Movement
5th Theme,
B — B965

Symphony No. 6, in F,
Op. 68, " Pastoral "

1st Movement
1st Theme — B966

1st Movement
2nd Theme — B967

1st Movement
3rd Theme
A — B968

1st Movement
3rd Theme,
B — B969

2nd Movement
1st Theme
A — B970

2nd Movement
1st Theme, A
Accompanying Motive — B971

2nd Movement
1st Theme,
B — B972

2nd Movement
2nd Theme — B973

2nd Movement
3rd Theme — B974

3rd Movement
1st Theme,
A — B975

3rd Movement
1st Theme,
B — B976

3rd Movement
2nd Theme — B977

3rd Movement
3rd Theme — B978

3rd Movement
4th Theme — B979

4th Movement
1st Theme,
A — B980

4th Movement
1st Theme,
B — B981

4th Movement
2nd Theme — B982

2nd Movement
3rd Theme,
B   B1023

3rd Movement
1st Theme   B1024

3rd Movement
2nd Theme   B1025

4th Movement
Intro.   B1026

4th Movement
1st Theme   B1027

4th Movement
2nd Theme   B1028

4th Movement
3rd Theme   B1029

4th Movement
4th Theme   B1030

Trio in B Flat,   1st Movement   B1031
Op.11, Cl., Cello & Pft.
Gassenhauer (Street Song)

2nd Movement   B1032

3rd Movement   B1033

Trio in C Minor,   1st Movement
Op.1 , No.3, Str.   1st Theme,
                         A   B1034

                         1st Movement
                         1st Theme,
                         B   B1035

                         1st Movement
                         2nd Theme   B1036

2nd Movement   B1037

3rd Movement
1st Theme   B1038

3rd Movement
2nd Theme   B1039

4th Movement
1st Theme   B1040

4th Movement
2nd Theme   B1041

Trio in D,   1st Movement   B1042
Op.70, No. 1   1st Theme
"Geister"
Vn, Cello, Pft.

1st Movement
2nd Theme — B1043

2nd Movement — B1044

3rd Movement — B1045

Trio in B Flat,
Op.97 "Archduke"
Vn, Cello, Pft.

1st Movement
1st Theme — B1046

1st Movement
2nd Theme — B1047

2nd Movement
1st Theme — B1048

2nd Movement
2nd Theme — B1049

2nd Movement
3rd Theme — B1050

3rd Movement — B1051

4th Movement — B1052

Trio, Vn, Cello, Pft.
(Little Trio in B Flat)

1st Theme — B1053

2nd Theme — B1054

Turkish March from Ruins
of Athens, Op.113
(Same Theme for Variations, Op. 76,) — B1055

Variations on "Nel Cor
Piu" of Paisiello, Pft. — B1056

Thirty-two Variations,
C Minor, Pft.   Theme — B1057

Variations on a Waltz
of Diabelli, Op.120, Pft.   Theme — B1058

BELLINI, Vincenzo (1801-1835)

Norma
Overture

1st Theme — B1059

2nd Theme — B1060

3rd Theme — B1061

BERLIOZ, Hector (1803-1869)

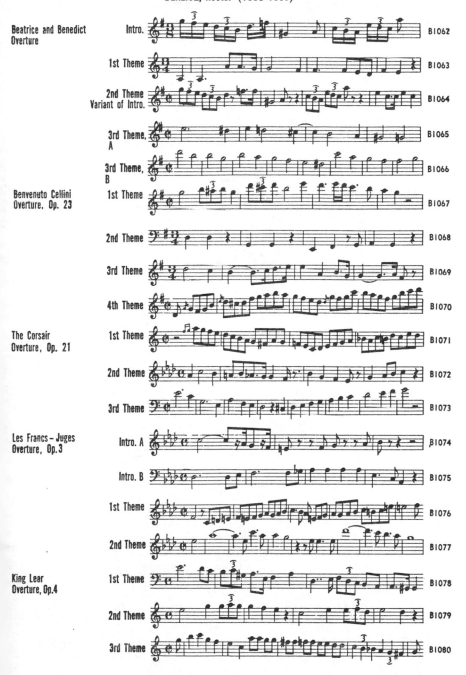

Beatrice and Benedict Overture	Intro.	B1062
	1st Theme	B1063
	2nd Theme Variant of Intro.	B1064
	3rd Theme, A	B1065
	3rd Theme, B	B1066
Benvenuto Cellini Overture, Op. 23	1st Theme	B1067
	2nd Theme	B1068
	3rd Theme	B1069
	4th Theme	B1070
The Corsair Overture, Op. 21	1st Theme	B1071
	2nd Theme	B1072
	3rd Theme	B1073
Les Francs-Juges Overture, Op. 3	Intro. A	B1074
	Intro. B	B1075
	1st Theme	B1076
	2nd Theme	B1077
King Lear Overture, Op. 4	1st Theme	B1078
	2nd Theme	B1079
	3rd Theme	B1080

4th Theme — B1081
5th Theme — B1082

Roman Carnival Overture, Op. 9
1st Theme — B1083
2nd Theme — B1084
3rd Theme — B1085
4th Theme — B1086

Romeo & Juliet, Overture Op. 17
1st Movement Combat, Tumult — B1087
2nd Movement Romeo Alone 1st Theme — B1088
2nd Movement Fête at the Capulets 2nd Theme — B1089
4th Movement Queen Mab Scherzo 1st Theme, A — B1090
4th Movement 1st Theme, B — B1091
4th Movement 2nd Theme — B1092

Fantastic Symphony, Op. 14
1st Movement Reveries, Passions Intro. A — B1093
1st Movement Intro. B — B1094
1st Movement 1st Theme — B1095
1st Movement 2nd Theme — B1096
2nd Movement A Ball 1st Theme — B1097
2nd Movement 2nd Theme — B1098
3rd Movement Scenes in the Country 1st Theme — B1099
3rd Movement 2nd Theme — B1100

4th Movement
March to the Scaffold
1st Theme — B1101

4th Movement
2nd Theme — B1102

5th Movement
Witches' Sabbath
1st Theme — B1103

5th Movement
2nd Theme
Dies Irae — B1104

5th Movement
3rd Theme — B1105

Harold in Italy, Op.16 1st Movement
Orch. Harold in the Mountains
Intro. A1 — B1106

1st Movement
Intro. A 2 — B1107

1st Movement
Intro. B — B1108

1st Movement
1st Theme — B1109

1st Movement
2nd Theme — B1110

1st Movement
3rd Theme — B1111

2nd Movement
March of the Pilgrims — B1112

3rd Movement
Serenade
1st Theme — B1113

3rd Movement
2nd Theme — B1114

4th Movement
Orgy of the Brigands
1st Theme — B1115

4th Movement
2nd Theme — B1116

4th Movement
3rd Theme — B1117

BERNSTEIN, Leonard (1918-)

Opening Dance — B1117a

At the Bar
Intro. — B1117b

Theme — BIII7c

Pas de Deux — BIII7d

Variation 1 / 1st Theme — BIII7e

2nd Theme — BIII7f

Variation 2 — BIII7g

Variation 3 / 1st Theme — BIII7h

2nd Theme — BIII7i

Finale — BIII7j

Jeremiah, Symphony
Copyright 1943 by
Harms, Inc.
Reprinted by
special permission.

1st Movement / Prophecy / 1st Theme — BIII7k

1st Movement / 2nd Theme — BIII7l

1st Movement / 3rd Theme — BIII7m

2nd Movement / 1st Theme — BIII7n

2nd Movement / 2nd Theme — BIII7o

3rd Movement / 1st Theme — BIII7p

3rd Movement / 2nd Theme — BIII7q

3rd Movement / 3rd Theme — BIII7r

BIZET, Georges (1838-1875)

L'Arlesienne
Suite No.1, Orch.

Overture / 1st Theme — BIII8

2nd Theme — BIII9

Minuetto / 1st Theme — BII20

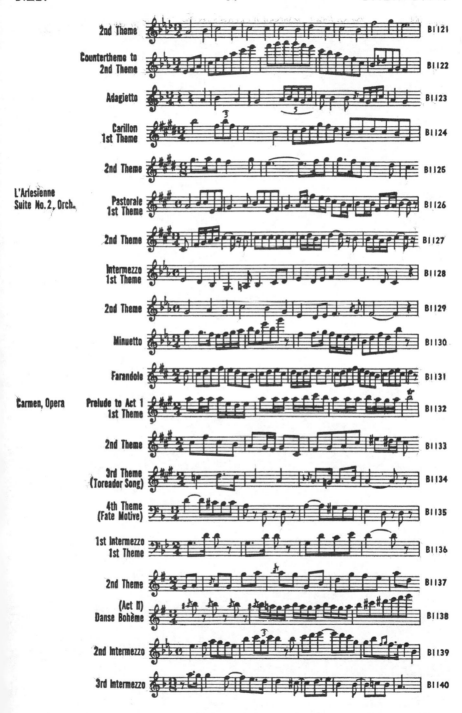

Petite Suite, Op. 22
"Jeux D'Enfants"
Orch.   Marche   B1141

Berceuse (Doll)   B1142

Impromptu   B1143

Duo (Petit Mari,
Petite Femme)   B1144

Galop (Le Bal)   B1145

Symphony No. 1.
in C   1st Movement
1st Theme,
A   B1146

1st Movement
1st Theme,
B   B1147

1st Movement
2nd Theme   B1148

2nd Movement
1st Theme   B1149

2nd Movement
2nd Theme   B1150

3rd Movement   B1151

4th Movement
1st Theme   B1152

4th Movement
2nd Theme   B1153

4th Movement
3rd Theme   B1154

BLOCH, Ernest (1880-1959)

Baal Shem, (Three
Pictures of Chassidic
Life) Vn. & Pft.   Vidui (Contrition)
Copyright 1924
by Carl Fischer,
Inc., N. Y.   B1155

Nigun (Improvisation)
1st Theme
Copyright 1924 by Carl Fischer,
Inc., N. Y.   B1156

2nd Theme   B1157

Simchas Torah
Copyright 1924 by Carl Fischer,
Inc., N. Y.   B1158

Concerto grosso
Str. Orch. & Pft.
Obbligato
By permission of C. C. Birchard &
Co., owners of the copyright.   1st Movement
(Prelude)   B1159

4th Movement / 2nd Theme — B1180

4th Movement / 3rd Theme — B1181

Quintet, Pft. & Str.
Copyright 1924
by G. Schirmer, Inc.

1st Movement / 1st Theme — B1182

1st Movement / 2nd Theme — B1183

2nd Movement / 1st Theme — B1184

2nd Movement / 2nd Theme — B1185

3rd Movement — B1186

Schelomo (Hebrew Rhapsody), Cello & Orch.
Copyright renewal assigned
1945 to G. Schirmer, Inc.

1st Theme — B1187

2nd Theme — B1188

3rd Theme — B1189

4th Theme — B1190

5th Theme — B1191

6th Theme — B1192

Sonata, Vn. & Pft.
Copyright 1922
by G. Schirmer, Inc.

1st Movement — B1193

2nd Movement — B1194

3rd Movement — B1195

Suite, Viola & Orch.
Copyright 1921
by G. Schirmer, Inc.

1st Movement / 1st Theme — B1196

1st Movement / 2nd Theme — B1197

1st Movement / 3rd Theme — B1198

2nd Movement / 1st Theme — B1199

2nd Movement
2nd Theme — B1200

3rd Movement — B1201

4th Movement — B1202

Israel, Symphony
Copyright 1925
by G. Schirmer, Inc.

1st Theme — B1203

2nd Theme — B1204

3rd Theme — B1205

4th Theme — B1206

5th Theme — B1207

Three Nocturnes,
Vn., Cello, & Pft.
Copyright by Carl Fischer, Inc., N. Y.
Reprinted by permisssion.

I — B1208

II — B1209

III — B1210

BOCCHERINI, Luigi (1743-1805)

Concerto in B Flat
Cello & Orch.

1st Movement
1st Theme — B1211

1st Movement
2nd Theme — B1212

2nd Movement — B1213

3rd Movement — B1214

Concerto No.2 in D
Cello & Orch.

1st Movement — B1215

2nd Movement
1st Theme — B1216

2nd Movement
2nd Theme — B1217

3rd Movement
1st Theme,
A — B1218

Quintet in D, Op.37, Str.	1st Movement	B1239
	2nd Movement	B1240
	3rd Movement 1st Theme	B1241
	3rd Movement 2nd Theme	B1242
Rondo, Cello & Pft.	1st Theme	B1243
	2nd Theme	B1244
	3rd Theme	B1245
Sonata No. 2 in C, Cello & Pft.	1st Movement	B1246
	2nd Movement	B1247
	3rd Movement	B1248
Sonata No. 6 in A, Cello & Pft.	1st Movement	B1249
	2nd Movement 1st Theme	B1250
	2nd Movement 2nd Theme	B1251
	3rd Movement 1st Theme	B1252
	3rd Movement 2nd Theme	B1253
Sonata in B Flat, Cello & Pft.	1st Movement	B1254
	2nd Movement	B1255
	3rd Movement 1st Theme	B1256
	3rd Movement 2nd Theme	B1257
Sonata in C, Cello & Pft.	1st Movement	B1258

2nd Movement   B1259

3rd Movement   B1260

BOËLLMANN, Leon (1862-1897)

Suite Gothique,   1st Movement
Op. 25, Organ   Introduction-Choral   B1261
Permission for reprint
granted by Durand
& Cie, Paris.   2nd Movement
Elkan-Vogel Co., Inc. Menuet Gothique   B1262
Philadelphia, Copyright
Owners

3rd Movement   B1263

4th Movement
Toccata   B1264

Variations Symphoniques,   Intro.   B1265
Op. 63, Cello & Orch.
Permission for reprint granted
by Durand & Cie, Paris.   Theme
Elkan-Vogel Co., Inc. Philadelphia,   B1266
Copyright Owners

BOÏELDIEU, François (1775-1834)

Le Calife De Bagdad   1st Theme
Overture   B1267

2nd Theme   B1268

3rd Theme   B1269

La Dame Blanche,   1st Theme
Overture,   B1270

2nd Theme   B1271

3rd Theme   B1272

BORODIN, Alexander (1833-1887)

On the Steppes of   1st Theme
Central Asia, Orch.   B127

2nd Theme   B127

Polovetsian Dances   1st Theme
from Prince Igor   B127

2nd Theme — B1276
3rd Theme — B1277
3rd Theme — B1278
4th Theme — B1279

Quartet No.1, in A,
Str.
1st Movement Intro. — B1280
1st Movement 1st Theme — B1281
1st Movement 2nd Theme — B1282
2nd Movement 1st Theme — B1283
2nd Movement 2nd Theme — B1284
2nd Movement 3rd Theme Fugato — B1285
3rd Movement 1st Theme — B1286
3rd Movement 2nd Theme — B1287
4th Movement 1st Theme — B1288
4th Movement 2nd Theme — B1289

Quartet No.2 in D,
Str.
1st Movement 1st Theme — B1290
1st Movement 2nd Theme — B1291
1st Movement 3rd Theme — B1292
2nd Movement 1st Theme — B1293
2nd Movement 2nd Theme — B1294
3rd Movement 1st Theme Notturno — B1295

3rd Movement 2nd Theme — B1316

3rd Movement 3rd Theme — B1317

4th Movement 1st Theme — B1318

4th Movement 2nd Theme — B1319

Symphony No. 3 in A Minor (Unfinished) — 1st Movement 1st Theme — B1320

1st Movement 2nd Theme — B1321

1st Movement 3rd Theme — B1322

2nd Movement 1st Theme — B1323

2nd Movement 2nd Theme — B1324

2nd Movement 3rd Theme — B1325

2nd Movement 4th Theme — B1326

BOYCE, William (1711-1779)

The Power of Music, Overture — 1st Theme — B1327

2nd Theme — B1328

BRAHMS, Johannes (1833-1897)

Ballade, in D Minor, Op.10, No.1, Pft. — B1329

Ballade, in D Op. 10, No. 2, Pft. — 1st Theme — B1330

2nd Theme — B1331

Ballade, in G Minor, Op.118, No. 3, Pft. — 1st Theme — B1332

2nd Theme — B1333

Capriccio, in B Minor, Op. 76, No. 2, Pft.   B1334

Capriccio, in C Sharp Minor, Op. 76, No. 5, Pft.   B1335

Capriccio, in D Minor, Op. 116, No. 1, Pft.   B1336

Concerto No. 1 in D Minor, Op. 15, Pft. & Orch.

1st Movement 1st Theme   B1337

1st Movement 2nd Theme   B1338

1st Movement 3rd Theme   B1339

1st Movement 4th Theme   B1340

2nd Movement   B1341

3rd Movement 1st Theme   B1342

3rd Movement 2nd Theme   B1343

3rd Movement 3rd Theme   B1344

Concerto No. 2, in B Flat Op. 83, Pft. & Orch.

1st Movement 1st Theme   B1345

1st Movement 2nd Theme   B1346

1st Movement 3rd Theme   B1347

2nd Movement 1st Theme   B1348

2nd Movement 2nd Theme   B1349

2nd Movement 3rd Theme   B1350

3rd Movement   B1351

4th Movement 1st Theme   B1352

4th Movement 2nd Theme   B1353

4th Movement 3rd Theme — B1354

4th Movement 4th Theme — B1355

Concerto in D, Op.77, Vn. & Orch. 1st Movement 1st Theme — B1356

1st Movement 2nd Theme — B1357

1st Movement 3rd Theme — B1358

2nd Movement — B1359

3rd Movement 1st Theme — B1360

3rd Movement 2nd Theme — B1361

Concerto in A Minor, Op. 102, Vn., Vcl. & Orch. 1st Movement 1st Theme — B1362

1st Movement 2nd Theme — B1363

2nd Movement 1st Theme — B1364

2nd Movement 2nd Theme — B1365

3rd Movement 1st Theme — B1366

3rd Movement 2nd Theme — B1367

3rd Movement 3rd Theme — B1368

Hungarian Dances Pft.-4 hands No. 1, in G Minor — B1369

No. 2, in D Minor 1st Theme — B1370

2nd Theme — B1371

No. 3, in F — B1372

No. 4, in F Minor 1st Theme — B1373

2nd Theme   B1374

No. 5, in F Sharp Minor
1st Theme   B1375

2nd Theme   B1376

No. 6, in D Flat   B1377

No. 7, in A   B1378

No.12, in D Minor   B1379

Intermezzo, in A Flat,
Op. 76, No.3, Pft.   B1380

Intermezzo, in A Minor,
Op. 76, No.7, Pft.   B1381

Intermezzo, in A Minor,
Op.116, No.2, Pft.   B1382

Intermezzo, in C Sharp
Minor, Op.116, No.3, Pft.   B1383

Intermezzo, in E,
Op.116, No.4, Pft.   B1384

Intermezzo, in E Flat,
Op.117, No. 1, Pft.   B1385

Intermezzo, in B Flat   1st Theme
Minor, Op.117. No.2, Pft.   B1386

2nd Theme   B1387

Intermezzo, in A Minor,
Op.118, No. 1, Pft.   B1388

Intermezzo, in A,   1st Movement
Op.118, No.2, Pft.   B1389

2nd Movement   B1390

Intermezzo, in E Flat   1st Movement
Minor, Op.118, No.6, Pft.   B1391

2nd Movement   B1392

Intermezzo, in B Minor,
Op.119, No.1, Pft.   B1393

Intermezzo, in E Minor, Op.119, No.2, Pft.   1st Theme — B1394

2nd Movement — B1395

Intermezzo, in C, Op.119, No.3, Pft. — B1396

Academic Festival, Overture, Op. 80   1st Theme — B1397

2nd Theme A — B1398

2nd Theme, B — B1399

3rd Theme — B1400

4th Theme — B1401

5th Theme Gaudeamus Igitur — B1402

Tragic Overture, Op. 81   1st Theme — B1403

2nd Theme — B1404

3rd Theme — B1405

Quartet in G Minor, Op.25, Pft. & Str.   1st Movement 1st Theme — B1406

1st Movement 2nd Theme — B1407

1st Movement 3rd Theme — B1408

1st Movement 4th Theme — B1409

2nd Movement 1st Theme — B1410

2nd Movement 2nd Theme — B1411

2nd Movement 3rd Theme Trio — B1412

3rd Movement 1st Theme — B1413

3rd Movement 2nd Theme — B1414

4th Movement 1st Theme — B1415

4th Movement 2nd Theme — B1416

4th Movement 3rd Theme — B1417

Quartet in A, Op. 26, Pft. & Str.

1st Movement 1st Theme — B1418

1st Movement 2nd Theme — B1419

2nd Movement — B1420

3rd Movement 1st Theme — B1421

3rd Movement 2nd Theme Trio — B1422

4th Movement — B1423

Quartet in C Minor Op. 51, No. 1, Str.

1st Movement 1st Theme — B1424

1st Movement 2nd Theme — B1425

2nd Movement — B1426

3rd Movement 1st Theme — B1427

3rd Movement 2nd Theme — B1428

4th Movement 1st Theme — B1429

4th Movement 2nd Theme — B1430

4th Movement 3rd Theme — B1431

4th Movement 4th Theme — B1432

Quartet in A Minor Op. 51, No. 2, Str.

1st Movement 1st Theme — B1433

1st Movement 2nd Theme   B1434

2nd Movement   B1435

3rd Movement 1st Theme   B1436

3rd Movement 2nd Theme   B1437

4th Movement 1st Theme   B1438

4th Movement 2nd Theme   B1439

Quartet in C Minor Op. 60, Pft. & Str.

1st Movement 1st Theme   B1440

1st Movement 2nd Theme   B1441

2nd Movement 1st Theme   B1442

2nd Movement 2nd Theme   B1443

3rd Movement   B1444

4th Movement 1st Theme   B1445

4th Movement 2nd Theme   B1446

Quartet in B Flat Op. 67, Str.

1st Movement 1st Theme   B1447

1st Movement 2nd Theme   B1448

2nd Movement 1st Theme   B1449

2nd Movement 2nd Theme   B1450

3rd Movement 1st Theme   B1451

3rd Movement 2nd Theme   B1452

4th Movement   B1453

Quintet in F Minor, Op.34, Pft. & Str.

1st Movement 1st Theme — B1454
1st Movement 2nd Theme — B1455
1st Movement 3rd Theme — B1456
1st Movement 4th Theme — B1457
2nd Movement 1st Theme — B1458
2nd Movement 2nd Theme — B1459
3rd Movement 1st Theme — B1460
3rd Movement 2nd Theme — B1461
3rd Movement 3rd Theme — B1462
4th Movement 1st Theme — B1463
4th Movement 2nd Theme — B1464

Quintet in F, Op.88, Str.

1st Movement — B1465
2nd Movement — B1466
3rd Movement 1st Theme — B1467
3rd Movement 2nd Theme — B1468

Quintet in G, Op.111, Str.

1st Movement 1st Theme — B1469
1st Movement 2nd Theme — B1470
2nd Movement — B1471
3rd Movement — B1472
4th Movement 1st Theme — B1473

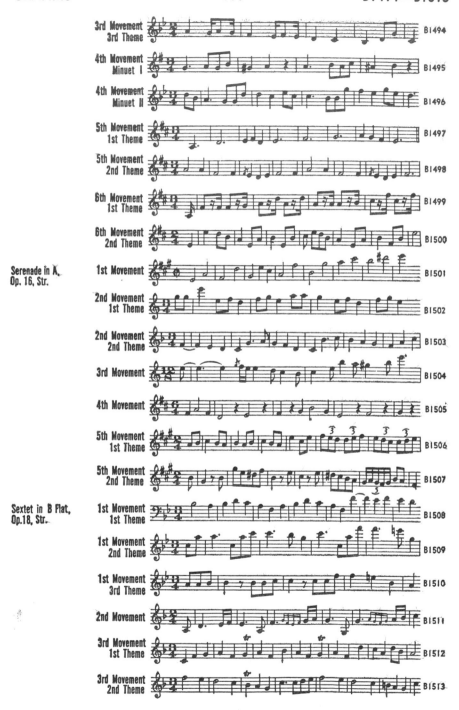

4th Movement B1514

Sextet, in G,
Op. 36, Str. 1st Movement 1st Theme B1515

1st Movement 2nd Theme B1516

2nd Movement 1st Theme B1517

2nd Movement 2nd Theme B1518

3rd Movement B1519

4th Movement 1st Theme B1520

4th Movement 2nd Theme B1521

Sonata in E Minor, Op.38, Cello & Pft. 1st Movement 1st Theme B1522

1st Movement 2nd Theme B1523

2nd Movement 1st Theme B1524

2nd Movement 2nd Theme B1525

3rd Movement 1st Theme B1526

3rd Movement 2nd Theme B1527

Sonata in F Op.99, Cello & Pft. 1st Movement 1st Theme B1528

1st Movement 2nd Theme B1529

2nd Movement 1st Theme B1530

2nd Movement 2nd Theme B1531

3rd Movement 1st Theme B1532

3rd Movement 2nd Theme B1533

Symphony No.1
in C Minor
Op.68

4th Movement — B1574

1st Movement
Intro. A 1 — B1575

Both Themes
Simultaneous
Intro. A 2 — B1576

1st Movement
Intro. B — B1577

1st Movement
1st Theme,
A — B1578

1st Movement
1st Theme,
B — B1579

1st Movement
1st Theme,
C — B1580

1st Movement
2nd Theme — B1581

1st Movement
3rd Theme — B1582

1st Movement
4th Theme — B1583

2nd Movement
1st Theme — B1584

2nd Movement
2nd Theme — B1585

2nd Movement
3rd Theme — B1586

2nd Movement
4th Theme — B1587

3rd Movement
1st Theme — B1588

3rd Movement
2nd Theme — B1589

3rd Movement
3rd Theme,
A — B1590

3rd Movement
3rd Theme,
B — B1591

3rd Movement
4th Theme — B1592

4th Movement
Intro. A — B1593

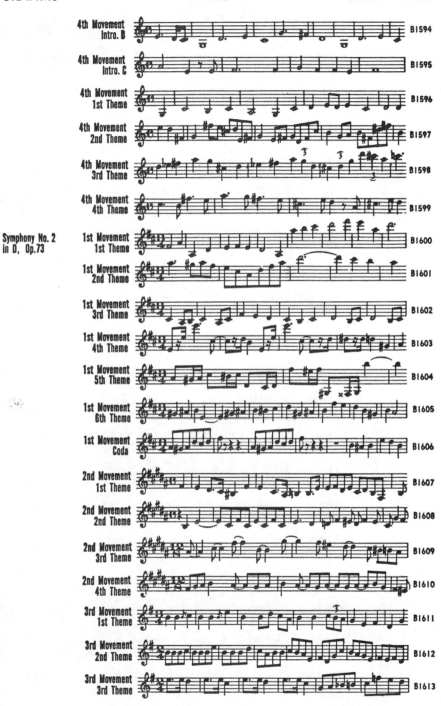

Symphony No. 2
in D, Op.73

4th Movement Intro. B — B1594

4th Movement Intro. C — B1595

4th Movement 1st Theme — B1596

4th Movement 2nd Theme — B1597

4th Movement 3rd Theme — B1598

4th Movement 4th Theme — B1599

1st Movement 1st Theme — B1600

1st Movement 2nd Theme — B1601

1st Movement 3rd Theme — B1602

1st Movement 4th Theme — B1603

1st Movement 5th Theme — B1604

1st Movement 6th Theme — B1605

1st Movement Coda — B1606

2nd Movement 1st Theme — B1607

2nd Movement 2nd Theme — B1608

2nd Movement 3rd Theme — B1609

2nd Movement 4th Theme — B1610

3rd Movement 1st Theme — B1611

3rd Movement 2nd Theme — B1612

3rd Movement 3rd Theme — B1613

3rd Movement
4th Theme — B1614

4th Movement
1st Theme,
A — B1615

4th Movement
1st Theme,
B — B1616

4th Movement
2nd Theme — B1617

4th Movement
3rd Theme — B1618

Symphony No. 3
in F Op. 90

1st Movement
1st Theme — B1619

1st Movement
2nd Theme — B1620

1st Movement
3rd Theme — B1621

1st Movement
4th Theme — B1622

2nd Movement
1st Theme — B1623

2nd Movement
2nd Theme — B1624

2nd Movement
3rd Theme — B1625

3rd Movement
1st Theme — B1626

3rd Movement
2nd Theme — B1627

3rd Movement
3rd Theme — B1628

4th Movement
1st Theme
A — B1629

4th Movement
1st Theme
B — B1630

4th Movement
2nd Theme — B1631

4th Movement
3rd Theme — B1632

4th Movement
4th Theme — B1633

Symphony No. 4
in E Minor, Op. 98

1st Movement
1st Theme
A   B1634

1st Movement
1st Theme
B   B1635

1st Movement
2nd Theme   B1636

1st Movement
3rd Theme   B1637

1st Movement
4th Theme   B1638

1st Movement
5th Theme   B1639

1st Movement
6th Theme   B1640

1st Movement
7th Theme   B1641

2nd Movement
1st Theme   B1642

2nd Movement
2nd Theme   B1643

2nd Movement
3rd Theme   B1644

3rd Movement
1st Theme
A   B1645

3rd Movement
1st Theme
B   B1646

3rd Movement
1st Theme
C   B1647

3rd Movement
2nd Theme   B1648

4th Movement
1st Theme   B1649

4th Movement
2nd Theme   B1650

4th Movement
3rd Theme   B1651

4th Movement
4th Theme   B1652

4th Movement
5th Theme   B1653

4th Movement / 6th Theme	B1654
4th Movement / 7th Theme	B1655
Trio in A Minor Op.114, Cl. or Viola, Cello & Pft. — 1st Movement / 1st Theme	B1656
1st Movement / 2nd Theme	B1657
2nd Movement	B1658
3rd Movement	B1659
4th Movement / 1st Theme	B1660
4th Movement / 2nd Theme	B1661
4th Movement / 3rd Theme	B1662
Trio in B Op.8 Vn., Cello & Pft. — 1st Movement / 1st Theme	B1663
1st Movement / 2nd Theme	B1664
2nd Movement / 1st Theme	B1665
2nd Movement / 2nd Theme	B1666
3rd Movement / 1st Theme	B1667
3rd Movement / 2nd Theme	B1668
4th Movement / 1st Theme	B1669
4th Movement / 2nd Theme	B1670
Trio in C Op.87, Vn., Cello & Pft. — 1st Movement / 1st Theme	B1671
1st Movement / 2nd Theme	B1672
1st Movement / 3rd Theme	B1673

3rd Movement 2nd Theme — B1694

4th Movement 1st Theme — B1695

4th Movement 2nd Theme — B1696

Variations on a Theme of Haydn, Op.56a, Orch. — Theme — B1697

Variations on a Theme of Schumann, Op.23, Pft. 4 Hands — B1698

Waltzes, Op. 39, Pft. — No. 1 — B1699

No. 2 — B1700

No. 3 — B1701

No. 4 — B1702

No. 7 — B1703

No. 8 — B1704

No. 9 — B1705

No.10 — B1706

No.11 — B1707

No.12 — B1708

No.14 — B1709

No.15 — B1710

No.16 — B1711

BRITTEN, Benjamin (1913-1976)

Peter Grimes, Four Sea Interludes, Op. 33a, Orch.

1st Interlude Dawn — B1711

By permission of the copyright owner, Boosey and Hawkes, Inc.

BRITTEN

2nd Interlude
Sunday Morning
1st Theme — B1711b

2nd Theme — B1711c

3rd Interlude
Moonlight — B1711d

4th Interlude
Storm
1st Theme — B1711e

4th Interlude
2nd Theme
A — B1711f

2nd Theme
B
(Simultaneous With A) — B1711g

3rd Theme — B1711h

4th Theme — B1711i

Phantasy-Quartet,
Oboe, Vn., Viola & Vcl.
By permission of the copyright owner,
Boosey and Hawkes, Inc.
1st Theme — B1711j

2nd Theme — B1711k

3rd Theme — B1711l

4th Theme — B1711m

Simple Symphony
Copyright by the
Oxford University Press
Reproduced
by permission.
1st Movement
(Boisterous Bourrée)
1st Theme — B1712

2nd Theme — B1713

2nd Movement
(Playful Pizzicato)
1st Theme — B1714

2nd Theme — B1715

3rd Movement
(Sentimental Sarabande)
1st Theme — B1716

2nd Theme — B1717

4th Movement
(Frolicsome Finale)
1st Theme — B1718

2nd Theme — B1719

Variations on a Theme of
Frank Bridge, Op. 10, Orch.
By permission
of the copyright owner,
Boosey and Hawkes, Inc.

Theme

B1719a

BRUCH, Max (1838-1920)

Concerto No. 1
in G Minor, Vn. & Orch.

Permission for reprint
granted by Durand
& Cie, Paris.
Elkan-Vogel Co.,Inc.
Philadelphia, Copyright
Owners.

1st Movement Intro.   B1720

1st Movement 1st Theme   B1721

1st Movement 2nd Theme   B1722

1st Movement 2nd Theme   B1723

2nd Movement 1st Theme, A   B1724

2nd Movement 1st Theme, B   B1725

3rd Movement 1st Theme   B1726

3rd Movement 2nd Theme   B1727

Concerto No. 2
in D Minor, Vn. & Orch.
By permission of Associated
Music Publishers, Inc.

1st Movement 1st Theme   B1728

1st Movement 2nd Theme   B1729

2nd Movement 1st Theme   B1730

2nd Movement 2nd Theme   B1731

3rd Movement 1st Theme, A   B1732

3rd Movement 1st Theme, B   B1733

3rd Movement 2nd Theme   B1734

Kol Nidrei (Based on
Traditional Hebrew Themes)
Vn. & Pft.
By permission of Associated
Music Publishers, Inc.

1st Theme   B1735

2nd Theme   B1736

3rd Theme   B1737

BRUCKNER, Anton (1824-1896)

Overture in G Minor
By permission of Associated Music Publishers, Inc.

- 1st Theme — B1738
- 2nd Theme — B1739
- 3rd Theme — B1740

Quintet in F, Str.
By permission of International Music Co.

- 1st Movement 1st Theme — B1741
- 1st Movement 2nd Theme — B1742
- 2nd Movement 1st Theme — B1743
- 2nd Movement 2nd Theme — B1744
- 3rd Movement — B1745
- 4th Movement — B1746

Symphony No. 3 in D Minor
Copyright by Lienau, Licensed by SESAC, Inc., N. Y.

- 1st Movement 1st Theme — B1747
- 1st Movement 2nd Theme — B1748
- 1st Movement 3rd Theme — B1749
- 1st Movement 4th Theme — B1750
- 2nd Movement 1st Theme — B1751
- 2nd Movement 2nd Theme — B1752
- 2nd Movement 3rd Theme — B1753
- 3rd Movement 1st Theme — B1754
- 3rd Movement 2nd Theme, A — B1755
- 3rd Movement 2nd Theme, B — B1756

4th Movement 1st Theme — B1757

4th Movement 2nd Theme — B1758

4th Movement 3rd Theme — B1759

Symphony No.4. in E Flat,"Romantic"
By permission of Associated Music Publishers, Inc.

1st Movement 1st Theme — B1760

1st Movement 2nd Theme — B1761

1st Movement 3rd Theme — B1762

2nd Movement 1st Theme — B1763

2nd Movement 2nd Theme — B1764

3rd Movement 1st Theme — B1765

3rd Movement 2nd Theme — B1766

3rd Movement 3rd Theme — B1767

4th Movement 1st Theme — B1768

4th Movement 2nd Theme — B1769

4th Movement 3rd Theme — B1770

4th Movement 4th Theme — B1771

Symphony No.5, in B Flat,
By permission of Associated Music Publishers, Inc.

1st Movement Intro. — B1772

1st Movement 1st Theme — B1773

1st Movement 2nd Theme — B1774

2nd Movement 1st Theme — B1775

2nd Movement 2nd Theme — B1776

1st Movement / 2nd Theme — B1797

1st Movement / 3rd Theme — B1798

2nd Movement / 1st Theme — B1799

2nd Movement / 2nd Theme — B1800

3rd Movement / 1st Theme — B1801

3rd Movement / 2nd Theme — B1802

BULL, John (1563-1628)

A Gigge (Doctor Bull's My Selfe) Pft.-Harpsi. — B1803

The King's Hunt, Pft.-Harpsi. — B1804

BUXTEHUDE, Dietrich (1637-1707)

Chaconne, in E Minor, Organ — B1805

Passacaglia, Organ — B1806

Prelude & Fugue, No.6 in E Minor, Organ / 1st Theme Prelude — B1807

2nd Theme Fugue 1 — B1808

3rd Theme Fugue 2 — B1809

4th Theme Fugue 3 — B1810

Prelude & Fugue, No.8 in E, Organ / 1st Theme Prelude — B1811

2nd Theme Fugue — B1812

Prelude & Fugue, No.14, in G Minor, Organ / 1st Theme Prelude — B1813

2nd Theme Fugue I — B1814

3rd Theme Fugue II — B1815

Toccata No. 20 in F, Organ — 1st Theme — B1816

2nd Theme — B1817

Toccata No. 21 in F, Organ — 1st Theme — B1818

2nd Theme — B1819

Toccata No. 22 in G Organ — B1820

BYRD, William (1543-1623)

The Bells
Fitzwilliam Virginal Book No. 69, Harpsi. — 1st Theme — B1821

2nd Theme — B1822

3rd Theme — B1823

The Carman's Whistle
Fitzwilliam Virginal Book, No. 58
Variations for Harpsi. — B1824

Galliard
Fitzwilliam Virginal Book No. 92
Harpsi. — B1825

Galliard, The Earl of Salisbury
from The Parthenia, Harpsi. — B1826

Sir John Grayes' Galliard
Fitzwilliam Virginal Book No. 191, Harpsi. — B1827

Miserere Fitzwilliam
Virginal Book No. 177
Organ or Harpsi. — 1st Theme — B1828

2nd Theme — B1829

O Mistris Myne Fitzwilliam Virginal
Book No. 66, Variations for Harpsi. — B1830

Pavan, The Earl of Salisbury
from The Parthenia
Harpsi. — Theme, A — B1831

Theme, B — B1832

Rowland, Harpsi.
Fitzwilliam Virginal Book No. 160 — B1833

Sellenger's Round, Harpsi.
Fitzwilliam Virginal Book No. 64   B1834

La Volta, Harpsi.
Fitzwilliam Virginal Book No. 155   B1835

Wolsey's Wilde, Harpsi.
Fitzwilliam Virginal Book No. 157   B1836

CABANILLAS, Juan (1644-1712)

Passacalles in D Minor, Organ   C1

Tiento De Falsas, Del 4° Tomo, Organ   C2

CABEZÓN, Antonio de (1510-1566)

Tiento, Del 1° Tomo, Organ   C3

Tiento, Del 4° Tomo, Organ   C4

Variations on "El Canto Del Caballero"   C5

CADMAN, Charles Wakefield (1881-1946)

Thunderbird Suite, Orch.
(Music for a Production
of Norman Bel Geddes)
(Based on American
Indian Tunes)
Copyright by
White-Smith
Music Publishers
Co., Boston.

1st Movement
From the
Village   C6

2nd Movement
Before the Sunrise   C7

3rd Movement
Nuwana's Love Song
(Blackfeet Indian Tune)   C8

4th Movement
Night Song (Blackfeet Indian Tune)   C9

5th Movement
Wolf Song (War Dance)   C10

CAIX d'HERVELOIS, Louis de (1670-1760)

Suite No. 1, in A,
Cello & Pft.

1st Movement
La Milanese   C11

2nd Movement
Sarabande   C12

3rd Movement
Minuet   C13

Pupazzetti, Orch.
By permission of the
copyright holders,
J. & W. Chester, Ltd., 11
Great Marlborough
Street, London, W. 1.

1st Movement
1st Theme
Marcietta — C51

1st Movement
2nd Theme — C52

2nd Movement
Berceuse — C53

3rd Movement
Serenata — C54

4th Movement
Notturnino — C55

5th Movement
1st Theme
Polka — C56

5th Movement
2nd Theme — C57

Serenata
Cl., Fg., Tpt., Vn. & Cello
By permission of Associated
Music Publishers, Inc.

1st Movement
Marcia — C58

2nd Movement
Minuet — C59

3rd Movement
1st Theme
Notturno — C60

3rd Movement
2nd Theme — C61

4th Movement
1st Theme
Gavotte — C62

4th Movement
2nd Theme
Musette — C63

5th Movement
Cavatina — C64

6th Movement
Finale-Tarantella — C65

Siciliana E Burlesca,
Vn., Cello, Pft.
Copyright 1919 by
G. Ricordi & Co., Inc.

1st Movement
Siciliana — C66

2nd Movement
Burlesca — C67

CHABRIER, Alexis Emmanuel (1841-1894)

Bourrée Fantasque,
Pft., Arr. for Orch., F. Mottl
By permission of
M M Enoch & Cie,
Music Publishers,
27 Boulevard
des Italiens, Paris

1st Theme — C68

2nd Theme,
A — C69

Espāna,
Rhapsody for Orch.
By permission of
M M Enoch & Cie.,
Music Publishers,
27 Boulevard
des Italiens, Paris.

Habañera, Pft. or Orch.
By permission of M M Enoch & Cie.,
Music Publishers,
27 Boulevard des Italiens, Paris.

Joyeuse Marche, Orch.
By permission of
M M Enoch & Cie.,
Music Publishers,
27 Boulevard
des Italiens, Paris.

Gwendoline,
Overture
By permission of
M M Enoch & Cie.,
Music Publishers,
27 Boulevard
des Italiens, Paris.

Pièces Pittoresques, Pft.

2nd Theme B — C70
1st Theme — C71[1]
2nd Theme — C72[2]
3rd Theme — C73
4th Theme — C74
5th Theme — C75[3]
— C76
Intro. — C77
1st Theme — C78
2nd Theme — C79
3rd Theme — C80
1st Theme — C81
2nd Theme — C82
3rd Theme — C83
No. 4 Sous Bois — C84
No. 6 Idylle — C85
No. 7 Danse Villageoise 1st Theme — C86
2nd Theme — C87
No. 8, Improvisation — C88
No. 10 Scherzo-Valse 1st Theme — C89

1. Same as W98.   2. Same as W99.   3. Same as W100.

Le Roi Malgré Lui, Orch.
By permission of
M M Enoch & Cie.,
Music Publishers,
27 Boulevard
des Italiens, Paris

2nd Theme — C90

3rd Theme — C91

Prelude — C92

Danse Slave
1st Theme — C93

2nd Theme — C94

Fête Polonaise
1st Theme — C95

2nd Theme — C96

3rd Theme — C97

CHADWICK, George W. (1854-1931)

Symphonic Sketches
Copyright renewal assigned
1935 to G. Schirmer, Inc.

I. Jubilee
1st Theme — C98

2nd Theme — C99

3rd Theme, A — C100

3rd Theme, B — C101

4th Theme — C102

II. Nöel — C103

CHAMINADE, Cécile (1857-1944)

Air de Ballet, Pft. — C104

Callirhoë, in G
Air de Ballet. Pft. — C105

The Flatterer, Pft. — C106

Scarf Dance, Pft.
1st Theme   2nd Theme — C107

3rd Theme (Orch. Version) — C108

Serenade, Pft. — C109

Spanish Serenade, Vn. & Pft. Arr. by Kreisler © Foley — C110

CHAUSSON, Ernest (1855-1899)

Concerto in D Pft., Vn. & Str. Quartet Op. 21
Copyright by Editions Salabert Editions Salabert, 22 Rue Chaucat, Paris Salabert, Inc., 1 East 57 St., N. Y.

1st Movement 1st Theme — C111
1st Movement 2nd Theme — C112
2nd Movement Sicilienne — C113
3rd Movement 1st Theme — C114
3rd Movement 2nd Theme — C115
4th Movement 1st Theme — C116
4th Movement 2nd Theme — C117

Poème, Op. 25, Vn. & Orch.
By permission of Associated Music Publishers, Inc.

Intro. — C118
1st Theme — C119
2nd Theme — C120
3rd Theme — C121

Quartet, Op. 30 Str. & Pft.
By permission of International Music Co.

1st Movement 1st Theme — C122
1st Movement 2nd Theme — C123
1st Movement 3rd Theme — C124
2nd Movement 1st Theme — C125
2nd Movement 2nd Theme — C126

3rd Movement / 1st Theme — C127
3rd Movement / 2nd Theme — C128
4th Movement / 1st Theme — C129
4th Movement / 2nd Theme — C130

Symphony in B Flat, Op. 20

1st Movement / 1st Theme — C131
1st Movement / 2nd Theme — C132
1st Movement / 3rd Theme — C133
1st Movement / 4th Theme — C134
2nd Movement / 1st Theme, A — C135
2nd Movement / 1st Theme, B — C136
2nd Movement / 2nd Theme — C137
3rd Movement / 1st Theme — C138
3rd Movement / 2nd Theme — C139

CHAVEZ, Carlos (1899-   )

Concerto
Pft. & Orch.
Copyright 1942
by G. Schirmer Inc

1st Movement / 1st Theme — C140
1st Movement / 2nd Theme — C141
2nd Movement — C142
3rd Movement / 1st Theme — C143
3rd Movement / 2nd Theme — C144

Sinfonia India
By permission of the
copyright owners,
G. Schirmer, Inc.

1st Theme, A — C145

1st Theme
B — C146

2nd Theme — C147

3rd Theme — C148

4th Theme — C149

5th Theme — C150

CHERUBINI, Maria Luigi (1760-1842)

Les Abencerages
Overture

Intro. — C151

1st Theme — C152

2nd Theme — C153

3rd Theme — C154

Anacreon
Overture

Intro. — C155

1st Theme — C156

2nd Theme — C157

Medea
Overture

1st Theme — C158

2nd Theme — C159

3rd Theme — C160

Der Wasserträger
(Les Deux Journées)
Overture

Intro. — C161

1st Theme — C162

2nd Theme — C163

CHOPIN, Frédéric (1810-1849)

Ballade I, Op. 23 — 1st Theme — C164

2nd Theme — C165

Ballade II, Op. 38 — C166

Ballade III, Op. 47 — 1st Theme — C167

2nd Theme — C168

Ballade IV, Op. 52 — C169

Barcarolle, Op. 60 — C170

Berceuse, Op. 57 — C171

Concerto No. 1, in E Minor, Op. 11 Pft. & Orch. — 1st Movement 1st Theme — C172

1st Movement 2nd Theme — C173

1st Movement 3rd Theme — C174

2nd Movement 1st Theme — C175

2nd Movement 2nd Theme — C176

3rd Movement 1st Theme — C177

3rd Movement 2nd Theme — C178

Concerto No. 2 in F Minor, Op. 21 Pft. & Orch. — 1st Movement 1st Theme — C179

1st Movement 2nd Theme — C180

2nd Movement — C181

3rd Movement 1st Theme — C182

3rd Movement 2nd Theme — C183

Ecossaise, No. 1, Op. 72, No. 3 — C184

Ecossaise, No. 2, Op. 72, No. 4 — C185

Études, Op. 10
No. 1 in C — C186

No. 2 in A Minor — C187

No. 3 in E — C188

No. 4 in C Sharp Minor — C189

No. 5 in G Flat "Black Key" — C190

No. 6 in E Flat Minor — C191

No. 7 in C — C192

No. 8 in F
Simultaneous
1st Theme — C193
2nd Theme — C194

No. 9 in F Minor — C195

No. 10 in A Flat — C196

No. 11 in E Flat — C197

No. 12 in C Minor "Revolutionary" — C198

Etudes, Op. 25
No. 1 in A Flat "Harp" — C198a

No. 2 in F Minor — C199

No. 3 in F — C200

No. 4 in A Minor — C201

No. 5 in E Minor   1st Theme   C202

2nd Theme   C203

No. 6 in G Sharp Minor   C204

No. 7 in C Sharp Minor   C205

No. 8 in D Flat   C206

No. 9 in G Flat "Butterfly"   C207

No. 10 in B Minor   Intro.   C208

1st Theme   C209

2nd Theme   C210

No. 11 in A Minor "Winter Wind"   C211

No. 12 in C Minor   C212

Posth. Etudes
No. 1 in F Minor   C213

No. 2 in D Flat   C214

No. 3 in A Flat   C215

Fantaisie in F Minor, Op. 49   1st Theme   C216

2nd Theme   C217

3rd Theme   C218

4th Theme   C219

Impromptu, Op. 29   1st Theme   C220

3rd Theme   C221

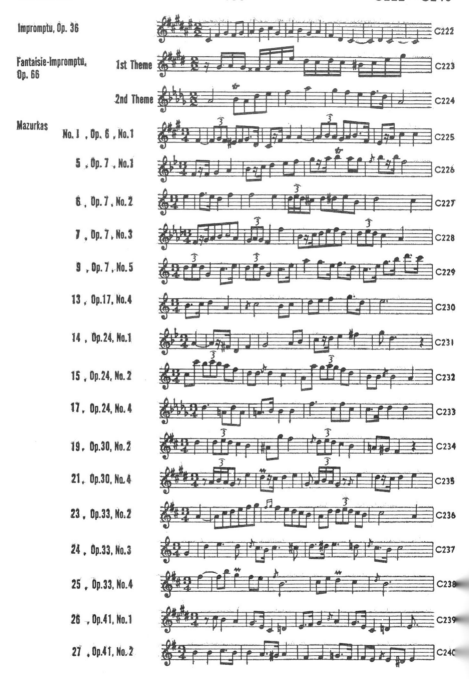

Impromptu, Op. 36 — C222

Fantaisie-Impromptu, Op. 66 — 1st Theme — C223

2nd Theme — C224

Mazurkas

No. 1 , Op. 6 , No. 1 — C225

5 , Op. 7 , No. 1 — C226

6 , Op. 7 , No. 2 — C227

7 , Op. 7 , No. 3 — C228

9 , Op. 7 , No. 5 — C229

13 , Op. 17, No. 4 — C230

14 , Op. 24, No. 1 — C231

15 , Op. 24, No. 2 — C232

17 , Op. 24, No. 4 — C233

19 , Op. 30, No. 2 — C234

21 , Op. 30, No. 4 — C235

23 , Op. 33, No. 2 — C236

24 , Op. 33, No. 3 — C237

25 , Op. 33, No. 4 — C238

26 , Op. 41, No. 1 — C239

27 , Op. 41, No. 2 — C240

No. 30 , Op.50, No.1   C241

31 ,Op.50, No.2 1st Theme   C242

2nd Theme   C243

32,Op.50, No.3 1st Theme   C244

2nd Theme   C245

36, Op.59, No.1   C246

38, Op.59, No.3   C247

39, Op.63, No.1   C248

41, Op.63, No.3   C249

42, Op.67, No.1   C250

43, Op. 67 No.2   C251

44, Op.67, No.3   C252

45 ,Op.67, No.4   C253

47 ,Op.68, No.2 1st Theme   C254

2nd Theme   C255

Nocturnes
  Op. 9, No.1
  in B Flat Minor   1st Theme   C256

2nd Theme   C257

Op. 9 , No.2
in E Flat   C258

Op. 9, No.3 in B   C259

Op.15 , No.1 in F — C260

Op.15 , No.2 in F Sharp — C261

Op.15 , No.3 in G Minor — C262

Op.27 , No.1 in C Sharp Minor — C263

Op.27 , No.2 in D Flat — C264

Op.32 , No.1 in B — C265

Op.32 , No.2 in A Flat — C266

Op.37 , No.1 in G Minor — C267

Op.37 , No.2 in G — C268

Op.48 , No.1 in C Minor — 1st Theme — C269

2nd Theme — C270

Op.48 , No.2 in F Sharp Minor — C271

Op.55 , No.1 in F Minor — C272

Op.55 , No.2 in E Flat — C273

Op.62 , No.1 in B — C274

Op.62 , No.2 in E — C275

Op.72 , No.1 in E Minor — C276

Andante Spianato & Polonaise, Op. 22 — 1st Theme Andante — C277

2nd Theme Polonaise — C278

Polonaises
Op. 26, No. 1 in C Sharp Minor   C279

Op. 40, No. 1 in A   1st Theme   C280

2nd Theme   C281

Op. 40, No. 2 in C Minor   C282

Op. 44 in F Sharp Minor   C283

Op. 53 in A Flat   1st Theme   C284

2nd Theme   C285

Preludes, Op. 28, No. 1   C286

2   C287

3   C288

4   C289

5   C290

6   C291

7   C292

8   C293

9   C294

10   C295

11   C296

12   C297

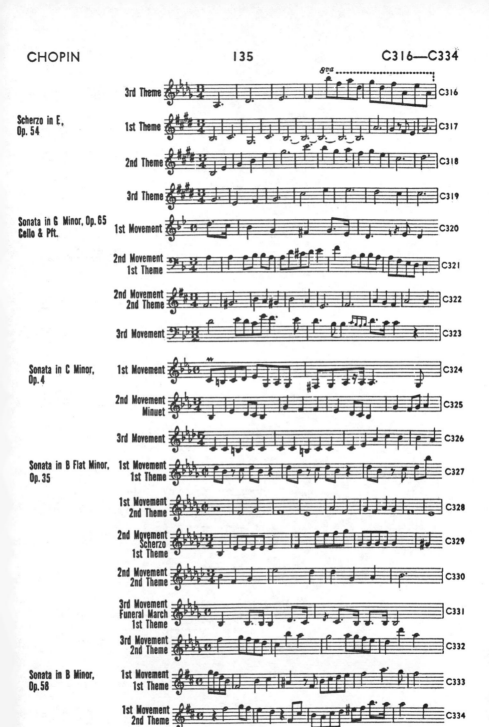

Scherzo in E, Op. 54

Sonata in G Minor, Op. 65 Cello & Pft.

Sonata in C Minor, Op. 4

Sonata in B Flat Minor, Op. 35

Sonata in B Minor, Op. 58

2nd Movement   C335

3rd Movement   C336

4th Movement   C337

Waltzes

Op.18 in E Flat   C338

  C339

Op.34, No.1 in A Flat   C340

  C341

  C342

Op.34, No.2 in A Minor   C343

  C344

Op.34, No.3 in F   C345

Op.42, in A Flat   C346

  C347

Op.64, No.1 in D Flat
"Minute"   C348

Op.64, No.2 in C Sharp Minor   C349

  C350

Op.64, No.3 in A Flat   C351

Op.69, No.1 in A Flat   C352

Op.69, No.2
in B Minor   1st Theme   C353

2nd Theme — C354

Op. 70, No. 1 in G Flat — 1st Theme — C355

2nd Theme — C356

Op. 70, No. 2 in F Minor — C357

Op. 70, No. 3 in D Flat — C358

Waltz in E Minor, Posth. — 1st Theme — C359

2nd Theme — C360

Waltz in E, Posth. — C361

CIMAROSA, Domenico (1749-1801)

Il Matrimonio Segreto Overture — 1st Theme — C362

2nd Theme — C363

CLEMENTI, Muzio (1752-1832)

Sonata in B Flat, Pft. Op. 47, No. 2 — 1st Movement — C364

2nd Movement — C365

3rd Movement 1st Theme — C366

3rd Movement 2nd Theme — C367

Sonata in G Minor, Pft. Didone Abbandonata Op. 50, No. 3 — 1st Movement Intro. — C368

1st Movement — C369

2nd Movement — C370

3rd Movement — C371

Sonata No. 1 in B Flat
2 Pianos, 4 Hands

1st Movement
1st Theme — C372

1st Movement
2nd Theme — C373

2nd Movement — C374

3rd Movement — C375

Sonata No. 2 in B Flat
2 Pianos, 4 Hands

1st Movement
1st Theme — C376

1st Movement
2nd Theme — C377

2nd Movement
Tempo Di Minuetto — C378

COLERIDGE-TAYLOR, Samuel (1875-1912)

Othello Suite, Orch.

1st Movement
Dance
1st Theme — C387

1st Movement
2nd Theme — C388

2nd Movement
Children's Intermezzo
1st Theme — C389

2nd Movement
2nd Theme — C390

3rd Movement
Funeral March
1st Theme — C391

3rd Movement
2nd Theme — C392

4th Movement
Willow Song — C393

5th Movement
Military March
1st Theme — C394

5th Movement
2nd Theme — C395

Petite Suite de Concert
Orch.
Le Caprice de Nanette

1st Movement
1st Theme — C396

By permission of the copyright
owner, Boosey and Hawkes, Inc.

1st Movement / 2nd Theme — C397

Demande et Réponse — 2nd Movement / 1st Theme — C398

2nd Movement / 2nd Theme — C399

Un Sonnet D'Amour — 3rd Movement / 1st Theme — C400

La Tarantelle Frétillante — 3rd Movement / 2nd Theme — C401

4th Movement — C402

COPLAND, Aaron (1900-   )

Appalachian Spring Ballet
By permission of the copyright owner, Boosey and Hawkes, Inc. — 1st Theme — C403

2nd Theme — C404

3rd Theme — C405

4th Theme, A — C406

4th Theme, B — C407

5th Theme — **Shaker Melody "The Gift To Be Simple"** — C408

6th Theme — C409

Billy the Kid, Ballet
The Open Prairie
By permission of the copyright owner, Boosey and Hawkes, Inc. — Intro. / 1st Theme — C410

Intro. / 2nd Theme — C411

Street in a Frontier Town (Cowboy Tune) — Scene I / 1st Theme — C412

The Streets of Laredo — 2nd Theme — C413

(Cowboy Tune) — 3rd Theme — C414

(Cowboy Tune) — 4th Theme — C415

COPLAND

The Card Game — Scene II, 1st Theme — C416

Macabre Dance — 3rd Theme — C417

Billy in Prison — 4th Theme — C418

Scene III — C419

Concerto for Orch. & Pft.
Copyright 1929,
Cos Cob Press, Inc.

1st Movement, 1st Theme, A — C420

1st Movement, 1st Theme, B — C421

1st Movement, 2nd Theme — C422

2nd Movement, 1st Theme — C423

2nd Movement, 2nd Theme — C424

2nd Movement, 3rd Theme — C425

2nd Movement, 4th Theme — C426

Dance Symphony
Copyright 1931,
Cos Cob Press, Inc.

Intro. — C427

1st Movement, 1st Theme — C428

1st Movement, 2nd Theme — C429

1st Movement, 3rd Theme — C430

2nd Movement, 1st Theme — C431

2nd Movement, 2nd Theme — C432

3rd Movement, 1st Theme — C433

3rd Movement, 2nd Theme — C434

3rd Movement, 3rd Theme — C435

Music for the Theatre, Small Orch.
Copyright 1932,
Cos Cob Press, Inc.

1st Movement
Prologue
1st Theme   C436

1st Movement
2nd Theme   C437

2nd Movement
Dance
1st Theme   C438

2nd Movement
2nd Theme   C439

3rd Movement
Interlude
1st Theme   C440

3rd Movement
2nd Theme   C441

4th Movement
Burlesque
1st Theme   C442

4th Movement
2nd Theme   C443

Nocturne, Vn. & Pft.
By permission of the copyright
owner, Boosey and Hawkes, Inc.

1st Theme   C444

2nd Theme   C445

Passacaglia, Pft.
By permission of the copyright
owner, Boosey and Hawkes, Inc.   C446

Piano Variations
Copyright 1932, Cos Cob Press, Inc.

Theme   C447

El Salon Mexico, Orch.
By permission of the copyright
owner, Boosey and Hawkes, Inc.

Intro.   C448

1st Theme   C449

2nd Theme
Trumpet Solo   C450

3rd Theme   C451

4th Theme   C452

5th Theme   C453

6th Theme   C454

7th Theme
Clarinet Solo   C455

Two Pieces, Str. Orch.
Copyright by Arrow
Music Press, Inc., N. Y.

1st Movement
Lento Molto
1st Theme   C456

1st Movement
2nd Theme   C457

2nd Movement
Rondino
1st Theme   C458

2nd Movement
2nd Theme   C459

Vitebsk, (Study on a Jewish Theme) Vn., Cello & Pft.
Copyright 1934,
Cos Cob Press, Inc.

Theme   C460

CORELLI, Arcangelo (1653-1713)

Concerto Grosso in G Minor, String & Harpsi. Op. 6, No.8 Christmas Concerto

1st Movement
Intro.   C461

1st Movement
1st Theme   C462

1st Movement
2nd Theme   C463

2nd Movement   C464

3rd Movement   C465

4th Movement   C466

5th Movement
Pastorale   C467

Concerto Grosso in B Flat, Op. 6, No.11 Str. Orch.

1st Movement
1st Theme
Preludio   C468

1st Movement
2nd Theme   C469

2nd Movement
Allemande,
A   C470

2nd Movement
Allemande,
B   C471

3rd Movement
Intro.   C472

3rd Movement   C473

4th Movement
Sarabande   C474

5th Movement Giga   C475

Sonata in G Minor, Op. 5 , No.5 Vn. & Harpsi.   1st Movement   C476

2nd Movement   C477

3rd Movement   C478

4th Movement   C479

5th Movement Gigue   C480

Sonata in E Minor, Op. 5 , No. 8 Vn. & Harpsi.   1st Movement Preludio   C481

2nd Movement Allemande   C482

3rd Movement Sarabande   C483

4th Movement Giga   C484

Sonata in D Minor, Op. 5, No. 12 "La Folia"   C485

Sonata Da Camera, B Flat, Op. 2, No.5 2 Vns., Viola Da Gamba, Harpsi.   1st Movement Preludio   C486

2nd Movement Allemande   C487

3rd Movement Sarabande   C488

4th Movement Tempo Di Gavotta   C489

Sonata Da Camera, G, Op. 2, No. 12 2 Vns., Viola Da Gamba, Harpsi.   C490

CORNELIUS, Peter (1824-1874)

Der Barbier Von Bagdad Overture   1st Theme   C491

2nd Theme   C492

3rd Theme   C493

COUPERIN, François (1668-1733)

Les Abeilles, Harpsi.   C494

La Bandoline, Harpsi.   C495

Les Baricades Misterieuses, Harpsi.   C496

Le Bavolet-Flotant, Harpsi.   C497

Les Bergeries, Harpsi.   Rondeau   C498

La Bersan, Harpsi.   C499

Les Calotins et Les Calotines, Harpsi.   C500

Le Carillon de Cythere, Harpsi.   C501

La Commére, Harpsi.   C502

Concert No. 8 in G,   1st Movement
Dans Le Goùt Théatral   Overture
1st Theme   C503

2nd Theme   C504

2nd Movement
Grande Retournele   C505

3rd Movement
Air No. 1   C506

4th Movement
Air Tendre No. 1   C507

5th Movement
Air Léger No. 1   C508

6th Movement
Loure   C509

7th Movement
Air No. 2   C510

8th Movement
Sarabande Brave
Et Tendre   C511

9th Movement
Air Léger No. 2   C512

Concert Royal, No. 4 1st Movement Prelude — C533
in E Minor, Chamber Orch.

2nd Movement Allemande — C534

3rd Movement Courante Françoise — C535

4th Movement Courante à L'Italiéne — C536

5th Movement Sarabande — C537

6th Movement Rigaudon — C538

7th Movement Forlane — C539

La Croûilli ou La Couperinéte, Harpsi. — C540

Le Dodo, Harpsi. — C541

Les Fastes de La Grande Et Ancienne Ménestrandises, Harpsi. — C542
Act I (Les Notables et Jurés-Ménestrandises)

Act II (Les Viéleux et Les Gueux) 1st Theme — C543

2nd Theme — C544

Act III (Les Jongleurs, Sauteurs, et Saltimbiques) — C545

Act IV (Les Invalides) — C546

Act V (Desordre et Deroute de Toute La Troupe) — C547

La Fleurie ou La Tendre Nanètte Harpsi. — C548

Les Folies Françaises Harpsi. 1st Movement La Virginité — C549

2nd Movement La Pudeur — C550

3rd Movement L'Ardeur — C551

4th Movement L'Esperance — C552

5th Movement
La Fidelité   C553

6th Movement
Le Perseverance   C554

7th Movement
La Langueur   C555

8th Movement
Le Coqueterie   C556

9th Movement
Les Vieux Galans   C557

10th Movement
Les Coucous Bénévoles   C558

11th Movement
La Jalousie Taciturne   C559

12th Movement
La Frénésie   C560

Le Gazouillement, Harpsi.   C561

L'Himen-Amour, Harpsi.   C562

La Julliet,
Harpsi. or Fl., Cello & Harpsi.   C563

Les Langueurs-Tendres, Harpsi.   C564

Les Moissonneurs, Harpsi.   C565

Le Moucheron, Harpsi.   C566

Musette de Choisi, Harpsi.   C567

Musette de Taverni, Harpsi.   C568

La Nanète, Harpsi.   C569

Passacaille, Harpsi.   Theme A   C570

Theme B   C571

Les Petits Moulins à Vent
Harpsi.   C572

Le Rossignol en Amour, Harpsi — C573

Soeur Monique, Harpsi. — C574

Les Tambourins, Harpsi. — C575

Le Tic-Toc-Chic ou Les Maillotins, Harpsi. — C576

Les Vergers Fleuris, Harpsi. — C577

Messe Pour Les Convents, Organ — Offertoire Sur Les Grands Jeux — C578

Recit de Chromhorne — C579

Messe Pour Les Paroisses, Organ — Fugue on the Kyrie — C580

Récit de Chromhorne — C581

Offertoire Sur Les Grands Jeux — 1st Theme — C582

2nd Theme — C583

CUI César (1835-1918)

Orientale, Op. 50, No.9, Vn. & Pft.
Copyright renewal assigned 1945 to G. Schirmer, Inc. — C584

Tarantella, Op. 12, Orch.
By permission of Associated Music Publishers, Inc. — 1st Theme — C585

2nd Theme — C586

3rd Theme — C587

4th Theme — C588

DAQUIN, Louis Claude (1694-1772)

Le Coucou, Harpsi. — 1st Theme — D1

2nd Theme — D2

La Guitarre, Harpsi. — D3

L'Hirondelle, Harpsi. — D4

Musette Et Tambourin Harpsi. — 1st Theme Musette — D5

2nd Theme Tambourin — D6

Noël No. 9, (Sur Les Flutes), Organ — D7

Noël No. 10, Organ — D8

DARGOMIJSKY, Alexander Sergeivich (1813-1869)

Roussalka, Opera

Danse Slave — D9

Gypsy Dance — D10

Dance of the Nymphs 1st Theme — D11

2nd Theme — D12

DEBUSSY, Claude (1862-1918)

Prélude A L'Après-Midi D'Un Faune (Afternoon of A Faun) Orch. — 1st Theme — D13

Permission for reprint granted by Jean Jobert, Paris. Elkan-Vogel Co. Inc., Philadelphia, Copyright Owners

2nd Theme — D14

Arabesque No. 1, in E, Pft. — 1st Theme, A — D15

Permission for reprint granted by Durand & Cie, Paris. Elkan-Vogel Co., Inc., Philadelphia, Copyright Owners

1st Theme, B — D16

2nd Theme — D17

Arabesque No. 2, in G, Pft. — 1st Theme — D18

Permission for reprint granted by Durand & Cie, Paris. Elkan-Vogel Co., Inc., Philadelphia, Copyright Owners.

2nd Theme — D19

Ballade, Pft. — 1st Theme — D20

Permission for reprint granted by Jean Jobert, Paris. Elkan-Vogel Co., Philadelphia, Inc. Copyright Owners.

2nd Theme — D21

Children's Corner Suite, Pft.
Permission for reprint granted by Durand & Cie, Paris. Elkan-Vogel Co., Inc., Philadelphia, Copyright Owners.

Doctor Gradus Ad Parnassum — D22

Jimbo's Lullaby — D23

Serenade of the Doll — D24

The Little Shepherd 1st Theme — D25

2nd Theme — D26

Golliwogg's Cake Walk 1st Theme — D27

2nd Theme — D28

3rd Theme (Parody on Tristan) — D29

Danses, Harp
Permission for reprint granted by Durand & Cie, Paris. Elkan-Vogel Co., Inc., Philadelphia, Copyright Owners.

I Danse Sacrée — D30

II Danse Profane — D31

Danse (Tarantelle Styrienne), Pft.
Permission for reprint granted by Jean Jobert, Paris. Elkan-Vogel Co., Inc. Philadelphia, Copyright Owners.

1st Theme — D32

2nd Theme — D33

Estampes, Pft.
Permission for reprint granted by Durand & Cie, Paris. Elkan-Vogel Co. Inc. Philadelphia Copyright Owners.

Pagodes — D34

La Soirée dans Grenade 1st Theme — D35

2nd Theme — D36

3rd Theme — D37

Jardins Sous La Pluie (Gardens in the Rain) 1st Theme — D38

2nd Theme — D39

L'Isle Joyeuse, Pft.
Permission for reprint granted by Durand & Cie, Paris. Elkan-Vogel Co., Inc., Philadelphia, Copyright Owners.

Intro. — D40

1st Theme — D41

2nd Theme — D42

3rd Theme — D43

Gigues, from Images, Orch., No. 1
Permission for reprint granted by Durand & Cie, Paris. Elkan-Vogel Co., Inc. Philadelphia, Copyright Owners.

1st Theme — D44

2nd Theme — D45

3rd Theme — D46

Iberia, from Images, Orch., No. 2
Par Les Rues et Par Les Chemins (Along the Streets and Roads)
Permission for reprint granted by Durand & Cie, Paris. Elkan-Vogel Co., Inc. Philadelphia, Copyright Owners.

1st Movement 1st Theme — D47

1st Movement 2nd Theme — D48

1st Movement 3rd Theme — D49

1st Movement 4th Theme — D50

1st Movement 5th Theme — D51

1st Movement 6th Theme — D52

Les Parfums de La Nuit (Perfumes of the Night)

2nd Movement Intro. — D53

2nd Movement 1st Theme — D54

2nd Movement 2nd Theme — D55

2nd Movement 3rd Theme — D56

2nd Movement 4th Theme — D57

2nd Movement 5th Theme — D58

2nd Movement 6th Theme — D59

Le Matin D'Un Jour De Fête (The Morning of a Holiday)

3rd Movement 1st Theme — D60

3rd Movement
2nd Theme — D61

3rd Movement
3rd Theme — D62

I Reflets Dans L'Eau   1st Theme — D63
from Images—1st Series, Pft.
Permission for reprint granted
by Durand & Cie, Paris.
Elkan-Vogel Co., Inc.   2nd Theme — D64
Philadelphia, Copyright Owners.

II Hommage à Rameau   1st Theme — D65
from Images—1st Series, Pft.
Permission for reprint granted
by Durand & Cie, Paris.
Elkan-Vogel Co., Inc.   2nd Theme — D66
Philadelphia, Copyright Owners.

Poissons D'Or (Goldfish)
from Images—2nd Series, Pft. — D67
Permission for reprint granted by Durand
& Cie, Paris. Elkan-Vogel Co., Inc.
Philadelphia, Copyright Owners.

Mazurka, Pft. — D68
Permission for reprint granted by Jean
Jobert, Paris. Elkan-Vogel Co., Inc.
Philadelphia, Copyright Owners.

La Mer, Orch.   1st Movement
1st Theme — D69
De L'Aube A
Midi Sur La Mer
(From Dawn to   1st Movement
Noon on the Sea)   2nd Theme — D70
Permission for reprint
granted by Durand & Cie,   1st Movement
Paris. Elkan-Vogel Co., Inc.   3rd Theme — D71
Philadelphia, Copyright
Owners,

1st Movement
4th Theme — D72

1st Movement
5th Theme — D73

1st Movement
6th Theme — D74

Jeux De Vagues   2nd Movement
(Play of the Waves)   1st Theme — D75

2nd Movement
2nd Theme — D76

2nd Movement
3rd Theme — D77

Dialogue du Vent   3rd Movement
et de la Mer   1st Theme — D78
(Dialogue of the
Wind and the Sea)   3rd Movement
2nd Theme — D79

Nocturnes, Orch.   Nuages (Clouds)
1st Theme — D80
Permission for reprint
granted by Jean Jobert, Paris.
Elkan-Vogel Co., Inc. Philadelphia,
Copyright Owners.

2nd Theme — D81
3rd Theme — D82
Fêtes 1st Theme — D83
2nd Theme — D84
3rd Theme — D85
4th Theme — D86
Sirènes 1st Theme — D87
2nd Theme — D88

Petite Suite, 2 Pianos
Permission for reprint granted by Durand & Cie, Paris. Elkan-Vogel Co., Inc. Philadelphia, Copyright Owners,

En Bateau 1st Theme — D89
2nd Theme — D90
Cortège 1st Theme — D91
2nd Theme — D92
Menuet 1st Theme — D93
2nd Theme — D94
Ballet 1st Theme — D95
2nd Theme — D96

Pour le Piano, Suite
Permission for reprint granted by Durand & Cie, Paris. Elkan-Vogel Co., Inc. Philadelphia, Copyright Owners,

Prélude 1st Theme — D97
2nd Theme — D98
Sarabande — D99
Toccata — D100

La Plus Que Lente, Waltz, Pft.
Permission for reprint granted by Durand & Cie, Paris. Elkan-Vogel Co., Inc. Philadelphia, Copyright Owners.
1st Theme — D101
2nd Theme — D102

Préludes, Book 1, Pft. Permission for reprint granted by Durand & Cie, Paris. Elkan-Vogel Co., Inc. Philadelphia, Copyright Owners.
No. 1 Danseuses De Delphes — D103
No. 2 Voiles (Veils) 1st Theme — D104
2nd Theme — D105

No. 5 Les Collines D'Anacapri (The Hills of Anacapri) — D106

No. 8 La Fille Aux Cheveux De Lin (The Girl With the Flaxen Hair) — D107

No. 10 La Cathédrale Engloutie (The Sunken Cathedral) 1st Theme — D108
2nd Theme — D109

No. 11 La Danse De Puck — D110

No. 12 Minstrels — D111

Préludes, Book II, Pft. Permission for reprint granted by Durand & Cie, Paris. Elkan-Vogel Co., Inc. Philadelphia, Copyright Owners.
No. 3 La Puerta Del Vino — D112
No. 5 Bruyères (Heather) — D113

No. 6 General Lavine-Eccentric — D114

No. 9, Hommage à S. Pickwick, Esq., P.P.M.P.C. (Parody on God Save the King) — D115

Printemps Symphonic Suite, Orch.
Permission for reprint granted by Durand & Cie, Paris. Elkan-Vogel Co., Inc. Philadelphia, Copyright Owners.
1st Movement 1st Theme — D116
1st Movement 2nd Theme — D117
2nd Movement 1st Theme — D118
2nd Movement 2nd Theme — D119

Quartet in G Minor, Str.
Permission for reprint granted by Durand & Cie, Paris. Elkan-Vogel Co., Inc. Philadelphia, Copyright Owners.
1st Movement 1st Theme, A — D120

1st Movement
1st Theme,
B   D121

1st Movement
2nd Theme   D122

2nd Movement
1st Theme,
A   D123

2nd Movement
1st Theme,
B   D124

3rd Movement
1st Theme   D125

3rd Movement
2nd Theme,
A   D126

3rd Movement
2nd Theme,
B   D127

4th Movement   D128

Rapsodie,
Saxophone & Orch.
Permission for reprint
granted by Durand & Cie,
Paris. Elkan-Vogel Co., Inc.
Philadelphia, Copyright
Owners.

1st Theme   D129

2nd Theme   D130

3rd Theme   D131

Rapsodie,
Clarinet & Orch.
Permission for reprint
granted by Durand & Cie,
Paris. Elkan-Vogel Co., Inc.
Philadelphia, Copyright
Owners.

1st Theme   D132

2nd Theme   D133

Rêverie, Pft.
By permisssion
of The Boston Music Co.,
copyright owner.

1st Theme   D134

2nd Theme   D135

Sonata in G Minor,
Vn. & Pft.
Permission for reprint
granted by Durand & Cie,
Paris. Elkan-Vogel Co., Inc.
Philadelphia, Copyright
Owners.

1st Movement
1st Theme   D136

1st Movement
2nd Theme   D137

2nd Movement
1st Theme   D138

2nd Movement
2nd Theme   D139

3rd Movement   D140

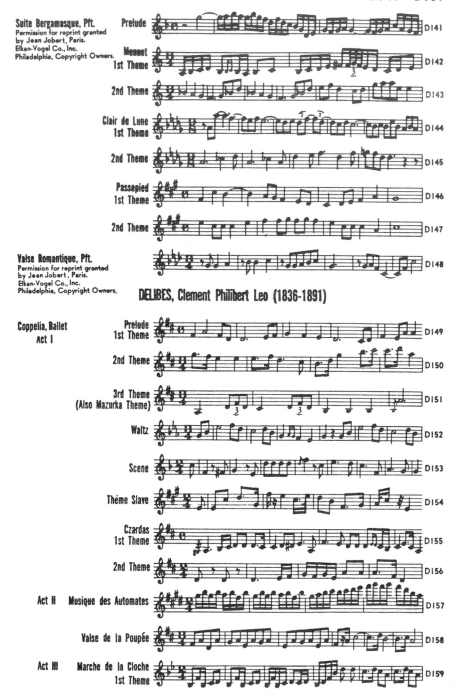

Suite Bergamasque, Pft.
Permission for reprint granted
by Jean Jobert, Paris.
Elkan-Vogel Co., Inc.
Philadelphia, Copyright Owners.

Prelude — D141

Menuet
1st Theme — D142

2nd Theme — D143

Clair de Lune
1st Theme — D144

2nd Theme — D145

Passepied
1st Theme — D146

2nd Theme — D147

Valse Romantique, Pft.
Permission for reprint granted
by Jean Jobert, Paris.
Elkan-Vogel Co., Inc.
Philadelphia, Copyright Owners,

— D148

DELIBES, Clement Philibert Leo (1836-1891)

**Coppelia, Ballet
Act I**

Prelude
1st Theme — D149

2nd Theme — D150

3rd Theme
(Also Mazurka Theme) — D151

Waltz — D152

Scene — D153

Thème Slave — D154

Czardas
1st Theme — D155

2nd Theme — D156

Act II   Musique des Automates — D157

Valse de la Poupée — D158

Act III   Marche de la Cloche
1st Theme — D159

2nd Theme — D160

Valse des Heures
1st Theme — D161

2nd Theme — D162

Danse de Fête — D163

Naïla Valse,
Pas des Fleurs

1st Theme — D164

2nd Theme — D165

3rd Theme — D166

4th Theme — D167

Le Roi L'A Dit,
Overture

1st Theme — D168

2nd Theme — D169

3rd Theme — D170

4th Theme — D171

Scene Du Bal from
Le Roi S'Amuse

Gaillarde — D172

Pavane — D173

Scène du Bouquet — D174

Lesquercarde — D175

Madrigal — D176

Passepied — D177

La Source, Ballet

Pas De Violes — D178

Danse Circassienne
1st Theme — D179

2nd Theme — D180

Scherzo—Polka — D181

Sylvia, Ballet

Prelude — D182

Les Chasseresses — D183

Valse Lente — D184

Marche de Bacchus
1st Theme — D185

2nd Theme — D186

Pizzicato — D187

DELIUS, Frederick (1862-1934)

Appalachia, Orch.
By permission of the
copyright owner,
Boosey and Hawkes, Inc.

Intro. — D188

1st Theme — D189

2nd Theme
(March Variant of
1st Theme) — D190

Brigg Fair, Orch.
By permission of the
copyright owner,
Boosey and Hawkes, Inc.

1st Theme — D191

2nd Theme — D192

Concerto, Vn. & Orch.
By permission of Augener,
Ltd., London

1st Theme — D193

2nd Theme — D194

3rd Theme — D195

4th Theme — D196

5th Theme — D197

6th Theme — D198

Eventyr
"Once Upon a Time", Orch.
By permission of Augener,
Ltd., London

1st Theme ... D199

2nd Theme ... D200

3rd Theme ... D201

Hassan,
Suite for Orch.
By permission of the
copyright owner,
Boosey and Hawkes, Inc.

Intermezzo ... D202

Serenade ... D203

In a Summer Garden, Orch.
By permission of Associated
Music Publishers, Inc.

1st Theme, A ... D204

1st Theme, B ... D205

2nd Theme ... D206

3rd Theme ... D207

4th Theme ... D208

Irmelin–Prelude, Orch.
By permission of the copyright
owner, Boosey and Hawkes, Inc. ... D209

Paris, Nocturne, Orch.
By permission of Associated
Music Publishers, Inc.

1st Theme ... D210

2nd Theme ... D211

3rd Theme ... D212

4th Theme ... D213

Sonata No. 2, Vn. & Pft.
By permission of the
copyright owner,
Boosey and Hawkes, Inc.

1st Theme ... D214

2nd Theme ... D215

3rd Theme ... D216

4th Theme ... D217

Two Pieces
for Small
Orchestra
Copyright by the
Oxford University Press
Reproduced by permission.

No. 1, On Hearing the
First Cuckoo in Spring ... D218

No.11 Summer Night on the River — D219

The Walk to the Paradise Garden, from A Village Romeo & Juliet, Orch.
By permission of the copyright owner, Boosey and Hawkes, Inc.
1st Theme — D220
2nd Theme — D221

DETT, Robert Nathaniel (1882-1943)

Juba Dance, Pft. from In the Bottoms
By permission of Clayton F. Summy Co., owners of the copyright.
1st Theme — D222
2nd Theme — D223

DIAMOND, David (1915-   )

Rounds, Str. Orch.
Permission granted by Elkan-Vogel Co., Inc. Philadelphia, Pa. Copyright 1946
1st Movement 1st Theme — D223a
1st Movement 2nd Theme — D223b
1st Movement 3rd Theme — D223c
2nd Movement — D223d
3rd Movement 1st Theme — D223e
3rd Movement 2nd Theme — D223f

DINICU, ARR. BY HEIFETZ

Hora Staccato, Vn. & Pft.
Copyright 1930 by Carl Fischer, Inc., N. Y.
1st Theme — D224
2nd Theme — D225

DITTERSDORF, Carl Ditters von (1739-1799)

Quartet, No. 5, in E Flat, Str.
1st Movement — D226
2nd Movement 1st Theme — D227
2nd Movement 2nd Theme — D228

3rd Movement — D229

Quartet, No. 6, in A, Str.

1st Movement — D230

2nd Movement — D231

3rd Movement — D232

DOHNÁNYI, Ernö von (1877-1960)

Capriccio, Op. 28, Pft. — D233

Rhapsody, Op. 11, No. 3, Pft.
By permission of Associated Music Publishers, Inc.

1st Theme — D234

2nd Theme — D235

Ruralia Hungarica, Op. 32a, No. 1 — D236

Ruralia Hungarica, Op. 32a, No. 2

1st Theme — D237

2nd Theme — D238

Ruralia Hungarica, Op. 32a, No. 7 — D239

Suite, Op. 19, Orch.
By permission of Associated Music Publishers, Inc.

Andante con Variazioni — D240

Scherzo 1st Theme — D241

2nd Theme — D242

Romance 1st Theme — D243

2nd Theme — D244

Rondo 1st Theme — D245

2nd Theme — D246

DONIZETTI, Gaetano (1797-1848)

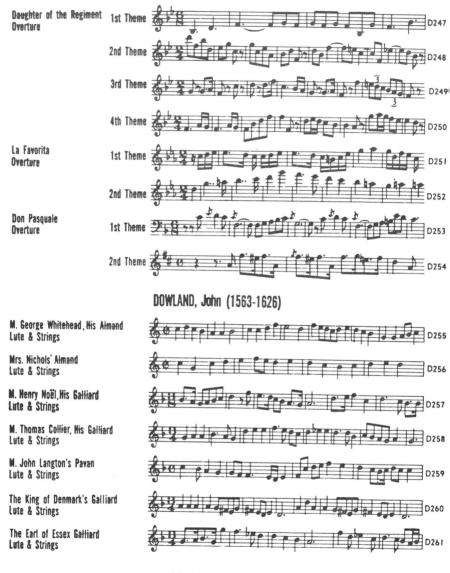

Daughter of the Regiment Overture — 1st Theme — D247

2nd Theme — D248

3rd Theme — D249

4th Theme — D250

La Favorita Overture — 1st Theme — D251

2nd Theme — D252

Don Pasquale Overture — 1st Theme — D253

2nd Theme — D254

DOWLAND, John (1563-1626)

M. George Whitehead, His Almand — Lute & Strings — D255

Mrs. Nichols' Almand — Lute & Strings — D256

M. Henry Noël, His Galliard — Lute & Strings — D257

M. Thomas Collier, His Galliard — Lute & Strings — D258

M. John Langton's Pavan — Lute & Strings — D259

The King of Denmark's Galliard — Lute & Strings — D260

The Earl of Essex Galliard — Lute & Strings — D261

DRDLA, Franz (1868-1944)

Souvenir, Vn. & Pft. — 1st Theme — D261a

2nd Theme — D261b

DRIGO, Riccardo (1846-1930)

Les Millions d'Arlequin, Serenade Vn. & Pft. — 1st Theme — D261c

2nd Theme — D261d

Valse Bluette, Vn. & Pft. — D261e

DUKAS, Paul (1865-1935)

L'Apprenti Sorcier (The Sorcerer's Apprentice) Scherzo for Orch.
Permission for reprint granted by Durand & Cie, Paris. Elkan-Vogel Co., Inc. Philadelphia, Copyright Owners. — Intro. — D262

1st Theme — D263

2nd Theme — D264

La Péri Dance Poem for Orch.
Permission for reprint granted by Durand & Cie, Paris. Elkan-Vogel Co., Inc. Philadelphia, Copyright Owners. — 1st Theme — D265

2nd Theme — D266

3rd Theme — D267

4th Theme — D268

DVOŘÁK, Antonin (1841-1904)

Bagatelles, Op. 47, Pft. & Str.
By permission of Associated Music Publishers, Inc. — 1st Movement — D269

2nd Movement — D270

4th Movement — D271

5th Movement 1st Theme — D272

5th Movement 2nd Theme — D273

Carnaval Overture, Op. 92
By permission of Associated Music Publishers, Inc. — 1st Theme — D274

2nd Theme — D275

3rd Theme — D276

4th Theme — D277

Concerto in B Minor,
Op.104, Cello & Orch.
Copyright 1930
by G. Schirmer, Inc.

1st Movement
1st Theme — D278

1st Movement
2nd Theme — D279

2nd Movement
1st Theme — D280

2nd Movement
2nd Theme — D281

3rd Movement
1st Theme — D282

3rd Movement
2nd Theme — D283

Concerto in A Minor,
Op. 53, Vn. & Orch.
By permission of Associated
Music Publishers, Inc.

1st Movement
1st Theme,
A — D284

1st Movement
1st Theme,
B — D285

1st Movement
2nd Theme — D286

2nd Movement
1st Theme — D287

2nd Movement
2nd Theme — D288

3rd Movement
1st Theme — D289

3rd Movement
2nd Theme — D290

3rd Movement
3rd Theme — D291

Humoresque, Op. 101,
No. 7, Pft.
By permission of Associated
Music Publishers, Inc.

1st Theme — D292

2nd Theme — D293

3rd Theme — D294

Quartet in D,
Op. 23, Pft. & Str.
By permission of Associated
Music Publishers, Inc.

1st Movement
1st Theme — D295

1st Movement / 2nd Theme — D296

2nd Movement — D297

3rd Movement / 1st Theme — D298

3rd Movement / 2nd Theme — D299

Quartet in E Flat, Op. 87, Pft. & Str.
By permission of Associated Music Publishers, Inc.

1st Movement / 1st Theme — D300

1st Movement / 2nd Theme — D301

2nd Movement — D302

3rd Movement / 1st Theme — D303

3rd Movement / 2nd Theme — D304

4th Movement / 1st Theme — D305

4th Movement / 2nd Theme — D306

Quart., in F, Op. 96 Str., "American"
By permission of Associated Music Publishers, Inc.

1st Movement / 1st Theme — D307

1st Movement / 2nd Theme — D308

2nd Movement — D309

3rd Movement / 1st Theme — D310

3rd Movement / 2nd Theme A — D311

3rd Movement / 2nd Theme B — D312

4th Movement / Intro. — D313

4th Movement / 1st Theme — D314

4th Movement / 2nd Theme — D315

**Quartet in
A Flat , Op. 105, Str.**
By permission of
Associated Music
Publishers, Inc.

1st Movement
1st Theme — D316

1st Movement
2nd Theme — D317

2nd Movement
1st Theme — D318

2nd Movement
2nd Theme — D319

3rd Movement — D320

4th Movement
1st Theme — D321

4th Movement
2nd Theme — D322

4th Movement
3rd Theme — D323

**Quartet in
G, Op. 106, Str.**
By permission of
Associated Music
Publishers, Inc.

1st Movement
1st Theme — D324

1st Movement
2nd Theme — D325

2nd Movement — D326

3rd Movement
1st Theme — D327

3rd Movement
2nd Theme — D328

3rd Movement
3rd Theme — D329

4th Movement
1st Theme — D330

4th Movement
2nd Theme — D331

4th Movement
3rd Theme — D332

**Quintet, Op. 81
Pft. & Str.**

1st Movement
1st Theme — D332a

1st Movement
2nd Theme — D332b

2nd Movement
Dumka
1st Theme, A — D332c

2nd Movement 1st Theme, B — D332d

2nd Movement 1st Theme, C — D332e

2nd Movement 2nd Theme — D332f

3rd Movement — D332g

4th Movement 1st Theme — D332h

4th Movement 2nd Theme — D332i

Quintet in E Flat, Op. 97, Str.
By permission of Associated Music Publishers, Inc.

1st Movement 1st Theme — D333

1st Movement 2nd Theme — D334

2nd Movement 1st Theme — D335

2nd Movement 2nd Theme — D336

3rd Movement — D337

4th Movement — D338

Scherzo Capriccioso, Op. 66, Orch.
By permission of Associated Music Publishers, Inc.

1st Theme — D339

2nd Theme — D340

3rd Theme — D341

4th Theme — D342

Serenade for Strings, in E, Op. 22
By permission of Associated Music Publishers, Inc.

1st Movement 1st Theme — D343

1st Movement 2nd Theme — D344

2nd Movement 1st Theme — D345

2nd Movement 2nd Theme — D346

Sextet, Op. 48, Str.
By permission of
Associated Music
Publishers, Inc.

3rd Movement — D347
4th Movement — D348
5th Movement — D349
1st Movement 1st Theme — D350
1st Movement 2nd Theme — D351
2nd Movement Dumka 1st Theme A — D352
2nd Movement 1st Theme, B — D353
2nd Movement 2nd Theme — D354
3rd Movement — D355
4th Movement (Theme for Variations) — D356

Slavonic Dances, Op. 46, Orch. No. 1
1st Theme — D357
2nd Theme — D358

No. 2
1st Theme — D359
2nd Theme — D360

No. 3
1st Theme — D361
2nd Theme — D362

No. 4
1st Theme — D363
2nd Theme — D364

No. 5
1st Theme — D365
2nd Theme — D366

No. 6   1st Theme   D367

2nd Theme   D368

No. 7   1st Theme   D369

2nd Theme   D370

3rd Theme   D371

No. 8   1st Theme   D372

2nd Theme   D373

Slavonic Dances, Op. 72,
Orch. No. 1   1st Theme   D374

2nd Theme   D375

3rd Theme   D376

No. 2   1st Theme   D377

2nd Theme   D378

3rd Theme   D379

No. 3   1st Theme   D380

2nd Theme   D381

3rd Theme   D382

4th Theme   D383

No. 4   1st Theme   D384

2nd Theme   D385

No. 5   1st Theme   D386

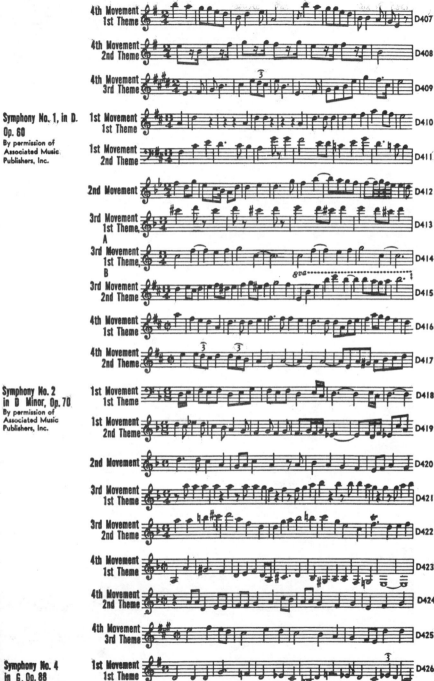

4th Movement, 1st Theme   D407

4th Movement, 2nd Theme   D408

4th Movement, 3rd Theme   D409

Symphony No. 1, in D.
Op. 60
By permission of
Associated Music
Publishers, Inc.

1st Movement, 1st Theme   D410

1st Movement, 2nd Theme   D411

2nd Movement   D412

3rd Movement, 1st Theme, A   D413

3rd Movement, 1st Theme, B   D414

3rd Movement, 2nd Theme   D415

4th Movement, 1st Theme   D416

4th Movement, 2nd Theme   D417

Symphony No. 2
in D Minor, Op. 70
By permission of
Associated Music
Publishers, Inc.

1st Movement, 1st Theme   D418

1st Movement, 2nd Theme   D419

2nd Movement   D420

3rd Movement, 1st Theme   D421

3rd Movement, 2nd Theme   D422

4th Movement, 1st Theme   D423

4th Movement, 2nd Theme   D424

4th Movement, 3rd Theme   D425

Symphony No. 4
in G, Op. 88
By permission of
Novello & Co., Ltd.,
London

1st Movement, 1st Theme   D426

1st Movement 2nd Theme — D427

1st Movement 3rd Theme — D428

2nd Movement — D429

3rd Movement 1st Theme — D430

3rd Movement 2nd Theme — D431

4th Movement 1st Theme — D432

4th Movement 2nd Theme — D433

Symphony No. 5, in E Minor, Op. 95 "From The New World" Published and Copyrighted 1928 by Oliver Ditson Co.

1st Movement 1st Theme — D434

1st Movement 2nd Theme — D435

1st Movement 3rd Theme — D436

2nd Movement 1st Theme — D437

2nd Movement 2nd Theme — D438

2nd Movement 3rd Theme — D439

3rd Movement 1st Theme — D440

3rd Movement 2nd Theme — D441

3rd Movement 3rd Theme — D442

4th Movement 1st Theme — D443

4th Movement 2nd Theme — D444

4th Movement 3rd Theme — D445

Trio in F Minor, Op. 65, 1st Movement Vn., Pft. & Cello 1st Theme — D446
By permission of Associated Music Publishers, Inc.

1st Movement
2nd Theme — D447

2nd Movement — D448

3rd Movement — D449

4th Movement
1st Theme — D450

4th Movement
2nd Theme — D451

Trio, Op. 90 Vn. Pft. & Cello, "Dumky"
By permission of Associated Music Publishers, Inc.

1st Movement
Intro. — D452

1st Movement
1st Theme,
A — D453

1st Movement
1st Theme,
B — D454

1st Movement
2nd Theme — D455

1st Movement
3rd Theme — D456

2nd Movement — D457

3rd Movement
1st Theme — D458

3rd Movement
2nd Theme — D459

4th Movement
1st Theme — D460

4th Movement
2nd Theme — D461

5th Movement
Intro. — D462

5th Movement — D463

Wedding Dance From Die Waldtaube, Op. 110, Orch.
By permission of Associated Music Publishers, Inc.

1st Theme — D464

2nd Theme — D465

Waltzes, Op. 54, Pft. No. 1
By permission of Associated Music Publishers Inc

— D466

No. 3 — 1st Theme — D467
2nd Theme — D468
No. 6 — D469

ELGAR, Sir Edward (1857-1934)

Chanson de Nuit, Op. 15, No. 1, Orch.
By permission of Novello & Co., Ltd., London. — E1

Cockaigne, In London Town Op. 40, Concert Overture, Orch.
By permission of the copyright owner, Boosey and Hawkes, Inc.
1st Theme — E2
2nd Theme — E3
3rd Theme — E4
4th Theme — E5

Concerto in E Minor, Op. 85, Cello & Orch.
By permission of Novello & Co., Ltd., London.
1st Movement Intro. — E6
1st Movement 1st Theme — E7
1st Movement 2nd Theme — E8
2nd Movement 1st Theme — E9
2nd Movement 2nd Theme — E10
3rd Movement — E11
4th Movement — E12

Concerto in B Minor, Op. 61, Vn. & Orch.
By permission of Novello & Co., Ltd., London.
1st Movement 1st Theme, A — E13
1st Movement 1st Theme, B — E14
1st Movement 2nd Theme — E15
2nd Movement 1st Theme — E16

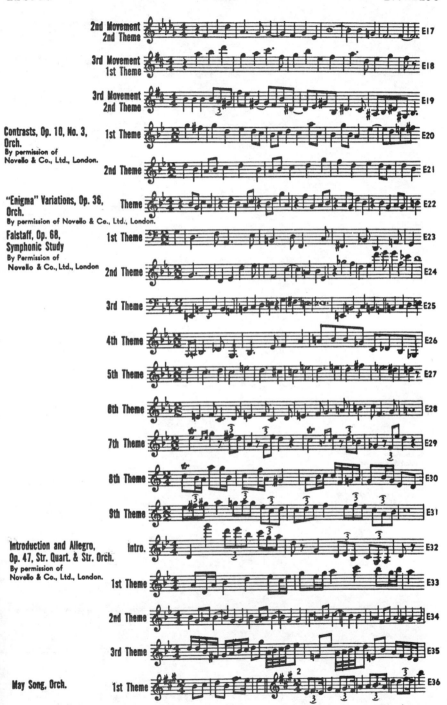

2nd Movement 2nd Theme — E17

3rd Movement 1st Theme — E18

3rd Movement 2nd Theme — E19

Contrasts, Op. 10, No. 3, Orch.
By permission of Novello & Co., Ltd., London.
1st Theme — E20

2nd Theme — E21

"Enigma" Variations, Op. 36, Orch.
By permission of Novello & Co., Ltd., London.
Theme — E22

Falstaff, Op. 68, Symphonic Study
By Permission of Novello & Co., Ltd., London
1st Theme — E23

2nd Theme — E24

3rd Theme — E25

4th Theme — E26

5th Theme — E27

6th Theme — E28

7th Theme — E29

8th Theme — E30

9th Theme — E31

Introduction and Allegro, Op. 47, Str. Quart. & Str. Orch.
By permission of Novello & Co., Ltd., London.
Intro. — E32

1st Theme — E33

2nd Theme — E34

3rd Theme — E35

May Song, Orch.
1st Theme — E36

Pomp and Circumstance, Military Marches, Op. 39
No. 1
By permission of the copyright owner, Boosey and Hawkes, Inc.

No. 2

No. 3

No. 4

Salut D'Amour, Op. 12, Orch.
By permission of Associated Music Publishers, Inc.

Serenade, Op. 20. Str. Orch.
By permission of Associated Music Publishers, Inc.

Sonata in E Minor, Op. 82, Vn. & Pft.
By permission of Novello & Co., Ltd., London.

Symphony No. 1,
in A Flat, Op. 55
By permission of
Novello & Co., Ltd.,
London.

2nd Movement
2nd Theme — E57

3rd Movement
1st Theme — E58

3rd Movement
2nd Theme — E59

1st Movement
Intro. — E60

1st Movement
1st Theme — E61

1st Movement
2nd Theme — E62

2nd Movement
1st Theme — E63

2nd Movement
2nd Theme — E64

2nd Movement
3rd Theme — E65

2nd Movement
4th Theme — E66

3rd Movement
1st Theme — E67

3rd Movement
2nd Theme,
A — E68

3rd Movement
2nd Theme,
B — E69

3rd Movement
3rd Theme — E70

4th Movement
1st Theme — E71

4th Movement
2nd Theme — E72

4th Movement
3rd Theme — E73

The Wand of Youth
Suite No. 1, Op. 1a, Orch.
By permission of
Novello & Co., Ltd., London.

Overture — E74

Serenade — E75

Minuet (Old Style) — E76

*For Symphony No. 2 E73a-E73k, see page xiv.

Sun Dance   E77

Fairy Pipers   E78

Slumber Scene   E79

ENESCO, Georges (1881-1955)

Poème Roumain, Op. 1
Symphonic Suite

By permission of
M M Enoch & Cie.,
Music Publishers,
27 Boulevard
des Italiens, Paris

1st Movement
1st Theme   E80

1st Movement
2nd Theme   E81

1st Movement
3rd Theme   E82

2nd Movement
1st Theme   E83

2nd Movement
2nd Theme   E84

2nd Movement
Roumanian Folk Song
3rd Theme   E85

2nd Movement
4th Theme   E86

2nd Movement
5th Theme   E87

2nd Movement
Roumanian National Anthem   E88

Roumanian Rhapsody No. 1,
Op. 11, Orch.

By permission of
M M Enoch & Cie.,
Music Publishers,
27 Boulevard
des Italiens, Paris

1st Theme,
A   E89

1st Theme,
B   E90

2nd Theme   E91

3rd Theme,
A   E92

3rd Theme,
B   E93

4th Theme   E94

5th Theme   E95

6th Theme — E96
7th Theme — E97
8th Theme — E98

Roumanian Rhapsody No. 2 Op. 11, Orch.
By permission of M M Enoch & Cie. Music Publishers, 27 Boulevard des Italiens, Paris.

1st Theme — E99
2nd Theme — E100
3rd Theme — E101
4th Theme — E102
5th Theme — E103

ERKEL, Franz (1810-1893)

Hunyadi László, Opera Overture

1st Theme — E104
2nd Theme — E105
3rd Theme — E106
4th Theme — E107

FALLA, Manuel de (1876-1946)

El Amor Brujo, Ballet
By permission of the copyright holders, J. & W. Chester, Ltd., 11 Great Marlborough Street, London, W. 1.

Introduction & Scene — F1
En La Cueva — F2
Canción del Amor Dolido — F3
Dance of Terror 1st Theme — F4
2nd Theme — F5
Ritual Fire Dance 1st Theme — F6

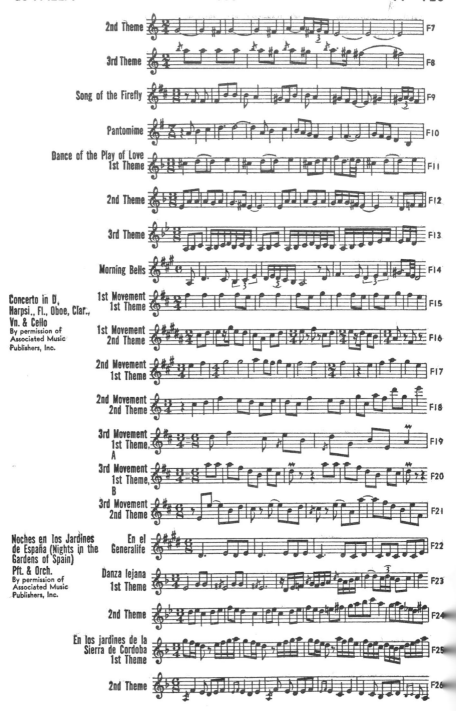

2nd Theme ... F7
3rd Theme ... F8
Song of the Firefly ... F9
Pantomime ... F10
Dance of the Play of Love 1st Theme ... F11
2nd Theme ... F12
3rd Theme ... F13
Morning Bells ... F14

Concerto in D, Harpsi., Fl., Oboe, Clar., Vn. & Cello
By permission of Associated Music Publishers, Inc.

1st Movement 1st Theme ... F15
1st Movement 2nd Theme ... F16
2nd Movement 1st Theme ... F17
2nd Movement 2nd Theme ... F18
3rd Movement 1st Theme, A ... F19
3rd Movement 1st Theme, B ... F20
3rd Movement 2nd Theme ... F21

Noches en los Jardines de España (Nights in the Gardens of Spain) Pft. & Orch.
By permission of Associated Music Publishers, Inc.

En el Generalife ... F22
Danza lejana 1st Theme ... F23
2nd Theme ... F24
En los jardines de la Sierra de Cordoba 1st Theme ... F25
2nd Theme ... F26

4 Pieces Espagñoles, Pft.
Permission for reprint
granted by Durand & Cie, Paris.
Elkan-Vogel Co., Inc.
Philadelphia, Copyright Owners.

Aragonesa — F27

Cubana — F28

Montañesa 1st Theme — F29

2nd Theme — F30

Andaluza 1st Theme — F31

2nd Theme — F32

3 Dances from El Sombrero de Tres Picos (The Three Cornered Hat), Orch.
By permission of the copyright holders, J. & W. Chester, Ltd., 11 Great Marlborough Street, London, W. 1.

Dance of the Neighbors 1st Theme — F33

2nd Theme — F34

Danse du Corregidor (Mayor's Dance) 1st Theme — F35

2nd Theme — F36

Jota 1st Theme — F37

2nd Theme — F38

3rd Theme — F39

4th Theme — F40

Miller's Dance — F41

Suite Populaire Espagñole, Vn. & Pft.
By permission of the copyright holders, J. & W. Chester, Ltd., 11 Great Marlborough Street, London, W. 1.

El Pano Moruno — F42

Nana — F43

Canción — F44

Polo — F45

Asturiana — F46

La Vida Breve
Orch.
By permission of Associated
Music Publishers, Inc.

Jota 1st Theme — F47

2nd Theme — F48

Dance, No. 1 1st Theme — F49

2nd Theme — F50

Dance No. 2 1st Theme — F51

2nd Theme — F52

FARNABY, Giles (1560-1600)

His Conceit, Fitzwilliam Virginal Book No. 273, Harpsi. — F53

His Dreame, Fitzwilliam Virginal Book No. 260, Harpsi. — F54

His Humour, Fitzwilliam Virginal Book No. 196, Harpsi. — F55

His Rest, Fitzwilliam Virginal Book No. 195, Harpsi. — F56

Rosa Solis, Fitzwilliam Virginal Book No. 143, Harpsi. — F57

Tower Hill, Fitzwilliam Virginal Book No. 245, Harpsi. — F58

A Toye, Fitzwilliam Virginal Book No. 270, Harpsi. — F59

FAURÉ, Gabriel (1845-1924)

Ballade, Op. 19, Pft. & Orch 1st Theme — F60
By permission of
J. Hamelle Music
Publishers, Paris.

2nd Theme — F61

3rd Theme — F62

4th Theme — F63

Barcarolle No. 5, Op. 66, Pft. — F64
By permission of J. Hamelle
Music Publishers, Paris.

Barcarolle No. 6, Op. 70, Pft.
By permission of
J. Hamelle Music
Publishers, Paris.

**Dolly, Op. 56, Pft.,
4 Hands**
By permission of
J. Hamelle Music
Publishers, Paris.

Berceuse — F66

Mi-a-ou
1st Theme — F67

2nd Theme — F68

Le Jardin de Dolly — F69

Kitty-Valse
1st Theme — F70

2nd Theme — F71

Tendresse — F72

Le Pas Espagnol
1st Theme — F73

2nd Theme — F74

**Elégie, Op. 24,
Cello & Orch.**
By permission of
J. Hamelle Music
Publishers, Paris.

1st Theme — F75

2nd Theme — F76

**Impromptu, No. 2,
Op. 34, Pft.**
By permission of
International Music Co.

1st Theme — F76a

2nd Theme — F76b

**Impromptu, No. 3,
Op. 34, Pft.**
By permission of
International Music Co.

1st Theme — F76c

2nd Theme — F76d

3rd Nocturne, Op. 33, No. 3, Pft.
By permission of
J. Hamelle Music
Publishers, Paris.

— F77

4th Nocturne, Op. 36, Pft.
By permission of
J. Hamelle Music
Publishers, Paris.

— F78

6th Nocturne, Op. 63, Pft. 1st Theme — F79
By permission of
J. Hamelle Music
Publishers, Paris.

2nd Theme — F80

Pelléas and Mélisande, Op. 80, Orch.
By permission of J. Hamelle Music Publishers, Paris.

Quartet in C Minor, Op. 15, Pft. & Str.
By permission of J. Hamelle Music Publishers, Paris.

Quartet in E Minor, Op. 121, Str.
Permission for reprint granted by Durand & Cie, Paris. Elkan-Vogel Co., Inc. Philadelphia, Copyright Owners,

Sicilienne, Op. 78, Cello & Pft.
By permission of J. Hamelle Music Publishers, Paris.
Sonata in A, Op. 13, Vn. & Pft.
By permission of The Boston Music Co., copyright owner.

2nd Movement 2nd Theme   F101

3rd Movement 1st Theme, A   F102

3rd Movement 1st Theme, B   F103

3rd Movement 2nd Theme   F104

4th Movement 1st Theme   F105

4th Movement 2nd Theme   F106

FIELD, John (1782-1837)

Nocturne No. 3, Pft.   F107

Nocturne No. 4, Pft.   1st Theme   F108

2nd Theme   F109

Nocturne No. 5, Pft.   F110

Sonata in C Minor, Op. 1, No. 3, Pft.   1st Movement   F111

2nd Movement 1st Theme   F112

2nd Movement 2nd Theme   F113

FLOTOW, Friedrich von (1812-1883)

Alessandro Stradella Overture   1st Theme   F114

2nd Theme   F115

3rd Theme   F116

4th Theme   F117

Fatme (Zilda) Overture   1st Theme   F118

Martha
Overture

FRANÇAIX, Jean (1912-   )

Sonatine, Vn. & Pft.
By permission of Associated
Music Publishers, Inc.

FRANCK, César (1822-1890)

Three Chorals, Organ
No. 1

No. 2

No. 3

Les Djinns, Symphonic
Poem, Pft. & Orch.

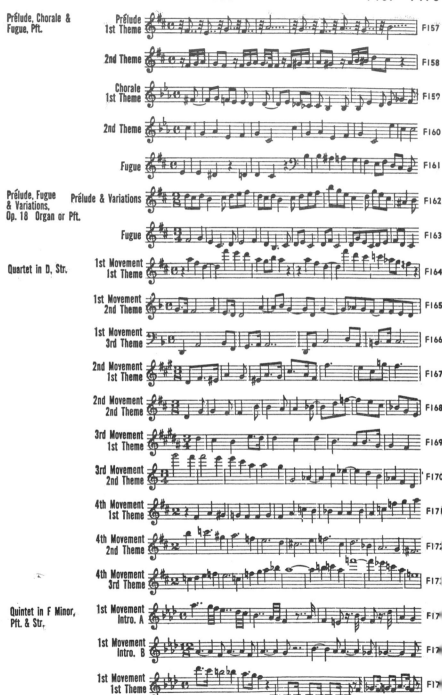

Prélude, Chorale & Fugue, Pft.

Prélude 1st Theme — F157

2nd Theme — F158

Chorale 1st Theme — F159

2nd Theme — F160

Fugue — F161

Prélude, Fugue & Variations, Op. 18 Organ or Pft. — Prélude & Variations — F162

Fugue — F163

Quartet in D, Str.

1st Movement 1st Theme — F164

1st Movement 2nd Theme — F165

1st Movement 3rd Theme — F166

2nd Movement 1st Theme — F167

2nd Movement 2nd Theme — F168

3rd Movement 1st Theme — F169

3rd Movement 2nd Theme — F170

4th Movement 1st Theme — F171

4th Movement 2nd Theme — F172

4th Movement 3rd Theme — F173

Quintet in F Minor, Pft. & Str.

1st Movement Intro. A — F174

1st Movement Intro. B — F175

1st Movement 1st Theme — F176

1st Movement / 2nd Theme   F177

1st Movement / 3rd Theme   F178

2nd Movement / 1st Theme   F179

2nd Movement / 2nd Theme   F180

2nd Movement / 3rd Theme   F181

3rd Movement / 1st Theme   F182

3rd Movement / 2nd Theme   F183

Sonata, Vn. & Pft.

1st Movement / Theme   F184

1st Movement / 2nd Theme   F185

2nd Movement / 1st Theme   F186

2nd Movement / 2nd Theme   F187

3rd Movement / (Recitative-Fantasia)   F188

3rd Movement / 2nd Theme / A   F189

3rd Movement / 2nd Theme / B   F190

3rd Movement / 3rd Theme   F191

4th Movement   F192

Symphonic Variations, Pft.

Intro.   F193

1st Theme   F194

2nd Theme   F195

Symphony in D Minor

1st Movement / Intro.   F196

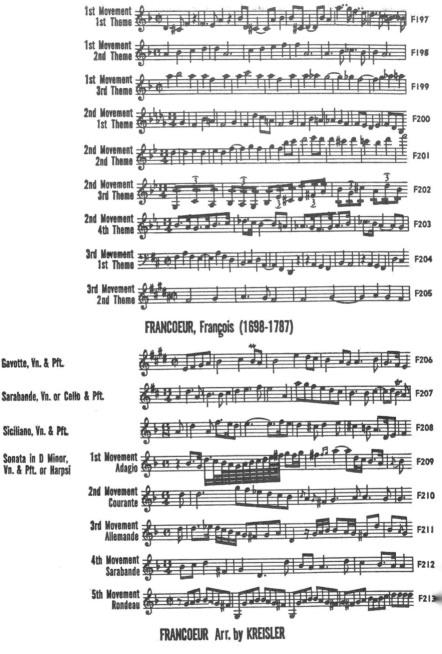

1st Movement 1st Theme — F197

1st Movement 2nd Theme — F198

1st Movement 3rd Theme — F199

2nd Movement 1st Theme — F200

2nd Movement 2nd Theme — F201

2nd Movement 3rd Theme — F202

2nd Movement 4th Theme — F203

3rd Movement 1st Theme — F204

3rd Movement 2nd Theme — F205

FRANCOEUR, François (1698-1787)

Gavotte, Vn. & Pft. — F206

Sarabande, Vn. or Cello & Pft. — F207

Siciliano, Vn. & Pft. — F208

Sonata in D Minor, Vn. & Pft. or Harpsi — 1st Movement Adagio — F209

2nd Movement Courante — F210

3rd Movement Allemande — F211

4th Movement Sarabande — F212

5th Movement Rondeau — F213

FRANCOEUR Arr. by KREISLER

Sicilienne et Rigaudon, Vn. & Pft. — Sicilienne — F214

Rigaudon  F215

FREDERICK II, King of Prussia (1712-1786)

Concerto No. 2, in
G, Flute & Str.

1st Movement
1st Theme  F216

1st Movement
2nd Theme F217

2nd Movement F218

3rd Movement F219

FRESCOBALDI, Girolamo (1583-1643)

Capriccio on the Cuckoo,
Harpsi.  F220

Capriccio on La Girolometa
Harpsi. F221

Capriccio on L'Aria di Ruggiero
Harpsi. F222

Capriccio: La Spagnoletta
Harpsi. F223

Fugue in G Minor, Organ & Str. F224

Ricercar Cromatico Post Il Credo
Organ F225

Toccata, Spinet or Lute F226

FUCÎK, Julius (1872-1916)

Entry of the Gladiators,
March

1st Theme F227

2nd Theme F228

3rd Theme F229

GABRIEL-MARIE (1852-1928)

La Cinquantaine, Air Dans
Le Style Ancien, Pft.   1st Theme GI

2nd Theme — G2

GADE, Niels (1817-1890)

Bridal Waltz from "Et Folkesagn," Ballet — 1st Theme — G3

2nd Theme — G4

Trio, Op. 42, Vn., Cello & Pft. — 1st Movement — G5

2nd Movement — G6

3rd Movement — G7

4th Movement Theme, A — G8

4th Movement Theme, B — G9

GALLOT, Jacques de (17th Cent.)

La Colombe (The Dove) Harpsi. — G10

GALUPPI, Baldassare (1706-1785)

Sonata in A, Pft. or Harpsi. — 1st Movement — G11

2nd Movement — G12

3rd Movement — G13

Sonata in C Minor, Pft. or Harpsi. — 1st Movement — G14

2nd Movement — G15

3rd Movement — G16

Sonata in D Harpsi. — 1st Movement — G17

2nd Movement — G18

3rd Movement  G19

4th Movement G20

GANNÉ, Louis (1862-1923)

La Czarina, Mazurka   **1st Theme** 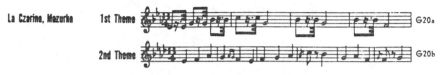 G20a

2nd Theme G20b

GAUTIER, Jean (1822-1878)

The Secret, Vn. & Pft.   **1st Theme**  G20c

2nd Theme G20d

GEMINIANI, Francesco (1687-1762)

Sonata in C Minor, Vn. & Pft.   **1st Movement**  G21

2nd Movement G22

3rd Movement Siciliano G23

4th Movement G24

GERMAN, Sir Edward (1862-1936)

As You Like It Incidental Music
By permission of Novello & Co., Ltd., London.   **1st Movement Woodland Dance**  G25

2nd Movement Children's Dance G26

3rd Movement Rustic Dance G27

Henry VIII Incidental Music
By permission of Novello & Co., Ltd., London   **Morris Dance 1st Theme** G28

2nd Theme G29

Shepherd's Dance G30

Torch Dance — G31

Romeo and Juliet Incidental Music, Orch.
By permission of Novello & Co., Ltd., London.
Pavane — G32

Welsh Rhapsody, Orch.
By permission of Novello & Co., Ltd., London.
1st Theme
Loudly Proclaim — G33

2nd Theme — G34

3rd Theme
Hunting the Hare — G35

4th Theme
Bells of Aberdovy — G36

5th Theme
David of the White Rock — G37

6th Theme
Men of Harlech — G38

GERSHWIN, George (1898-1937)

An American in Paris, Orch.
Copyright 1930 by New World Music Corp. Reprinted by special permission.
1st Theme — G39

2nd Theme — G40

3rd Theme
Blues Theme — G41

4th Theme — G42

Concerto in F, Pft. & Orch.
Copyright 1927 by Harms, Inc. Reprinted by special permission.
1st Movement
1st Theme — G43

1st Movement
2nd Theme — G44

1st Movement
3rd Theme — G45

2nd Movement
1st Theme, A — G46

2nd Movement
1st Theme, B — G47

2nd Movement
2nd Theme — G48

2nd Movement
3rd Theme — G49

3rd Movement 1st Theme — G50

3rd Movement 2nd Theme — G51

Prelude No. 1, Pft.
Copyright 1927 by New
World Music Corp.
Reprinted by special permission. — G52

Prelude No. 2, Pft.
Copyright 1927 by New
World Music Corp.
Reprinted by special permission. — 1st Theme G53

2nd Theme — G54

Prelude No. 3, Pft.
Copyright 1927 by New
World Music Corp.
Reprinted by special permission. — G55

**Rhapsody in Blue,
Pft. & Orch.**
Copyright 1924 by
Harms, Inc.
Reprinted by special permission — 1st Theme G56

2nd Theme — G57

3rd Theme — G58

4th Theme — G59

5th Theme — G60

GIBBONS, Orlando (1583-1625)

**The Lord of Salisbury, His Pavane,
Harpsi.** — G61

The Queen's Command, Harpsi. — G62

GLAZUNOFF, Alexander (1865-1936)

**Carnaval, Overture,
Op. 45, Orch.**
By permission of Associated
Music Publishers, Inc. — 1st Theme G63

2nd Theme — G64

3rd Theme — G65

4th Theme — G66

5th Theme — G67

Concerto in A Minor, Op. 82, Vn. & Orch.
By permission of Associated Music Publishers, Inc.
1st Theme — G68
2nd Theme — G69
3rd Theme — G70
4th Theme — G71
5th Theme — G72

Une Fête Slave, from Slav Str. Quartet Op. 26, No. 4, Orch.
By permission of Associated Music Publishers, Inc.
1st Theme — G73
2nd Theme — G74
3rd Theme — G75

Méditation, Op. 32, Vn. & Pft.
By permission of Associated Music Publishers, Inc.
— G76

Mélodie Arabe, Op. 20, No. 1, Cello & Pft.
By permission of Associated Music Publishers, Inc.
1st Theme — G77
2nd Theme — G78

Novelettes, Op. 15, Str. Quart.
By permission of Associated Music Publishers, Inc.
1st Movement Alla Spagnuola 1st Theme — G78a
1st Movement 2nd Theme — G78b
2nd Movement Orientale 1st Theme — G78c
2nd Movement 2nd Theme — G78d
3rd Movement Interludium in Modo Antico — G78e
4th Movement Waltz 1st Theme — G78f
4th Movement 2nd Theme — G78g
5th Movement All 'Ungherese — G78h

Ouverture Solennelle
By permission of Associated Music Publishers, Inc.
1st Theme — G79

2nd Theme — G80

3rd Theme — G81

4th Theme — G82

Rêverie, Op. 24
Fr. Horn & Pft.
By permission of Associated
Music Publishers, Inc.
— G83

The Seasons (Ballet), Bacchanal
Op. 67
By permission of Associated
Music Publishers, Inc.
— G84

Stenka Razin, Op. 13,   1st Theme
Symphonic Poem,   Volga Boat Song
Orch.
By permission of Associated
Music Publishers, Inc.
— G85

2nd Theme — G86

Valsa de Concert,   1st Theme
Op. 47, Orch.
By permission of Associated
Music Publishers, Inc.
— G87

2nd Theme — G88

3rd Theme — G89

GLIÈRE, Reinhold (1875-1956)

Russian Sailors' Dance
from the Red Poppy, Ballet
— G90

Symphony No. 3, Op. 42   Scherzo
"Ilia Mourometz"   1st Theme
— G91

2nd Theme — G92

GLINKA, Michael (1804-1857)

Capriccio Brilliant on the   1st Theme
Jota Aragonesa, Orch.
— G92a

2nd Theme — G93

Kamarinskaya, Orch.   1st Theme
— G94

2nd Theme,
A
— G95

2nd Theme,
B
— G96

The Lark, (Arr. by Balakirev), Pft. — G97

A Life for the Czar or Ivan Soussanine, Overture — Intro. — G98

1st Theme — G99

2nd Theme — G100

3rd Theme — G101

4th Theme — G102

Quartet in F, Str. — 1st Movement 1st Theme — G103

1st Movement 2nd Theme — G104

2nd Movement — G105

3rd Movement 1st Theme — G106

3rd Movement 2nd Theme — G107

4th Movement — G108

Romance, Pft., Vn. & Cello (Also as Song) — G109

Russlan and Ludmilla, Overture — 1st Theme — G110

2nd Theme — G111

Souvenir of a Night in Madrid, Orch. — 1st Theme Jota — G112

2nd Theme Punto Muruno — G113

3rd Theme Seguidillas Manchegas — G114

4th Theme Seguidillas Manchegas — G115

GLUCK, Christoph (1714-1787)

Act I — Air Gai — G135

Lento — G136

Act II — March — G137

(Theme used by Brahms) — Gavotte 1st Theme — G138

2nd Theme — G139

Act III — Danse des Esclaves — G140

(Also in Orpheus) — Chaconne — G141

Orpheus and Eurydice, Overture — G142

Dance of the Furies — G143

Dance of the Happy Spirits — G144

Melody — G145

GODARD, Benjamin (1849-1895)

Au Matin, Op. 83, Pft. — G146

Berceuse from Jocelyn — 1st Theme, A — G147
Published and Copyrighted
(renewal 1933) by Oliver
Ditson Co. Used by permission.

1st Theme, B — G148

2nd Theme — G149

2nd Mazurka, Pft. — G150

GODOWSKY, Leopold (1870-1938)

Alt-Wien, Pft. — G151
Copyright 1920 by G. Schirmer, Inc.

GOLDMARK, Karl (1830-1915)

Im Frühling, Op. 36, Overture
By permission of Associated Music Publishers, Inc.
- 1st Theme — G152
- 2nd Theme — G153

Sakuntala, Op. 13, Overture
By permission of Associated Music Publishers, Inc.
- 1st Theme — G154
- 2nd Theme — G155
- 3rd Theme — G156
- 4th Theme — G157

Symphony, Op. 26, "Rustic Wedding"
By permission of Associated Music Publishers, Inc.
- 1st Movement Wedding March — G158
- 2nd Movement Bridal Song — G159
- 3rd Movement Serenade 1st Theme — G160
- 3rd Movement 2nd Theme — G161
- 4th Movement In the Garden 1st Theme — G162
- 4th Movement 2nd Theme — G163
- 5th Movement Dance 1st Theme — G164
- 5th Movement 2nd Theme — G165

GOOSSENS, Eugene (1893-1962)

The Hurdy-Gurdy Man, Op. 18, No. 3, Pft.
By permission of the copyright holders, J. & W. Chester, Ltd., 11 Great Marlborough Street, London, W. 1.
- G166

GOSSEC, François Joseph (1734-1829)

Gavotte in D, Vn. & Pft.
- 1st Theme — G167
- 2nd Theme — G168

Tambourin, Vn. & Pft. — G169

GOTTSCHALK, Louis (1829-1869)

The Dying Poet, Pft. — G169a

GOUNOD, Charles François (1818-1893)

Faust, Ballet Music, Act V   1st Theme — G170

2nd Theme — G171

3rd Theme — G172

4th Theme — G173

5th Theme — G174

6th Theme — G175

Funeral March of a Marionette, Orch.   1st Theme — G176

2nd Theme — G177

The Queen of Sheba   Cortège — G178

GRAENER, Paul (1872-1944)

Die Flöte von Sans-Souci, Op. 88, Orch.   Intro. 1st Theme — G179
Copyright by Eulenburg, Licensed by SESAC, Inc., N. Y.

Intro. 2nd Theme — G180

1st Movement Sarabande — G181

2nd Movement Gavotte — G182

3rd Movement Air — G183

4th Movement Rigaudon — G184

GRAINGER, Percy (1882-1961)

Colonial Song, Orch. or Pft. 1st Theme — G185

2nd Theme — G186

Country Gardens, Eng. Morris Dance
Pft. Copyright renewed 1946
by Percy Grainger — G187

Handel in the Strand,
Clog Dance, Pft. or Orch. — G188

In A Nutshell, Suite   Arrival
Pft. & Orch.   Platform Humlet
Copyright renewal assigned   1st Theme — G189
1944 to G. Schirmer, Inc.

2nd Theme — G190

3rd Theme — G191

Gay But Wistful
1st Theme — G192

2nd Theme — G193

Pastoral — G194

"Gum Suckers" March
1st Theme — G195

2nd Theme — G196

Londonderry Air,
Irish Folk Song Setting
Pft. or Orch. — G197

Mock Morris, Pft. or Orch. — G198

Molly on the Shore
Irish Reel, Orch. or Pft.   1st Theme — G199

2nd Theme — G200

Shepherd's Hey, Eng. Morris Dance, Pft. — G201
Copyright 1922
by G. Schirmer, Inc.

GRANADOS, Enrique (1867-1916)

Goyescas, Opera   Intermezzo
Copyright renewal assigned   1st Theme — G202
1944 to G. Schirmer, Inc.

2nd Theme   G203

3rd Theme   G204

The Maiden and the Nightingale,
Goyescas No. 4, Pft.
Copyright renewal assigned
1944 to G. Schirmer, Inc.   G205

Spanish Dance, No. 2, Pft.   **1st Theme**   G206
Copyright renewal assigned
1943 to G. Schirmer, Inc.

                                 2nd Theme   G207

Spanish Dance, No. 4,   **1st Theme**   G208
Villanesca, Pft.
Copyright renewal assigned
1943 to G. Schirmer, Inc.   **2nd Theme**   G209

Spanish Dance, No. 5,   **1st Theme**   G210
Playera-Andaluza, Pft.
Copyright renewal assigned
1943 to G. Schirmer, Inc.   **2nd Theme**   G211

Spanish Dance, No. 6,   **1st Theme**   G212
Rondalla Aragonesa
Copyright renewal assigned
1943 to G. Schirmer, Inc.   **2nd Theme**   G213

GRETRY, André (1741-1813)

Ballet Suite from   **Gavotte**   G214
Cephale et Procris

                                 Tambourin   G215
                                 1st Theme,
                                 A

                                 1st Theme,   G216
                                 B

                                 2nd Theme   G217

Minuet   G218
Nymphes de Diane

                                 Gigue   G219

Colinette à la Cour   **Tambourin**   G220
Opera

                                 Gavotte   G221

Richard Coeur-de-Lion Opera — Rustic Dance — G222

La Rosière de Salency Opera — 1st Entr'acte 1st Theme — G223

2nd Theme — G224

2nd Entr'acte — G225

Ballet Suite from La Rosière Républicaine — Danse Légère — G226

Gavotte Gracieuse — G227

Contre Danse — G228

Romance — G229

Danse Générale — G230

Carmagnole — G231

Ballet Suite From Zémire et Azor — 1st Movement Air — G232

2nd Movement Pantomime — G233

3rd Movement Passepied — G234

GRIEG, Edvard (1843-1907)

Album Leaf, Op. 12, No. 7, Pft. — G235

Ballade, Op. 24, Pft.
By Permission of C. F. Peters, Clayton F. Summy Co., Chicago, Agents in the U. S. — G236

Concerto, Op. 16, Pft. & Orch. — 1st Movement Intro. — G237

1st Movement 1st Theme, A — G238

1st Movement 1st Theme, B — G239

1st Movement 2nd Theme — G240

1st Movement 3rd Theme, A — G241

1st Movement 3rd Theme B — G242

2nd Movement 1st Theme — G243

2nd Movement 2nd Theme — G244

3rd Movement 1st Theme — G245

3rd Movement 2nd Theme — G246

Cradle Song, Op. 66, No. 5, Pft.
By Permission of C. F. Peters,
Clayton F. Summy Co., Chicago,
Agents in the U. S. — G247

Dance Caprice, Op. 28, No. 3, Pft.   1st Theme — G248

2nd Theme — G249

Elfin Dance, Op. 12, No. 4, Pft. — G250

Erotic, Op. 43, No. 5, Pft.
By Permission of C. F. Peters,
Clayton F. Summy Co., Chicago,
Agents in the U. S. — G251

French Serenade, Op. 62, No. 3, Pft.
By Permission of C. F. Peters, Clayton F.
Summy Co., Chicago, Agents in the U. S. — G252

Holberg Suite, Op. 40, Str. Orch.   1st Movement Prelude — G253

2nd Movement Sarabande — G254

3rd Movement 1st Theme Gavotte — G255

3rd Movement 2nd Theme Musette — G256

4th Movement Air — G257

5th Movement Rigaudon — G258

In Der Heimat, Op. 43, No. 3, Pft. — G259

Little Bird, Op. 43, No. 4, Pft. — G260

The Lonely Wanderer, Op. 43, No. 2, Pft. — G261

Lyric Suite, Op. 54, Pft.   Shepherd Boy — G262
By Permission of C. F. Peters,
Clayton F. Summy Co., Chicago,
Agents in the U. S.
    Norwegian Rustic March — G263

March of the Dwarfs
1st Theme — G264

2nd Theme — G265

Nocturne — G266

Melancholy, Op. 65, No. 3, Pft. — G267
By Permission of C. F. Peters,
Clayton F. Summy Co., Chicago,
Agents in the U. S.
Melodie, Op. 47, No. 3, Pft. — G268
By Permission of C. F. Peters, Clayton F.
Summy Co., Chicago, Agents in the U. S.
Norwegian Bridal Procession,
Op. 19, No. 2, Pft. — G269
By Permission of C. F. Peters, Clayton F.
Summy Co., Chicago, Agents in the U. S.
Norwegian Dances,   No. 1
Op. 35, Pft. or Str. Orch.   1st Theme — G270
By Permission of C. F. Peters,
Clayton F. Summy Co., Chicago,
Agents in the U. S.   2nd Theme — G271

No. 2
1st Theme — G272

2nd Theme — G273

No. 3 — G274

No. 4
1st Theme — G275

2nd Theme — G276

Norwegian Melody, Op. 12,
No. 7, Pft.   1st Theme — G277
Copyright 1899
by G. Schirmer, Inc.
    2nd Theme — G278

Norwegian Melodies,   1st Movement
Op. 63, Str. Orch.   Popular Song — G279
By Permission of C. F.
Peters, Clayton F. Summy   2nd Movement
Co., Chicago,   1st Theme — G280
Agents in the U. S.   Cow Keeper's Tune

GRIEG

2nd Movement / 2nd Theme / Peasant Dance — G281

Papillon (Butterfly), Op. 43, No. 1, Pft. — G282

Peer Gynt, Suite No. 1, Op. 46, Orch. / 1st Movement Morning Mood — G283

2nd Movement Ase's Death — G284

3rd Movement Anitra's Dance 1st Theme — G285

3rd Movement 2nd Theme — G286

4th Movement In the Hall of the Mountain King — G287

Peer Gynt, Suite No. 2, Op. 55 Orch. Copyright 1899 by G. Schirmer, Inc. / 1st Movement Ingrid's Complaint 1st Theme — G288

1st Movement 2nd Theme — G289

2nd Movement Arabian Dance 1st Theme — G290

2nd Movement 2nd Theme — G291

3rd Movement Peer Gynt's Return Home — G292

4th Movement Solvejg's Song Intro. — G293

4th Movement 1st Theme — G294

4th Movement 2nd Theme — G295

Puck, Op. 71, No. 3, Pft. By Permission of C. F. Peters, Clayton F. Summy Co., Chicago, Agents in the U. S. — G296

Quartet in G Minor, Op. 27, Str. By permission of International Music Co. / 1st Movement 1st Theme — G297

1st Movement 2nd Theme — G298

2nd Movement Romanze 1st Theme — G299

2nd Movement 2nd Theme — G299

3rd Movement
Intermezzo
1st Theme — G300

3rd Movement
2nd Theme — G301

4th Movement
1st Theme — G302

4th Movement
2nd Theme — G303

Scherzo-Impromptu, Op. 73, No. 2, Pft.
By Permission of C. F. Peters, Clayton
F. Summy Co., Chicago, Agents in the U. S. — G304

Sigurd Jorsalfar, Orch.   1st Movement
Op. 56,   In the King's Hall (Prelude)
(Incidental Music),
By Permission of C. F.
Peters, Clayton F. Summy   1st Movement
Co., Chicago,   2nd Theme
Agents in the U. S. — G305 / G306

2nd Movement
Borghild's Dream (Intermezzo) — G307

3rd Movement
Triumphal March
1st Theme — G308

3rd Movement
2nd Theme — G309

Sonata in A Minor,
Op. 36, Cello & Pft.   1st Movement
By Permission of   1st Theme
C. F. Peters, Clayton
F. Summy Co., Chicago, 1st Movement
Agents in the U. S.   2nd Theme — G310 / G311

2nd Movement — G312

3rd Movement
1st Theme — G313

3rd Movement
2nd Theme — G314

3rd Movement
3rd Theme — G315

Sonata in E Minor,   1st Movement
Op. 7, Pft.   1st Theme
Published and Copyrighted
(renewal 1936)   1st Movement
by Oliver Ditson Co.   2nd Theme — G316 / G317
Used by permission.

1st Movement
3rd Theme — G318

2nd Movement — G319

3rd Movement   G320

4th Movement   G321

Sonata in G, Op. 13,
No. 2, Vn. & Pft.   1st Movement
Intro.   G322

1st Movement
1st Theme   G323

1st Movement
2nd Theme   G324

1st Movement
3rd Theme   G325

2nd Movement   G326

3rd Movement
1st Theme   G327

3rd Movement
2nd Theme   G328

Sonata in C Minor,
Op. 45, No. 3, Vn. & Pft.   1st Movement
Intro.   G329
Copyright 1917 by
Carl Fischer, Inc., N. Y.

1st Movement
1st Theme   G330

1st Movement
2nd Theme   G331

2nd Movement
1st Theme   G332

2nd Movement
2nd Theme   G333

3rd Movement
1st Theme   G334

3rd Movement
2nd Theme   G335

Summer's Eve, Op. 71, No. 2, Pft.   G336
By Permission of C. F. Peters, Clayton F.
Summy Co., Chicago, Agents in the U. S.

Symphonic Dances,
Op. 64, Orch.   No. 1   G337
By Permission of C. F. Peters,
Clayton F. Summy Co., Chicago,
Agents in the U. S.   No. 2
1st Theme,
A   G338

1st Theme,
B   G339

2nd Theme — G340

No. 3 — G341

No. 4
1st Theme — G342

2nd Theme — G343

To Spring, Op. 43, No. 6, Pft. — G344

Two Elegaic Melodies,
Op. 34, Str. Orch.
By Permission of C. F.
Peters, Clayton F. Summy Co.,
Chicago, Agents in the U. S.
No. 1
Heart Wounds — G345

No. 2
Springtime — G346

Two Melodies, Op. 53,
Str. Orch.
By Permission of C. F.
Peters, Clayton F. Summy Co.,
Chicago, Agents
in the U. S.
No. 1
Norwegian — G347

No. 2
The First Meeting — G348

Waltz, Op. 12, No. 2, Pft.
By Permission of C. F.
Peters, Clayton F. Summy Co.,
Chicago, Agents in the U. S.
1st Theme — G349

2nd Theme — G350

Wedding Day at Troldhaugen,
Op. 65, No. 6, Pft.
By Permission of C. F.
Peters, Clayton F. Summy Co.,
Chicago, Agents in the U. S. — G351

GRIFFES, Charles Tomlinson (1884-1920)

The Pleasure Dome of
Kubla Khan, Orch.
Copyright 1920
by G. Schirmer, Inc.
1st Theme — G352

2nd Theme — G353

3rd Theme — G354

4th Theme — G355

Two Sketches (Based on
Indian Themes),
Str. Quart.
Copyright 1922
by G. Schirmer, Inc.
1st Movement
Farewell Song of
Chippewa Indians — G356

2nd Movement
1st Theme — G357

2nd Movement
2nd Theme — G358

2nd Movement
3rd Theme — G359

The White Peacock, Op. 7, No. 1, Pft.
Copyright renewal assigned
1945 to G. Schirmer, Inc. — G362

GROFÉ, Ferde (1892-1972)

**Grand Canyon Suite,
Orch.**
Copyright 1932 Robbins
Music Corp.
Used by special
permission Copyright
Proprietor.

1st Movement
Sunrise — G361

2nd Movement
Painted Desert — G362

3rd Movement
On the Trail
1st Theme — G363

3rd Movement
2nd Theme — G364

**Mississippi Suite,
Orch.**
Copyright 1926
Leo Feist, Inc.
Used by Special
Permission Copyright
Proprietor.

1st Movement
Father of Waters — G365

2nd Movement
Huckleberry Finn — G366

3rd Movement
Old Creole Days — G367

4th Movement
Mardi Gras
1st Theme — G368

4th Movement
2nd Theme — G369

HALVORSEN, Johan (1864-1935)

**Andante Religioso
Vn. & Orch.**
By permission of Associated
Music Publishers, Inc.

1st Theme — H1

2nd Theme — H2

**Triumphal Entry
of the Boyars
Orch.**
By permission of Associated
Music Publishers, Inc.

1st Theme — H3

2nd Theme — H4

HANDEL, George Frideric (1685-1759)

**Concerto No. 1 in B
Flat, Oboe & Orch.**

1st Movement — H5

2nd Movement
Fugue — H6

3rd Movement — H7

4th Movement — H8

Concerto No. 3 in G Minor, Oboe & Orch. — 1st Movement — H9

2nd Movement — H10

3rd Movement — H11

4th Movement — H12

Concerto No. 1 in G Minor, Organ & Orch., Op. 4, No. 1 — 1st Movement, 1st Theme — H13

1st Movement, 2nd Theme — H14

2nd Movement, 1st Theme — H15

2nd Movement, 2nd Theme — H16

3rd Movement — H17

Concerto No. 2 in B Flat, Organ & Orch., Op. 4, No. 2 — 1st Movement — H18

2nd Movement — H19

3rd Movement — H20

4th Movement — H21

Concerto No. 4 in F Organ & Orch., Op. 4, No. 4 — 1st Movement — H22

2nd Movement — H23

3rd Movement — H24

4th Movement, 1st Theme — H25

4th Movement, 2nd Theme — H26

Concerto No. 6 in B Flat Organ & Orch., Op. 4, No. 6 — 1st Movement — H27

2nd Movement — H28

3rd Movement — H29

Concerto No. 7 in B Flat Organ & Orch., Op. 7, No. 1 — 1st Movement 1st Theme — H30

1st Movement 2nd Theme — H31

2nd Movement 1st Theme — H32

2nd Movement 2nd Theme — H33

3rd Movement — H34

4th Movement Bourée — H35

Concerto No. 10 in D Minor, Organ & Orch. Op. 7, No. 4 — 1st Movement — H36

2nd Movement — H37

3rd Movement — H38

Concerto No. 11, in G Minor, Op. 7, No. 5 — 1st Movement 1st Theme — H39

1st Movement 2nd Theme — H40

2nd Movement 1st Theme — H41

2nd Movement 2nd Theme — H42

3rd Movement Minuet — H43

4th Movement Gavotte — H44

Concerto in F Double Wind Choir & Str. — 1st Movement — H45

2nd Movement 1st Theme — H46

Concerto Grosso in A Minor, Op. 6, No. 4 Str. Orch. — 1st Movement — H67

2nd Movement — H68

3rd Movement — H69

4th Movement 1st Theme — H70

4th Movement 2nd Theme — H71

Concerto Grosso in D, Op. 6, No. 5 Str. Orch. — 1st Movement — H72

2nd Movement — H73

3rd Movement — H74

4th Movement — H75

5th Movement 1st Theme — H76

5th Movement 2nd Theme — H77

6th Movement — H78

Concerto Grosso in G Minor Op. 6, No. 6 Str. Orch. — 1st Movement — H79

2nd Movement — H80

3rd Movement 1st Theme — H81

3rd Movement 2nd Theme — H82

4th Movement — H83

5th Movement — H84

Concerto Grosso in B flat Op. 6, No. 7 Str. Orch. — 1st Movement — H85

2nd Movement — H86

5th Movement 1st Theme — H107

5th Movement 2nd Theme — H108

6th Movement — H109

Concerto Grosso in A Op. 6, No. 11 Str. Orch. — 1st Movement — H110

2nd Movement — H111

3rd Movement — H112

4th Movement — H113

5th Movement — H114

Concerto Grosso in B Minor Op. 6, No. 12 Str. Orch. — 1st Movement — H115

2nd Movement — H116

3rd Movement — H117

4th Movement — H118

5th Movement — H119

Fireworks Music Orch. — 1st Movement Overture 1st Theme — H120

1st Movement Overture 2nd Theme — H121

2nd Movement Bourrée — H122

3rd Movement Largo alla Siciliana "La Paix" — H123

4th Movement La Rejouissance — H124

5th Movement Minuet No. 1 — H12

6th Movement Minuet No. 2 — H12

Alcina, Opera — Overture 1st Theme — H127
Overture 2nd Theme — H128
Musette — H129
Minuet — H130
Gavotte From Ballet — H131
Sarabande From Ballet — H132
Minuet From Ballet — H133
Gavotte No. 2 From Ballet — H134
Tamburino — H135

Oratorios — March from Joseph — H136
March from Judas Maccabeus — H137
Dead March from Saul — H138

Messiah — Overture 1st Theme — H139
2nd Theme — H140
Pt. 1 (Pastoral Symphony) — H141

Sonata in G, Flute & Fig. Bass Op. 1, No.5 — 1st Movement — H142
2nd Movement — H143
3rd Movement — H144
4th Movement — H145
5th Movement — H146

Sonata in C,
Flute & Fig. Bass
Op. 1, No. 7

Sonata in B Minor,
Flute & Fig. Bass
Op. 1, No. 9

Sonata in F,
Flute & Fig. Bass
Op. 1, No. 11

Sonata in C Minor,
Fl., Vn., & Fig. Bass
Op. 2, No. 1

1st Movement — H147
2nd Movement — H148
3rd Movement — H149
4th Movement — H150
5th Movement — H151
1st Movement — H152
2nd Movement — H153
3rd Movement — H154
4th Movement — H155
5th Movement — H156
6th Movement — H157
7th Movement — H158
1st Movement — H159
2nd Movement — H160
3rd Movement — H161
4th Movement — H162
1st Movement — H163
2nd Movement — H164
3rd Movement — H165
4th Movement — H166

Sonata, G Minor,
2 Fls. or 2 Vns.
& Fig. Bass, Op. 2, No. 2
    1st Movement   H167
    2nd Movement   H168
    3rd Movement   H169
    4th Movement   H170

Sonata in G Minor,
Oboe & Fig. Bass
Op. 1, No. 6
    1st Movement   H171
    2nd Movement   H172
    3rd Movement   H173
    4th Movement   H174

Sonata in E,
Oboe or Vn. & Fig. Bass
Op. 1, No. 15
    1st Movement   H175
    2nd Movement   H176
    3rd Movement   H177
    4th Movement   H178

Sonata in E Flat
2 Vns. or 2 Oboes
& Fig. Bass
    1st Movement   H179
    2nd Movement   H180
    3rd Movement   H181
    4th Movement   H182

Sonata in A
Op. 1, No. 3
Vn. & Fig. Bass
    1st Movement   H183
    2nd Movement   H184
    3rd Movement   H185
    4th Movement   H186

Sonata in F Op. 1, No. 12 Vn. & Fig. Bass — 1st Movement — H187

2nd Movement — H188

3rd Movement — H189

4th Movement — H190

Sonata in D Op. 1, No. 13 Vn. & Fig. Bass — 1st Movement — H191

2nd Movement — H192

3rd Movement — H193

4th Movement — H194

Sonata in A Op. 1, No. 14 Vn. & Fig. Bass — 1st Movement — H195

2nd Movement — H196

3rd Movement — H197

4th Movement — H198

Suite No. 1 in B Flat Pft., 2nd Set. — Air and Variations — H199

Suite No. 2 in F Pft. — 1st Movement — H200

2nd Movement — H201

3rd Movement — H202

4th Movement — H203

Suite No. 3 in D Minor Pft. — 1st Movement Allemande — H204

2nd Movement — H205

3rd Movement Air — H206

4th Movement
Gigue — H207

5th Movement
Minuet — H208

Suite No. 4 in E Minor
Pft.
1st Movement — H209

2nd Movement
Allemande — H210

3rd Movement
Courante — H211

4th Movement
Sarabande — H212

5th Movement
Gigue — H213

Suite No. 5 in E
Pft.
1st Movement
Prelude — H214

2nd Movement
Allemande — H215

3rd Movement
Courante — H216

Air (The
Harmonious
Blacksmith)
4th Movement
1st Theme,
A — H217

4th Movement
1st Theme,
B — H218

Suite No. 7 in G Minor
Pft.
1st Movement
Overture
1st Theme — H219

1st Movement
Overture
2nd Theme — H220

2nd Movement — H221

3rd Movement — H222

4th Movement
Sarabande — H223

5th Movement
Gigue — H224

6th Movement — H225

Suite No. 8 in F Minor
Pft.
1st Movement — H226

2nd Movement — H227

3rd Movement
Allemande — H228

4th Movement
Courante — H229

5th Movement
Gigue — H230

Suite in G
Pft., 2nd Set — Chaconne No. 2 — H231

Suite No. 4 in D Minor
Pft., 2nd Set — 1st Movement
Allemande — H232

2nd Movement
Courante — H233

3rd Movement
Sarabande — H234

4th Movement
Gigue — H235

Suite No. 8 in G
Pft., 2nd Set — 1st Movement
Allemande — H236

2nd Movement — H237

3rd Movement
Courante — H238

4th Movement
Aria — H239

5th Movement
Minuet — H240

6th Movement
Gavotte — H241

7th Movement — H242

Chaconne No.9 in G
from 2nd Set of Piano Suites — H243

Capriccio No. 3 in G Minor
from 3rd Collection of Piano Works — H244

Fantasia in C
No.4 from 3rd Collection of
Piano Works — H245

Water Music
Orch. — 1st Movement
Overture — H246

2nd Movement — H247

3rd Movement — H248

4th Movement — H249

5th Movement
Andante — H250

6th Movement — H251

7th Movement
Air — H252

8th Movement — H253

9th Movement
Bourée — H254

10th Movement
Hornpipe — H255

11th Movement — H256

12th Movement — H257

13th Movement
1st Theme — H258

13th Movement
2nd Theme — H259

14th Movement — H260

15th Movement
Aria — H261

16th Movement — H262

17th Movement
Air — H263

18th Movement
Minuet
1st Theme — H264

18th Movement
2nd Theme — H265

19th Movement — H266

20th Movement
Coro — H267

HANSON, Howard (1896-   )

Merry Mount Suite
Copyright 1933 by Harms, Inc.
Reprinted by special permission.
Overture — H268

Children's Dance
1st Theme — H269

2nd Theme — H270

Prelude to Act II
& Maypole Dances
1st Theme — H271

2nd Theme — H272

3rd Theme — H273

Chorale for Strings, Op. 3
Copyright 1932 by
Eastman School of Music,
Rochester, N. Y.
1st Movement
Intro. — H274

Sonata Op. 1, Pft.
Copyright 1931
Cos Cob Press, Inc.
1st Movement
1st Theme — H275

1st Movement
2nd Theme — H276

1st Movement
3rd Theme,
A — H277

1st Movement
3rd Theme,
B — H278

2nd Movement — H279

3rd Movement
1st Theme — H280

3rd Movement
2nd Theme — H281

HARRIS, Roy (1898-   )

Symphony No. 2
"Romantic"
Copyright 1934 by
Harold Flammer, Inc.
Used by permission.
— H282

1st Movement
Prelude — H283

2nd Movement
Andante Ostinato — H284

3rd Movement Scherzo — H285

Symphony No. 3

1st Theme — H286

2nd Theme — H287

3rd Theme — H288

4th Theme — H289

5th Theme — H290

6th Theme, A — H291

6th Theme, B — H292

Three Variations on a Theme St. Quartet — H293

HAYDN, Franz Josef (1732-1809)

Andante & Variations, Pft. Op. 83, F. Minor 1st Theme — H294

2nd Theme — H295

Arietta (Theme & Variations) E Flat Pft. — H296

Capriccio in G, Pft. — H297

Fantasia in C, Pft. 1st Theme — H298

2nd Theme — H299

Concerto in D Cello & Orch. Op.101 1st Movement 1st Theme — H300

1st Movement 2nd Theme — H301

2nd Movement — H302

3rd Movement 1st Theme — H303

Concerto in D
Pft. & Orch.

Concerto in E Flat
Trumpet & Orch.

Quartet in B Flat
Op. 1, No. 1, Str.
"La Chasse"

Quartet in C
Op. 1, No. 6 Str.

3rd Movement
2nd Theme — H304

1st Movement — H305

2nd Movement
1st Theme — H306

2nd Movement
2nd Theme — H307

3rd Movement
1st Theme — H308

3rd Movement
2nd Theme — H309

1st Movement
1st Theme — H310

1st Movement
2nd Theme — H311

2nd Movement — H312

3rd Movement — H314

1st Movement — H315

2nd Movement — H316

3rd Movement — H317

4th Movement — H318

5th Movement — H319

1st Movement — H320

2nd Movement — H321

3rd Movement — H32

4th Movement
1st Theme — H32

4th Movement
2nd Theme — H32

5th Movement — H325

Quartet in B Flat
Op. 3, No. 4, Str.
1st Movement 1st Theme — H326

1st Movement 2nd Theme — H327

2nd Movement 1st Theme — H328

2nd Movement 2nd Theme — H329

Quartet in F
Op. 3, No. 5, Str.
1st Movement 1st Theme — H330

1st Movement 2nd Theme — H331

2nd Movement — H332

3rd Movement 1st Theme — H333

3rd Movement 2nd Theme — H334

4th Movement — H335

Quartet in E Flat
Op. 20, No. 1, Str.
1st Movement — H336

2nd Movement — H337

3rd Movement — H338

4th Movement — H339

Quartet in C
Op. 20, No. 2, Str.
1st Movement — H340

2nd Movement 1st Theme — H341

2nd Movement 2nd Theme — H342

3rd Movement — H343

4th Movement — H344

4th Movement / 2nd Theme — H365

Quartet in D
Op. 33, No. 6, Str.

1st Movement — H366

2nd Movement — H367

3rd Movement — H368

4th Movement — H369

Quartet in E Flat
Op. 50, No. 3, Str.

1st Movement — H370

2nd Movement — H371

3rd Movement — H372

4th Movement — H373

Quartet in D
Op. 50, No. 6, Str.
"The Frog"

1st Movement — H374

2nd Movement — H375

3rd Movement / 1st Theme — H376

3rd Movement / 2nd Theme — H377

4th Movement / 1st Theme — H378

4th Movement / 2nd Theme — H379

Quartet in G
Op. 54, No. 1, Str.

1st Movement — H380

2nd Movement — H381

3rd Movement — H382

4th Movement — H383

Quartet in C
Op. 54, No. 2, Str.

1st Movement / 1st Theme — H384

Quartet in B Flat
Op.64, No.3, Str.

1st Movement / 1st Theme — H405

1st Movement / 2nd Theme — H406

2nd Movement — H407

3rd Movement / 1st Theme — H408

3rd Movement / 2nd Theme — H409

4th Movement / 1st Theme — H410

4th Movement / 2nd Theme — H411

Quartet in G
Op.64, No.4, Str.

1st Movement / 1st Theme — H412

1st Movement / 2nd Theme — H413

1st Movement / 3rd Theme — H414

2nd Movement — H415

3rd Movement — H416

4th Movement — H417

Quartet in D
Op.64 No.5, Str.
"The Lark"

1st Movement / 1st Theme — H418

1st Movement / 2nd Theme — H419

1st Movement / 3rd Theme — H420

2nd Movement — H421

3rd Movement / 1st Theme — H422

3rd Movement / 2nd Theme — H423

4th Movement — H424

Quartet in E Flat
Op.64 No.6, Str.   1st Movement   H425

2nd Movement   H426

3rd Movement
1st Theme   H427

3rd Movement
2nd Theme   H428

4th Movement   H429

Quartet in B Flat
Op.71 No.1, Str.   1st Movement   H430

2nd Movement   H431

3rd Movement   H432

4th Movement   H433

Quartet in C
Op.74 No.1, Str.   1st Movement   H434

2nd Movement
1st Theme   H435

2nd Movement
2nd Theme   H436

3rd Movement
1st Theme   H437

3rd Movement
1st Theme   H438

4th Movement
1st Theme   H439

4th Movement
2nd Theme   H440

4th Movement
3rd Theme   H44

Quartet in F
Op.74, No.2, Str.   1st Movement   H44

2nd Movement   H44

3rd Movement
1st Theme   H44

3rd Movement 2nd Theme — H444a

4th Movement 1st Theme — H445

4th Movement 2nd Theme — H446

Quartet in G Minor Op.74, No. 3, Str. "Horseman"

1st Movement 1st Theme — H447

1st Movement 2nd Theme — H448

2nd Movement 1st Theme — H449

2nd Movement 2nd Theme — H450

3rd Movement 1st Theme — H451

3rd Movement 2nd Theme — H452

4th Movement 1st Theme — H453

4th Movement 2nd Theme — H454

Quartet in G Op. 76, No.1, Str.

1st Movement 1st Theme — H455

1st Movement 2nd Theme — H456

2nd Movement — H457

3rd Movement 1st Theme — H458

3rd Movement 2nd Theme — H459

4th Movement — H460

Quartet in D Op. 76, No. 2, Str. "Quinten"

1st Movement — H461

2nd Movement 1st Theme — H462

2nd Movement 2nd Theme — H463

4th Movement / 2nd Theme	H504
Sonata in C Minor / B. & H. No. 20, Pft. — 1st Movement	H505
2nd Movement	H506
3rd Movement	H507
Sonata in F / B. & H. No. 23, Pft. — 1st Movement	H508
2nd Movement	H509
3rd Movement	H510
Sonata in E Minor / B. & H. No. 34, Pft. — 1st Movement / 1st Theme	H511
1st Movement / 2nd Theme	H512
2nd Movement	H513
3rd Movement	H514
Sonata in C / B. & H. No. 35, Pft. — 1st Movement / 1st Theme	H515
1st Movement / 2nd Theme	H516
2nd Movement	H517
3rd Movement / 1st Theme	H518
3rd Movement / 2nd Theme	H519
Sonata in C Sharp Minor Pft. B. & H. No. 36 — 1st Movement	H520
2nd Movement / 1st Theme	H521
2nd Movement / 2nd Theme	H522
3rd Movement / 1st Theme	H523

Sonata in D, Pft.
B. & H. No.37

3rd Movement
2nd Theme — H524

1st Movement — H525

2nd Movement — H526

3rd Movement
1st Theme — H527

3rd Movement
2nd Theme — H528

3rd Movement
3rd Theme — H529

Symphony in A
B. & H. No.28

1st Movement — H530

2nd Movement — H531

3rd Movement
1st Theme — H532

3rd Movement
2nd Theme — H533

4th Movement
1st Theme — H534

4th Movement
2nd Theme — H535

Symphony in
F Sharp Minor
B. & H. No.45, "Farewell"

1st Movement
1st Theme — H536

1st Movement
2nd Theme — H537

2nd Movement — H538

3rd Movement
1st Theme — H539

3rd Movement
2nd Theme — H540

4th Movement — H541

5th Movement — H542

Symphony in D
B. & H No.73
"La Chasse"

1st Movement
Intro. — H543

1st Movement / 2nd Theme   H584

2nd Movement   H585

3rd Movement / 1st Theme   H586

3rd Movement / 2nd Theme   H587

4th Movement / 1st Theme   H588

4th Movement / 2nd Theme   H589

Symphony in D / B. & H. No. 93 / London 2

1st Movement / Intro.   H590

1st Movement / 1st Theme   H591

1st Movement / 2nd Theme   H592

2nd Movement   H593

3rd Movement / 1st Theme   H594

3rd Movement / 2nd Theme, A   H595

3rd Movement / 2nd Theme, B   H596

4th Movement / 1st Theme   H597

4th Movement / 2nd Theme   H598

Symphony in G / B. & H. No. 94 / "Surprise"

1st Movement / Intro.   H599

1st Movement / 1st Theme   H600

1st Movement / 2nd Theme   H601

2nd Movement   H602

3rd Movement / 1st Theme   H603

HAYDN

3rd Movement 2nd Theme — H604

4th Movement 1st Theme — H605

4th Movement 2nd Theme — H606

Symphony in C Minor B. & H. No.95 London 5

1st Movement 1st Theme — H607

1st Movement 2nd Theme — H608

2nd Movement — H609

3rd Movement 1st Theme — H610

3rd Movement 2nd Theme — H611

4th Movement — H612

Symphony in C B. & H. No.97 London 1

1st Movement Intro. — H613

1st Movement 1st Theme — H614

1st Movement 2nd Theme — H615

2nd Movement — H616

3rd Movement 1st Theme — H617

3rd Movement 2nd Theme — H618

4th Movement 1st Theme — H619

4th Movement 2nd Theme — H620

Symphony in B Flat B. & H. No.98 London 4

1st Movement Intro. — H621

1st Movement 1st Theme — H622

1st Movement 2nd Theme — H623

2nd Movement 1st Theme — H624
2nd Movement 2nd Theme — H625
3rd Movement 1st Theme — H626
3rd Movement 2nd Theme — H627
4th Movement 1st Theme — H628
4th Movement 2nd Theme — H629
4th Movement 1st Theme — H630

Symphony in E Flat
B. & H. No.99
London 10
"Imperial"

1st Movement Intro. — H631
1st Movement 1st Theme — H632
1st Movement 2nd Theme — H633
2nd Movement 1st Theme — H634
2nd Movement 2nd Theme — H635
3rd Movement 1st Theme — H636
3rd Movement 2nd Theme — H637
4th Movement 1st Theme — H638
4th Movement 2nd Theme — H639
4th Movement 3rd Theme — H640

Symphony in G
B. & H. No.100
"Military"

1st Movement Intro. — H641
1st Movement 1st Theme — H642
1st Movement 2nd Theme — H643

Symphony in D
B. & H. No. 101
"Clock"

Symphony in B Flat
B. & H. No.102
London 9

Symphony in E Flat
B. & H. No.103
"Drum Roll"

Symphony in D
B. & H. No 104
"London"

Symphony in C
"Toy Symphony"

1st Movement 3rd Theme — H684
1st Movement 4th Theme — H685
2nd Movement 1st Theme — H686
2nd Movement 2nd Theme — H687
3rd Movement — H688

Trio No. 1 in G
Vn. Pft. & Cello

1st Movement — H689
2nd Movement 1st Theme — H690
2nd Movement 2nd Theme — H691
3rd Movement "Gypsy" Rondo 1st Theme — H692
3rd Movement 2nd Theme — H693
3rd Movement 3rd Theme — H694
3rd Movement 4th Theme — H695
3rd Movement 5th Theme — H696
3rd Movement 6th Theme — H697

Trio No. 2 in F Sharp
Minor Vn., Pft. & Cello

1st Movement 1st Theme — H698
1st Movement 2nd Theme — H699
2nd Movement — H700
3rd Movement 1st Theme — H701
3rd Movement 2nd Theme — H702

Trio No. 3 in C
Vn., Pft. & Cello

1st Movement 1st Theme — H703

1st Movement / 2nd Theme — H704

2nd Movement — H705

3rd Movement — H706

Trio No. 5 in E Flat
Vn., Pft. & Cello
1st Movement — H707

2nd Movement — H708

3rd Movement — H709

Trio No. 1 in C
2 Flutes and Cello
"London"
1st Movement / 1st Theme — H710

1st Movement / 2nd Theme — H711

2nd Movement — H712

3rd Movement — H713

Trio No. 2 in G
2 Flutes and Cello
"London"
1st Movement — H714

2nd Movement — H715

3rd Movement — H716

HERBERT, Victor (1859-1924)

Babes in Toyland, Orch.
Copyright 1903 by
M. Witmark & Sons
Copyright renewed.
Reprinted by
special permission.
March / 1st Theme — H717

2nd Theme — H718

Natoma,
Opera
Copyright renewal assigned
1938 to G. Schirmer, Inc.
Dagger Dance — H719

Habañera — H720

HEROLD, Louis (1791-1833)

Zampa
Overture
1st Theme — H721

2nd Theme   H722

HINDEMITH, Paul (1895-1963)

Kleine Kammermusik
Op.24 No.2
Ob., Fl., Cl., Hn., Fag.
By permission of
Associated Music
Publishers, Inc.

1st Movement / 1st Theme   H723

1st Movement / 2nd Theme   H724

2nd Movement / Waltz / 1st Theme   H725

2nd Movement / 2nd Theme   H726

2nd Movement / 3rd Theme   H727

3rd Movement / 1st Theme   H728

3rd Movement / 2nd Theme   H729

4th Movement   H730

5th Movement / 1st Theme   H731

5th Movement / 2nd Theme   H732

5th Movement / 3rd Theme   H733

5th Movement / 4th Theme   H734

Mathis der Mahler
Symphony
By permission of
Associated Music
Publishers, Inc.

1st Movement / Concert of Angels / Intro.   H735

1st Movement / 1st Theme, A   H736

1st Movement / 1st Theme, B   H737

1st Movement / 2nd Theme   H738

1st Movement / 3rd Theme   H739

1st Movement / 4th Theme   H740

2nd Movement
Entombment
1st Theme — H741

2nd Movement
2nd Theme — H742

Temptation of St. Anthony

3rd Movement
Intro. — H743

3rd Movement
1st Theme — H744

3rd Movement
2nd Theme — H745

3rd Movement
3rd Theme — H746

3rd Movement
4th Theme — H747

3rd Movement
5th Theme — H748

3rd Movement
6th Theme — H749

Quartet
Op. 22, No. 3, Str.
By permission of
Associated Music
Publishers, Inc.

1st Movement — H750

2nd Movement
1st Theme — H751

2nd Movement
2nd Theme — H752

3rd Movement
1st Theme — H753

3rd Movement
2nd Theme — H754

4th Movement — H755

5th Movement
1st Theme — H756

5th Movement
2nd Theme — H757

5th Movement
3rd Theme — H758

Der Schwanendreher
Concerto, Vla. & Orch.
On Old Folk Tunes
By permission
of Associated Music
Publishers, Inc.

1st Movement
"Zwischen Berg
und Tiefem Tal"
1st Theme — H759

1st Movement
2nd Theme — H760

2nd Movement 1st Theme — H761

2nd Movement 2nd Theme — H762

2nd Movement 3rd Theme (theme for Fugato) "Der Gutzgauch Auf Dem Zaune Sass" — H763

3rd Movement Theme for Variations "Seid Ihr Der Schwanendreher" — H764

Sonata No.2 Pft. By permission of Associated Music Publishers, Inc.

1st Movement 1st Theme — H765

1st Movement 2nd Theme — H766

2nd Movement 1st Theme — H767

2nd Movement 2nd Theme — H768

3rd Movement — H769

3rd Movement 2nd Theme Rondo — H770

Sonata No.3 Pft. By permission of Associated Music Publishers, Inc.

1st Movement 1st Theme — H771

1st Movement 2nd Theme — H772

2nd Movement — H773

3rd Movement — H774

4th Movement Fugue theme — H775

Sonata Pft., 4 Hands By permission of Associated Music Publishers, Inc.

1st Movement 1st Theme — H776

1st Movement 2nd Theme — H777

2nd Movement 1st Theme — H778

2nd Movement 2nd Theme — H779

3rd Movement — H780

Trauermusik, Orch. (Funeral Music) For George V of England — 1st Movement — H781
By permission of Associated Music Publishers, Inc.

2nd Movement — H782

3rd Movement — H783

4th Movement Choral Für deinen Thron Tret' Ich Hiermit — H784

Trio No. 2 Vn., Viola, Cello — 1st Movement 1st Theme — H785
By permission of Associated Music Publishers, Inc.

1st Movement 2nd Theme — H786

2nd Movement 1st Theme — H787

2nd Movement 2nd Theme — H788

3rd Movement 1st Theme — H789

3rd Movement 2nd Theme — H790

3rd Movement 3rd Theme — H791

HOLBROOKE, Josef (1878-1958)

Bronwen Overture — 1st Theme — H792
Copyright by Lienau, Licensed by SESAC, Inc., N. Y.

2nd Theme — H793

3rd Theme — H794

Quintet, Op. 27, No. 1 Cl. & Str. — 1st Movement Cavatina — H795
By Permission of Novello & Co., Ltd., London

2nd Movement Variations — H796

HOLST, Gustav Theodore (1874-1934)

The Planets, Op. 32 Orch. — 1st Movement 1st Theme — H797

Mars, the Bringer of War — 1st Movement 2nd Theme — H798
Copyright 1921 by Goodwin & Tabb, Ltd., London.

3rd Movement / 2nd Theme   H819

4th Movement / The Dargason / Finale   H820

Two Songs without Words
Op. 22, Orch.
Copyright 1925
by E.C Schirmer, Boston.

I Country Song / 1st Theme   H821

2nd Theme   H822

II Marching Song / 1st Theme   H823

2nd Theme   H824

3rd Theme   H825

HONEGGER, Arthur (1892-1955)

Chant de Nigamon
Orch.
Copyright by Editions Salabert
Editions Salabert,
22 Rue Chaucat, Paris
Salabert, Inc.,
1 East 57 St., N. Y.

1st Theme   H826

2nd Theme   H827

3rd Theme   H828

4th Theme   H829

Concertino
Pft. & Orch.
Copyright by Editions
Salabert Editions Salabert,
22 Rue Chaucat, Paris
Salabert, Inc.,
1 East 57 St., N. Y.

1st Movement / 1st Theme   H830

1st Movement / 2nd Theme   H831

1st Movement / 3rd Theme   H832

2nd Movement   H833

3rd Movement / 1st Theme   H834

3rd Movement / 2nd Theme   H835

King David
Symphonic Psalm

1st Movement / Intro.   H836

Cortège
By permission of
Novello & Co.,
Ltd., London.

1st Theme   H837

2nd Theme

March of the Philistines

March of the Israelites

**Pastorale D'Été
Orch.**
Copyright by Editions Salabert
Editions Salabert,
22 Rue Chaucat, Paris
Salabert, Inc.,
I East 57 St., N. Y.

1st Theme

2nd Theme

3rd Theme

4th Theme

**Rugby,
Orch.**
Copyright by Editions Salabert
Editions Salabert,
22 Rue Chaucat, Paris
Salabert, Inc.,
I East 57 St., N. Y.

1st Theme

2nd Theme

HOWELLS, Herbert (1892-   )

**Puck's Minuet, Op. 20,
No. 1, Orch.**
Copyright 1919 by
Goodwin & Tabb,
Ltd., London.

1st Theme

2nd Theme

HUBAY, Jeno (1858-1937)

**Hejre Kati, Op. 32, No. 4,
Vn. & Orch., from
Hungarian Czardas Scenes**
Copyright 1901
by Carl Fischer, Inc., N. Y.

1st Theme

2nd Theme

3rd Theme

**Poème Hongrois, Op. 27, No. 1
Vn. & Orch.**

**Poème Hongrois, Op. 27,
No. 9 Vn. & Orch.**
By permission of J. Hamelk
Music Publishers, Paris.

1st Theme

2nd Theme

H838
H839
H840
H841
H842
H843
H844
H845
H846
H847
H848
H849
H850
H851
H852
H853
H854

HUMMEL, Johann (1778-1837)

Rondo in E Flat, Op.11   H855

HUMPERDINCK, Engelbert (1854-1921)

Hansel & Gretel, Opera
Prelude to Act 1   1st Theme   H856
Copyright 1895
by B. Schott's Söhne

   2nd Theme   H857

Prelude to Act 2 "Witch's Ride"   H858

Pantomine   H859

Prelude "The Gingerbread House"
to Act 3   1st Theme   H860

2nd Theme   H861

"Gingerbread Waltz"   H862

Königskinder, Opera
Prelude   1st Theme, A   H863

1st Theme, B   H864

Prelude
to Act 2   "Children's Rounds"
1st Theme   H865

2nd Theme   H866

3rd Theme   H867

IBERT, Jacques (1890-1962)

Concerto, Alto Sax
& Small Orch.   1st Movement
1st Theme   I1
Copyright by A. Leduc
Music Publishers, Paris

1st Movement
2nd Theme   I2

2nd Movement   I3

3rd Movement
1st Theme   I4

IBERT

Divertissement, Chamber Orch.
Permission for reprint granted by Durand & Cie, Paris. Elkan-Vogel Co.,Inc. Philadelphia, Copyright Owners.

3rd Movement / 2nd Theme — i5

1st Movement / Intro. — i6

2nd Movement / Cortege / 1st Theme — i7

2nd Movement / 2nd Theme — i8

3rd Movement / Nocturne — i9

4th Movement / Waltz / 1st Theme — i10

4th Movement / 2nd Theme — i11

5th Movement / Parade / 1st Theme — i12

5th Movement / 2nd Theme — i13

6th Movement / Finale — i14

Entr'Acte, Flute & Guitar
Copyright by A. Leduc Music Publishers, Paris

1st Theme — i15

2nd Theme — i16

Escales (Ports of Call) Orch.
Copyright by A. Leduc Music Publishers, Paris

1st Movement / Rome—Palerme / 1st Theme — i17

1st Movement / 2nd Theme — i18

2nd Movement / Tunis—Nefta — i19

3rd Movement / Valencia / 1st Theme — i20

3rd Movement / 2nd Theme — i21

Histoires, Pft.
Copyright by A. Leduc Publishers, Paris

No. 1 / La Meneuse de Tortues D'Or / (The Keeper of the Golden Tortoises) — i22

No. 2 / Le Petit Ane Blanc / (The Little White Donkey) — i23

No. 3 / Le Vieux Mendicant / (The Old Beggar) — i24

No. 4
A Giddy Girl   125

No. 8
Le Cage de Crystal
(The Crystal Cage)   126

Pièce, flûte alone
Copyright by A. Leduc
Music Publishers, Paris   127

ILYINSKY, Alexander (1859-1919)

Berceuse, Pft.   128

D'INDY, Vincent (1851-1931)

Le Camp de Wallenstein,
Op. 12, Orch.
Permission for reprint
granted by Durand & Cie,
Paris. Elkan-Vogel Co., Inc.
Philadelphia, Copyright
Owners.

1st Theme   129
2nd Theme   130
3rd Theme   131
4th Theme   132
5th Theme   133

Istar, Op. 42,
Symphonic Variations
Permission for reprint granted
by Durand & Cie, Paris.
Elkan-Vogel Co., Philadelphia,
Inc. Copyright Owners.

1st Theme   134
2nd Theme   135
3rd Theme   136
4th Theme   137
5th Theme   138
6th Theme   139

Sonata in C,
Op. 59, Vn. &, Pft.
Permission for reprint
granted by Durand & Cie,
Paris. Elkan-Vogel Co., Inc.
Philadelphia, Copyright
Owners.

1st Movement
1st Theme   140
1st Movement
2nd Theme   141
1st Movement
3rd Theme   142

D'INDY (continued)

- 2nd Movement, 1st Theme — i43
- 2nd Movement, 2nd Theme — i44
- 3rd Movement, 1st Theme, A — i45
- 3rd Movement, 1st Theme, B — i46
- 3rd Movement, 2nd Theme — i47
- 4th Movement — i48

Suite en Parties, Op. 91,
Fl., Vn., Viola, Cello,
Harp

By permission of the copyright owner, Heugel Ltd., London.

- 1st Movement, Entrée en Sonate — i49
- 2nd Movement, Air Désuet — i50
- 3rd Movement, Sarabande, 1st Theme — i51
- 3rd Movement, 2nd Theme — i52
- 3rd Movement, 3rd Theme — i53
- 4th Movement, Farandole — i54

Symphony on a French
Mountain Theme, Op. 25

By permission of J. Hamelle Music Publishers, Paris.

- 1st Movement, 1st Theme — i55
- 1st Movement, 2nd Theme — i56
- 2nd Movement — i57
- 3rd Movement, 1st Theme — i58
- 3rd Movement, 2nd Theme — i59

INFANTE, Manuel (1883-   )

Pochades Andalouses,
Pft.

- No. 1, Canto Flamenco — i60
- No. 2, Danse Gitane — i61

No. 3
Aniers sur la Route de Seville   162

No. 4
Tientos   163

INGHELBRECHT, D. E. (1880-1965)

Four Fanfares, Brass   **No. 1** Pour une Fête   164
Copyright by Editions
Salabert Editions Salabert,
22 Rue Chaucat, Paris   **No. 2**
Salabert, Inc.,
1 East 57 St., N. Y.   Pour le Président   165

No. 3
Funèbre Pour des Mineurs Ensevelis   166

No. 4
Dédicatoire   167

Nurseries (3rd Set),   **No. 1**
Orch.   Nous N'irons Plus au Bois   168
Copyright by A. Leduc
Music Publishers, Paris

No. 2
Le Tour Prends Garde!   169

No. 3
Bon Voyage Monsieur Dumollet   170

No. 4
Sur le Pont d'Avignon   171

No. 5
Où est la Marguerite?   172

No. 6
Arlequin marie sa Fille   173

IPPOLITOFF-IVANOFF, Michael (1859-1935)

Caucasian Sketches,   **1st Movement**
Op. 10, Orch.   In the Mountain Pass
By permission of   **1st Theme**   174
International Music Co.

1st Movement
2nd Theme   175

1st Movement
3rd Theme   176

2nd Movement
In the Village
Intro.   177

2nd Movement
1st Theme   178

2nd Movement
2nd Theme   179

3rd Movement
In the Mosque — 180

4th Movement
Procession of the Sardar
1st Theme — 181

4th Movement
2nd Theme — 182

Quartet, Op. 13, Str.   1st Movement
Intro. — 183

1st Movement
1st Theme — 184

1st Movement
2nd Theme — 185

2nd Movement
(Humoresca—Scherzando)
1st Theme — 186

2nd Movement
2nd Theme — 187

3rd Movement
Intermezzo — 188

4th Movement
1st Theme — 189

4th Movement
2nd Theme — 190

4th Movement
3rd Theme — 191

IRELAND, John (1879-1962)

April, Pft. — 192

Concertino Pastorale,
Str. Orch.
By permission of the
copyright owner, Boosey
and Hawkes, Inc.   1st Movement
Eclogue
1st Theme — 193

1st Movement
2nd Theme — 194

2nd Movement
Threnody — 195

Concerto in E Flat
Pft. & Orch.
By permission of the
copyright holders,
J. & W. Chester, Ltd.,
11 Great Marlborough
Street, London, W. 1.   1st Movement
1st Theme — 196

1st Movement
2nd Theme — 197

2nd Movement
1st Theme — 198

2nd Movement / 2nd Theme — ı99

3rd Movement / 1st Theme — ı100

3rd Movement / 2nd Theme — ı101

The Holy Boy, Pft. — ı102

A London Overture, Orch. / 1st Theme
By permission of the copyright owner, Boosey and Hawkes, Inc. — ı103

2nd Theme — ı104

3rd Theme — ı105

Phantasy in A Minor, Vn., Pft. & Cello / 1st Theme
By permission of Augener, Ltd., London — ı106

2nd Theme — ı107

3rd Theme — ı108

Sonata in G Minor, Cello & Pft. / 1st Movement / 1st Theme
By permission of Augener, Ltd., London — ı109

1st Movement / 2nd Theme — ı110

2nd Movement / 1st Theme — ı111

2nd Movement / 2nd Theme — ı112

3rd Movement / 1st Theme — ı113

3rd Movement / 2nd Theme — ı114

Trio No. 3 in E Minor & Major, Vn., Cello & Pft. / 1st Movement / 1st Theme — ı115

1st Movement / 2nd Theme — ı116

2nd Movement / 1st Theme — ı117

2nd Movement / 2nd Theme, A — ı118

2nd Movement 2nd Theme, B — I119
3rd Movement 1st Theme — I120
3rd Movement 2nd Theme — I121
4th Movement 1st Theme — I122
4th Movement 2nd Theme — I123

IVANOVICI, J. (1845-1902)

Waves of the Danube, Waltzes, Orch.

No. 1 1st Theme — I124
No. 1 2nd Theme — I125
No. 2 1st Theme — I126
No. 2 2nd Theme — I127
No. 3 — I128
No. 4 — I129

IVES, Charles (1874-1954)

New England Holidays, Orch.
Washington's Birthday (Barn Dance) 1st Theme — I130

Copyright 1937 by New Music Society of California, San Francisco, California.

2nd Theme — I131

JACOBI, Frederick (1891-1952)

Indian Dances, Orch.

Buffalo Dance Intro. — J1
Theme — J2
Butterfly Dance — J3
War Dance 1st Theme — J4

2nd Theme — J5

Corn Dance — J6

Scherzo, Woodwind Quintet — 1st Theme — J7
Copyright 1938
by Carl Fischer, Inc., N. Y.

2nd Theme — J8

JANÁČEK, Leoš (1854-1928)

Lásské Tance, Bohemian Folk Dances, Orch. — Starodavny 1st Theme — J9

2nd Theme — J10

3rd Theme — J11

Sinfonietta — 1st Movement — J12

2nd Movement 1st Theme — J13

2nd Movement 2nd Theme — J14

3rd Movement — J15

4th Movement — J16

5th Movement — J17

JÄRNEFELT, Armas (1869-1958)

Praeludium, Pft. or Orch. — J18
By permission of the copyright holders,
J. & W. Chester, Ltd.,
11 Great Marlborough Street, London, W. 1.

JENSEN, Adolf (1837-1879)

Murmuring Zephyrs, Pft. — J19

Reigen (Elfin Dance), Op. 33, No. 5, Pft. or Orch. — J20

JONGEN, Joseph (1873-1953)

Légende Naïve, Op. 59, No. 1, Vn. & Pft.
By permission of the copyright holders,
J. & W. Chester, Ltd., 11 Great Marlborough
Street, London, W. 1.

Petite Suite, Pft.

Légende Naïve ... J21

1st Movement / Petite Marche Militaire ... J22

2nd Movement / Conte Plaisant ... J23

3rd Movement / Nostalgie ... J24

4th Movement / Valse Gracieuse ... J25

5th Movement / Tambourin / 1st Theme ... J26

5th Movement / 2nd Theme ... J27

JUON, Paul (1872-1940)

Ärva (Valse Mignonne), Op. 52, No. 2, Vn. & Pft.
Copyright by Lienau, Licensed
by SESAC, Inc., N. Y.

1st Theme ... J28

2nd Theme ... J29

Berceuse, Op. 28, No. 3, Vn. & Pft.
Copyright by Lienau, Licensed
by SESAC, Inc., N. Y.

... J30

Chamber Symphony in B Flat, Op. 27
Copyright by Lienau, Licensed
by SESAC, Inc., N. Y.

1st Movement / 1st Theme ... J31

1st Movement / 2nd Theme ... J32

2nd Movement ... J33

3rd Movement / 1st Theme, A ... J34

3rd Movement / 1st Theme, B ... J35

3rd Movement / 2nd Theme ... J36

4th Movement ... J37

KABALEVSKY, Dmitri (1904-   )

Colas Breugnon, Op. 24, Overture — 1st Theme — K1
Copyright 1946 by Leeds Music Corp., N. Y. Reprinted here by permisssion of the copyright owner. — 2nd Theme — K2

Symphony No. 2 in C Minor, Op. 19 — 1st Movement 1st Theme — K3
Copyright 1945 by Leeds Music Corp., N. Y. Reprinted here by permisssion of the copyright owner. — 1st Movement 2nd Theme — K4

2nd Movement Intro. — K5
2nd Movement 1st Theme — K6
2nd Movement 2nd Theme — K7
3rd Movement 1st Theme — K8
3rd Movement 2nd Theme — K9
3rd Movement 3rd Theme — K10
3rd Movement 4th Theme — K11

KALINNIKOFF, Basil (1866-1901)

Symphony No. 1 in G Minor — 1st Movement 1st Theme — K12
1st Movement 2nd Theme — K13
2nd Movement 1st Theme — K14
2nd Movement 2nd Theme — K15
3rd Movement 1st Theme — K16
3rd Movement 2nd Theme — K1
4th Movement 1st Theme — K1

4th Movement
2nd Theme  K19

KETELBEY, Albert W. (1880-1959)

1st Theme 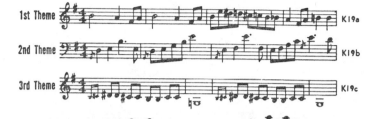 K19a

2nd Theme K19b

3rd Theme K19c

4th Theme K19d

1st Theme K20

2nd Theme K21

3rd Theme  K22

1st Theme K22a

2nd Theme  K22b

3rd Theme  K22c

4th Theme K22d

5th Theme K22e

6th Theme K22f

KHACHATURIAN, Aram (1903-   )

1st Movement
1st Theme  K23

1st Movement
2nd Theme K24

2nd Movement
Intro. K25

2nd Movement
Theme K26

Concerto, Vn. & Orch.

Gayane, Ballet

3rd Movement 1st Theme A — K27
3rd Movement 1st Theme B — K28
3rd Movement 2nd Theme — K29
1st Movement 1st Theme A — K30
1st Movement 1st Theme B — K31
1st Movement 2nd Theme — K32
2nd Movement — K33
3rd Movement 1st Theme — K34
3rd Movement 2nd Theme — K35
3rd Movement 3rd Theme — K36
Dance of the Rose Maidens — K37
Ayshe's Awakening and Dance 1st Theme — K38
2nd Theme — K39
Dance of the Kurds — K40
Lullaby — K41
Lezghinka — K42
Dance of the Young Kurds 1st Theme — K43
2nd Theme — K44
Variations — K45
Sword Dance 1st Theme — K46

Masquerade
Suite for Orch.

2nd Theme — K47

1st Movement
Waltz
1st Theme — K48

1st Movement
2nd Theme — K49

2nd Movement
Nocturne — K50

3rd Movement
Mazurka — K51

4th Movement
Romance — K52

5th Movement
Galop — K53

Toccata, Pft.

1st Theme — K54

2nd Theme — K55

KHRENNIKOFF, Tikhon (1913-   )

Symphony No. 1, Op. 4
Copyright 1945 by Leeds
Music Corp., N. Y.
Reprinted here by
permission of the
copyright owner.

1st Movement
1st Theme — K56

1st Movement
2nd Theme — K57

1st Movement
3rd Theme — K58

2nd Movement
1st Theme — K59

2nd Movement
2nd Theme — K60

3rd Movement
1st Theme — K61

3rd Movement
2nd Theme — K62

KODÁLY, Zoltán (1882-1967)

Galanta Dances
Orch.
By permission of the copyright owner,
Boosey and Hawkes, Inc.

Intro. — K63

1st Movement — K64

2nd Movement   K65

3rd Movement   K66

4th Movement
1st Theme   K67

4th Movement
2nd Theme   K68

5th Movement
1st Theme   K69

5th Movement
2nd Theme   K70

**Háry János, Op. 15,
Suite from Opera**
By permission of the
copyright owner,
Boosey and Hawkes, Inc.

Kezdodik a Mese
(The Fairy Tale
Begins)   K71

Bécsi Harangjáték
(Viennese Musical Clock)   K72

Dal (Song)   K73

(Battle and Defeat of Napoleon)
1st Theme
Franciak Indulója   K74

2nd Theme
Napoleon Bevonulása   K75

3rd Theme
Gyászinduló   K76

Közjáték
1st Theme   K77

2nd Theme   K78

3rd Theme   K79

Piros Alma   K80

Bordal-Ó Melysok Hal   K81

Hogyan Tudtal Rozsám   K82

Hej Két Tikom   K83

Toborzó
1st Theme   K84

2nd Theme — K103

3rd Theme — K104

**Liebeslied,
Old Viennese Song**
Vn. & Pft.
Copyright by Charles Foley,
New York   1st Theme — K105

2nd Theme — K106

**The Old Refrain
Viennese Popular Song**
Vn. & Pft.
Copyright by Charles Foley, New York   — K107

Polichinelle, Serenade
Vn. & Pft.
Copyright by Charles Foley, New York   — K108

**Praeludium and Allegro
(Style of Pugnani)**
Vn. & Pft.
Copyright by Charles Foley, New York   Praeludium — K109

Allegro — K110

**La Précieuse
(Style of Couperin)**
Vn. & Pft.
Copyright by Charles Foley,
New York   1st Theme — K111

2nd Theme — K112

Rondino on a Theme by Beethoven
Vn. & Pft.
Copyright by Charles Foley, New York   — K113

Schön Rosmarin
Vn. & Pft.
Copyright by Charles Foley, New York   1st Theme — K114

2nd Theme — K115

Tambourin Chinois, Op. 3
Vn. & Pft.
Copyright by Charles Foley, New York   1st Theme — K116

2nd Theme — K117

**Tempo di Minuetto
(Style of Pugnani), Vn. & Pft.**
Copyright by Charles Foley, New York   — K118

KREUTZER, Conradin (1780-1849)

**Das Nachtlager in Granada,
Overture**   1st Theme — K119

2nd Theme — K120

3rd Theme — K121

KUHNAU, Johann (1660-1722)

Sonata, The Combat Between David and Goliath, Pft.
1st Theme — The Bravado of Goliath — K122
2nd Theme — The Prayer of the Israelites — K123
3rd Theme — The Courage of David — K124
4th Theme — The Contest — K125
5th Theme — Joy of the Israelites Over the Victory — K126

LACK, Théodore (1846-1921)

Idilio, Op. 134, Pft. — L1
Arlequin, Vn. & Orch.
1st Theme — L2
2nd Theme — L3

LALO, Edouard (1823-1892)

Concerto in D Minor, Vcl. & Orch.
1st Movement 1st Theme — L4
1st Movement 2nd Theme — L5
2nd Movement Intermezzo 1st Theme — L6
2nd Movement 2nd Theme — L7
3rd Movement — L8

Concerto Russe, Op. 29, Vn. & Orch.
1st Movement Intro. — L9
1st Movement 1st Theme — L10
1st Movement 2nd Theme — L11
2nd Movement Chant Russe — L12

3rd Movement
Intermezzo
1st Theme   L13

3rd Movement
2nd Theme   L14

4th Movement
Intro.   L15

4th Movement
Chant Russe   L16

Namouna, Ballet Suite   Prelude
                         1st Theme   L17

                         2nd Theme   L18

Theme Varié   L19

Parades de Foire
1st Theme   L20

2nd Theme   L21

Fête Foraine
1st Theme   L22

2nd Theme   L23

Rapsodie Norvégienne,   1st Movement
Orch.   Intro.   L24

1st Movement
1st Theme   L25

1st Movement
2nd Theme   L26

2nd Movement
1st Theme,
A   L27

2nd Movement
1st Theme,
B   L28

2nd Movement
2nd Theme   L29

2nd Movement
3rd Theme   L30

Le Roi D'Ys, Overture   Intro.   L31

1st Theme   L32

2nd Theme — L33

Symphonie Espagnole, Op. 21, Vn. & Orch.

1st Movement 1st Theme, A — L34

1st Movement 1st Theme, B — L35

1st Movement 2nd Theme — L36

2nd Movement 1st Theme — L37

2nd Movement 2nd Theme — L38

3rd Movement Intermezzo Intro. — L39

3rd Movement Intermezzo 1st Theme — L40

3rd Movement 2nd Theme — L41

4th Movement Intro. — L42

4th Movement — L43

5th Movement Intro. — L44

5th Movement 1st Theme — L45

5th Movement 2nd Theme — L46

LANGE, Gustav (1830-1889)

Flower Song, Pft. — L47

LASSEN, Eduard (1830-1904)

Fest-Overtüre Op. 51, Orch.
By permission of Associated Music Publishers, Inc.

Intro. — L48

1st Theme — L49

2nd Theme — L50

3rd Theme   L51

4th Theme   L52

5th Theme   L53

LECLAIR, Jean-Marie (1697-1764)

Sonata in D,
Op. 8, No. 3,
Vn. & Pft.

1st Movement   L54

2nd Movement   L55

3rd Movement
Sarabande   L56

4th Movement
Tambourin
1st Theme, A   L57

4th Movement
1st Theme, B   L58

4th Movement
2nd Theme   L59

Trio-Sonata in D,
Op. 2, No. 8,
Fl., Viola di Gamba & Harpsi.

1st Movement   L60

2nd Movement   L61

3rd Movement
Sarabande   L62

4th Movement   L63

LECUONA, Ernesto (1896-1963)

Suite Andalucia, Pft.
Copyright 1929 by
Ernesto Lecuono
Copyright assigned 1931
to Edward B. Marks Co.
Copyright Assigned 1932
to Edward B. Marks Corp.
Used by Permission

Andalucia
1st Theme   L64

2nd Theme   L65

Gitanerias
1st Theme   L66

2nd Theme   L67

Malaguena
1st Theme   L68

2nd Theme   L69

3rd Theme   L70

LEKEU, Guillaume (1870-1894)

Adagio, Op. 3, Str. Orch.   1st Theme   L75

2nd Theme   L76

Quartet in B Minor, (Unfinished), Pft. & Str.   1st Movement 1st Theme   L77

1st Movement 2nd Theme   L78

2nd Movement 1st Theme   L79

2nd Movement 2nd Theme   L80

Sonata in G, Vn. & Pft.   1st Movement 1st Theme   L81

1st Movement 2nd Theme   L82

2nd Movement 1st Theme   L83

2nd Movement 2nd Theme   L84

3rd Movement 1st Theme   L85

3rd Movement 2nd Theme   L86

LIADOFF, Anatol (1855-1914)

Baba Yaga, Op. 56, Orch.,
By permission of Associated
Music Publishers, Inc.

The Enchanted Lake
Op. 62, Orch.
By permission of Associated
Music Publishers, Inc.

  L87

1st Theme   L88

2nd Theme   L89

Kikimora, Op. 63, Orch.
By permission of Associated
Music Publishers, Inc.
1st Theme, A — L90

1st Theme, B — L91

2nd Theme — L92

3rd Theme — L93

The Music Box, Op. 32, Pft. 1st Theme — L94
(or The Musical Snuff Box)
By permission of Associated
Music Publishers, Inc.
2nd Theme — L95

3rd Theme — L96

Russian Folk Dances, Op. 58, Orch.
By permission of
Associated Music   Legend of the Birds — L97
Publishers, Inc.

I Danced With a Mosquito — L98

Cradle Song — L99

Village Dance — L100

LISZT, Franz (1811-1886)

Ballade No. 2,
in B Minor, Pft.   1st Theme — L101

2nd Theme — L102

Bénédiction de Dieu Dans la Solitude
Pft. — L10

Berceuse, Pft. — L10

Concerto No. 1 in E Flat
Pft. & Orch.   1st Theme — L10

2nd Theme — L1

3rd Theme — L1

LISZT

4th Theme — L108

Concerto No. 2 in A
Pft. & Orch.   1st Theme — L109

2nd Theme — L110

3rd Theme — L111

4th Theme — L112

5th Theme — L113

Consolation No. 2, Pft. — L114

Consolation No. 3, Pft. — L115

Etude No. 2 in F Minor, Pft. — L116

Etude No. 3 in D Flat — L117

(6) Grandes Etudes de Paganini
    Etude No. 1 in G Minor, Pft.
    (Paganini Caprice, No. 6) — L118

Etude No. 2 in E Flat, 1st Theme — L119
Pft. (Paganini Caprice,
No. 17)
                        2nd Theme — L120

Etude No. 3 in G Sharp
Minor, La Campanella, 1st Theme — L121
Pft. (Paganini, Vn.
Concerto No. 7, B Min.)
                        2nd Theme — L122

Etude No. 5 in E, Pft.
("La Chasse" Paganini
Caprice, No. 9) — L123

Etude No. 6 in A Minor, Pft.
(Paganini Caprice, No. 24)
(Theme also used by Brahms
 and Rachmaninoff) — L124

Transcendental Etude No. 7, Eroica, Pft. — L125

Faust Symphony   1st Movement
                      Faust
                      1st Theme — L126

1st Movement 2nd Theme — L127

1st Movement 3rd Theme — L128

1st Movement 4th Theme — L129

1st Movement 5th Theme — L130

2nd Movement Gretchen 1st Theme — L131

2nd Movement 2nd Theme — L132

2nd Movement 3rd Theme — L133

(Variant of 1st Movement, 2nd Theme) — 2nd Movement 4th Theme — L134

(Variant of 1st Movement, 3rd Theme) — 3rd Movement Mephistopholes 1st Theme — L135

3rd Movement 2nd Theme — L136

3rd Movement 3rd Theme — L137

Les Funérailles Pf¹ — 1st Theme — L138

2nd Theme — L139

3rd Theme — L140

Grand Galop Chromatique, Pft. — 1st Theme — L141

2nd Theme — L142

Gnomenreigen, Etude, Pft. — 1st Theme — L143

2nd Theme — L144

3rd Theme — L145

LISZT   281   L146—L164

Hungarian Rhapsody No. 1
in E, Pft.   1st Theme   L146

2nd Theme   L147

3rd Theme   L148

Hungarian Rhapsody No. 2
in C Sharp Minor, Pft.   1st Theme   L149

2nd Theme   L150

3rd Theme   L151

4th Theme   L152

5th Theme   L153

6th Theme   L154

7th Theme   L155

Hungarian Rhapsody No. 4
in E Flat, Pft.   1st Theme   L156

2nd Theme   L157

Hungarian Rhapsody No. 5
in E Minor, Pft.   1st Theme   L158

2nd Theme   L159

3rd Theme   L160

Hungarian Rhapsody No. 6
in D Flat, Pft.   1st Theme   L161

2nd Theme   L162

3rd Theme   L163

4th Theme   L164

Hungarian Rhapsody No. 8 in F Sharp Minor, Pft.   L165

Hungarian Rhapsody No. 9 in E Flat, Pft. "Carnival in Pesth"   1st Theme   L166

2nd Theme   L167

3rd Theme   L168

4th Theme   L169

Hungarian Rhapsody No. 10 in E, Pft.   1st Theme   L170

2nd Theme   L171

Hungarian Rhapsody No. 12 in C Sharp Minor, Pft.   1st Theme   L172

2nd Theme   L173

3rd Theme   L174

4th Theme   L175

5th Theme   L176

Hungarian Rhapsody No. 13 in A Minor, Pft.   1st Theme   L177

2nd Theme   L178

3rd Theme   L179

Hungarian Rhapsody No. 14 in F Minor (same material as for Hungarian Fantasie, Pft. & Orch.)   1st Theme   L180

2nd Theme   L181

3rd Theme   L182

4th Theme   L183

Hungarian Rhapsody No. 15 in A Minor, Pft. "Rakóczy March"   1st Theme   L184

2nd Theme — L185

3rd Theme — L186

Liebestraum No. 1, Pft. — L187

Liebestraum No. 2, Pft. — L188

Liebestraum No. 3, Pft. — L189

Mazeppa, Transcendental Etude No. 4, Pft. or Orch. — 1st Theme — L190

2nd Theme — L191

Mephisto Waltz, Pft. — 1st Theme — L192

2nd Theme — L193

3rd Theme — L194

Polonaise No. 1 in C Minor, Pft. — 1st Theme — L195

2nd Theme — L196

Polonaise No. 2 in E, Pft. — 1st Theme — L197

2nd Theme — L198

3rd Theme — L199

Rapsodie Espagnole, Pft. & Orch. — 1st Theme Folies d'Espagne — L200

2nd Theme Jota Aragonesa — L201

3rd Theme — L202

4th Theme — L203

Sonata in B Minor, Pft. — 1st Theme — L204

2nd Theme ... L205

3rd Theme ... L206

4th Theme ... L207

5th Theme ... L208

6th Theme ... L209

Funeral Triumph of Tasso, Symphonic Poem No. 2A — 1st Theme ... L210

2nd Theme ... L211

3rd Theme ... L212

Les Préludes, Symphonic Poem No. 3 — 1st Theme ... L213

2nd Theme ... L214

3rd Theme ... L215

4th Theme ... L216

5th Theme ... L217

Totentanz, (paraphrase on "Dies Irae"), Pft. & Orch. ... L218

Two Legends, Pft.
St. François d'Assise Prédicant aux Oiseaux — 1st Theme ... L219

2nd Theme ... L220

St. François De Paule Marchant Sur Les Flots ... L221

Valse-Impromptu, Pft. — 1st Theme ... L222

2nd Theme ... L223

Valse Mélancolique, Pft. — 1st Theme ... L224

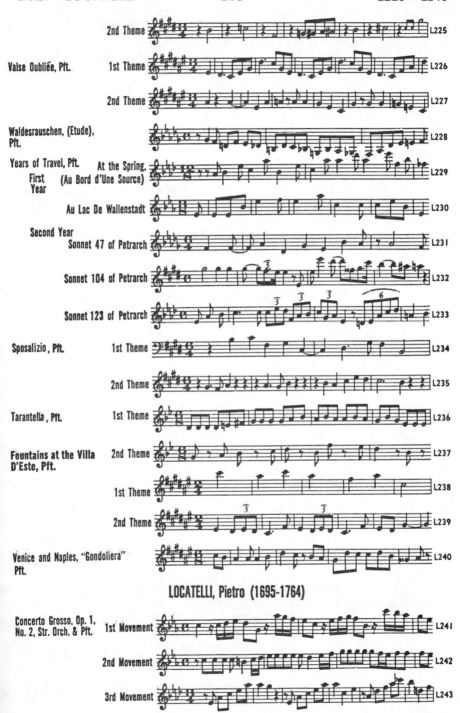

2nd Theme — L225

Valse Oubliée, Pft.   1st Theme — L226

2nd Theme — L227

Waldesrauschen, (Etude), Pft. — L228

Years of Travel, Pft.   At the Spring,
First   (Au Bord d'Une Source) — L229
Year

Au Lac De Wallenstadt — L230

Second Year
    Sonnet 47 of Petrarch — L231

    Sonnet 104 of Petrarch — L232

    Sonnet 123 of Petrarch — L233

Sposalizio, Pft.   1st Theme — L234

2nd Theme — L235

Tarantella, Pft.   1st Theme — L236

Fountains at the Villa D'Este, Pft.   2nd Theme — L237

1st Theme — L238

2nd Theme — L239

Venice and Naples, "Gondoliera" Pft. — L240

LOCATELLI, Pietro (1695-1764)

Concerto Grosso, Op. 1, No. 2, Str. Orch. & Pft.   1st Movement — L241

2nd Movement — L242

3rd Movement — L243

4th Movement ... L244

5th Movement ... L245

LOEFFLER, Charles Martin (1861-1935)

La Mort de Tintagiles,
Op. 6, Orch.
Copyright renewal assigned
1933 to G. Schirmer, Inc.

1st Theme, A ... L246

1st Theme, B ... L247

2nd Theme ... L248

3rd Theme ... L249

4th Theme ... L250

5th Theme ... L251

A Pagan Poem (after Virgil),
Op. 14, Pft. & Orch.
Copyright renewal assigned
1937 to G. Schirmer, Inc.

Intro. ... L252

1st Theme ... L253

2nd Theme ... L254

3rd Theme ... L255

4th Theme ... L256

5th Theme ... L257

Quintet, Str.
(In One Movement)
Copyright 1938
by G. Schirmer, Inc.

1st Theme ... L258

2nd Theme ... L259

3rd Theme ... L260

4th Theme ... L261

5th Theme ... L262

Two Rhapsodies, Oboe, Vla. & Pft.   L'Étang,(The Pool)   L263
Copyright renewal assigned 1932 to G. Schirmer, Inc.

La Cornemuse,(The Bagpipe) 1st Theme   L264

2nd Theme   L265

LOEILLET, Jean Baptiste (1653-1728)

Sonata No. 7 in F, Fl. & Pft.   1st Movement   L266

2nd Movement   L267

3rd Movement   L268

4th Movement Gavotte   L269

5th Movement Aria   L270

6th Movement   L271

Suite No. 1 in G Minor, Harpsi.   1st Movement Allemande   L272

2nd Movement Minuet   L273

3rd Movement Sarabande   L274

4th Movement   L275

LORTZING, Gustav Albert (1801-1851)

Czar und Zimmerman, Overture   1st Theme   L276

2nd Theme   L277

3rd Theme   L278

4th Theme, A Clog Dance   L279

4th Theme, B   L280

Undine, Overture — 1st Theme — L281
2nd Theme — L282
3rd Theme — L283

LOUIS XIII (1601-1643)

Amaryllis, Pft. — 1st Theme — L284
2nd Theme — L285
3rd Theme — L286

LUIGINI, Alexandre (1850-1906)

Ballet Egyptien, Orch.
By permission of
The Boston Music Co.,
copyright owner.
— 1st Movement — L287
2nd Movement — L288

LULLY, Jean Baptiste (1632-1687)

Alceste, Opera — Overture 1st Theme — L289
2nd Theme — L290

Amadis de Gaule Opera — Minuet — L291

L'Amour Médecin, (Comedy-Ballet), Opera — Overture — L292

Atys Opera — Entrée des Songes Agréables — L293

Les Songes Agréables — L294

Gavotte Air Pour la Suite de Flore — L295

Le Bourgeois Gentilhomme, Opera — Overture 1st Theme — L296

2nd Theme — L297

Ballet, Act 1
1st Theme   L298

2nd Theme
Sarabande   L299

3rd Theme
Gaillarde   L300

4th Theme   L301

Act IV
Cérémonie Turque   L302

Proserpine, Menuet
des Ombres Heureuses
Opera   1st Movement   L303

2nd Movement   L304

Le Temple de la Paix
Orch.   Intro.
1st Theme   L305

Intro.
2nd Theme   L306

Minuet
1st Theme   L307

2nd Theme   L308

Thésée
Opera   Overture
1st Theme   L309

2nd Theme   L310

Marche des Sacrificateurs   L311

Le Triomphe de L'Amour,
Ballet   Nocturne   L312

MacDOWELL, Edward (1861-1908)

Concerto No. 1,
in A Minor, Op. 15,
Pft. & Orch.
By permission of
Associated Music
Publishers, Inc.

1st Movement
1st Theme   M1

1st Movement
2nd Theme   M2

2nd Movement   M3

3rd Movement
1st Theme   M4

3rd Movement
2nd Theme — M5

3rd Movement
3rd Theme — M6

3rd Movement
4th Theme — M7

**Concerto No. 2.
in D Minor, Op. 23.
Pft. & Orch.**
Copyright 1922 by
G. Schirmer, Inc.

1st Movement
1st Theme — M8

1st Movement
2nd Theme — M9

2nd Movement
1st Theme — M10

2nd Movement
2nd Theme — M11

2nd Movement
3rd Theme — M12

3rd Movement
1st Theme — M13

3rd Movement
2nd Theme — M14

Marionettes, Pft. Witch, Op. 38. No. 4
Revised and Augmented Edition,
Copyright 1929 by The Arthur P. Schmidt
Co. Used by Permission. — M15

Clown, Op. 38, No. 5
Revised and Augmented Edition,
Copyright 1929 by The Arthur P. Schmidt
Co. Used by Permission. — M16

Villain, Op. 38, No. 6
Revised and Augmented Edition,
Copyright 1929 by The Arthur P. Schmidt Co.
Used by Permission — M17

Of Br'er Rabbit, Op. 61, No. 2, Pft.
Copyright 1930 by The Arthur
P. Schmidt Co. Used by Permission — M18

Of a Tailor and a Bear, Pft.
Copyright 1925 and 1942 by The
Arthur P. Schmidt Co. Used by Permission. — M19

An Old Garden. Op. 62. No. 1. Pft.,
Copyright 1930 by The Arthur P.
Schmidt Co. Used by Permission. — M2

**Polonaise,
Op. 46, No. 12, Pft.** — M2

Scotch Poem, Op. 31, No. 2, Pft.
Revised Edition, Copyright 1923 by The
Arthur P. Schmidt Co. Used by Permission — M2

Sea Pieces, Pft.
To the Sea. Op. 55, No. 1
Copyright 1926 by The Arthur P. Schmidt
Co. Used by Permission. — M2

A. D. 1620, Op. 55, No. 3
Copyright 1926 by The Arthur P. Schmidt
Co. Used by Permission. — M

Starlight, Op. 55, No. 4
Copyright 1926 by The Arthur P.
Schmidt Co. Used by Permission.
M25

Nautilus, Op. 55, No. 7
Copyright 1926 by The Arthur P.
Schmidt Co. Used by Permission.
M26

Suite No. 2, (Indian)
Orch.
By permission of Associated
Music Publishers, Inc.
I. Legend, Intro.
M27

1st Theme
M28

2nd Theme
M29

II. Love Song
1st Theme
M30

2nd Theme
M31

III. In War-Time
M32

IV. Elegy
M33

V. Village Festival
1st Theme
M34

2nd Theme
M35

Witches' Dance, Op. 17, No. 2, Pft.
Revised Edition, Copyright 1918 by The
Arthur P. Schmidt Co. Used by Permission.
M36

Woodland Sketches, Pft. To a Wild Rose,
Copyright 1924 by   Op. 51, No. 1
The Arthur P. Schmidt Co.
Used by Permission.
M37

Will O'the Wisp, Op. 51, No. 2
Copyright 1924 by The Arthur P. Schmidt
Co. Used by Permission.
M38

In Autumn, Op. 51, No. 4
Copyright 1924 by The Arthur P. Schmidt
Co. Used by Permission.
M39

From an Indian Lodge, Op. 51, No. 5
Copyright 1924 by   1st Theme
The Arthur P. Schmidt Co.
Used by Permission.
M40

2nd Theme
M41

To a Water Lily, Op. 51, No. 6
Copyright 1924 by 1st Theme
The Arthur P. Schmidt Co.
Used by Permission.
M42

2nd Theme
M43

From Uncle Remus, Op. 51, No. 7
Copyright 1924 by The Arthur P.
Schmidt Co. Used by Permission.
M44

Op. 51, No. 8

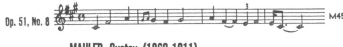

MAHLER, Gustav (1860-1911)

Symphony No. 1
in D

1st Movement
Intro.

1st Movement
1st Theme

1st Movement
2nd Theme

1st Movement
3rd Theme

2nd Movement
1st Theme

2nd Movement
2nd Theme

3rd Movement
1st Theme

3rd Movement
2nd Theme

4th Movement
1st Theme,
A

4th Movement
1st Theme,
B

4th Movement
2nd Theme

Symphony No. 2
in C Minor
"Resurrection"

1st Movement
1st Theme,
A

1st Movement
1st Theme,
B

1st Movement
2nd Theme

1st Movement
3rd Theme

2nd Movement
1st Theme

2nd Movement
2nd Theme

2nd Movement
3rd Theme

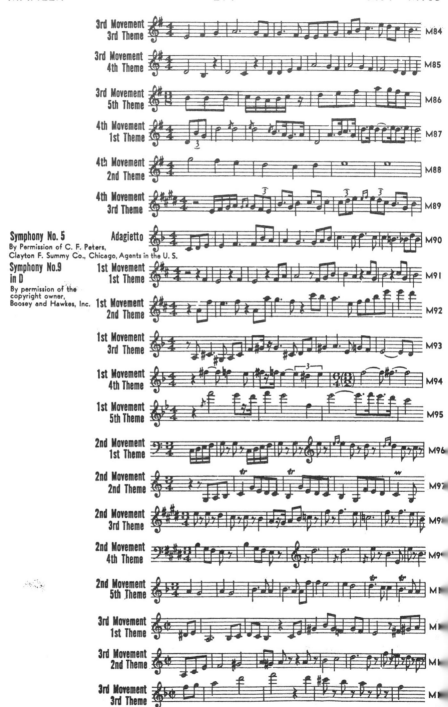

3rd Movement 3rd Theme — M84

3rd Movement 4th Theme — M85

3rd Movement 5th Theme — M86

4th Movement 1st Theme — M87

4th Movement 2nd Theme — M88

4th Movement 3rd Theme — M89

Symphony No. 5
By Permission of C. F. Peters,
Clayton F. Summy Co., Chicago, Agents in the U. S.

Adagietto — M90

Symphony No.9
in D
By permission of the
copyright owner,
Boosey and Hawkes, Inc.

1st Movement 1st Theme — M91

1st Movement 2nd Theme — M92

1st Movement 3rd Theme — M93

1st Movement 4th Theme — M94

1st Movement 5th Theme — M95

2nd Movement 1st Theme — M96

2nd Movement 2nd Theme — M97

2nd Movement 3rd Theme — M98

2nd Movement 4th Theme — M99

2nd Movement 5th Theme — M100

3rd Movement 1st Theme — M101

3rd Movement 2nd Theme — M102

3rd Movement 3rd Theme — M103

3rd Movement 4th Theme — M104

3rd Movement 5th Theme — M105

4th Movement Intro. — M106

4th Movement 1st Theme — M107

4th Movement 2nd Theme — M108

4th Movement 3rd Theme — M109

MAILLART, Louis (1817-1871)

Les Dragons De Villars Overture

1st Theme — M110

2nd Theme — M111

3rd Theme — M112

MALIPIERO, Francesco (1882-1973)

Cantari Alla Madrigalesca, Str. Quartet

1st Theme — M113

2nd Theme — M114

3rd Theme — M115

4th Theme — M116

La Cimarosiana, Orch.
By permission of the copyright holders, J. & W. Chester, Ltd., 11 Great Marlborough Street, London, W. 1.

1st Movement — M117

2nd Movement — M118

3rd Movement 1st Theme — M119

3rd Movement 2nd Theme — M120

4th Movement 1st Theme — M121

MALIPIERO (cont.)

4th Movement 2nd Theme — M122

5th Movement — M123

Impressioni Dal Vero
Orch.
By permission of the copyright
holders, J. & W. Chester, Ltd.,
11 Great Marlborough Street,
London, W. 1.

Il Capinero
1st Theme — M124

2nd Theme — M125

Il Picchio
1st Theme — M126

2nd Theme — M127

Il Chiù — M128

Rispetti E Strambotti
Quartet, Str.
By permission of the copyright
holders, J. & W. Chester, Ltd.,
11 Great Marlborough Street,
London, W. 1.

1st Theme — M129

2nd Theme — M130

3rd Theme — M131

MARGIS, Alfred (1874-   )

Valse Bleue,
Vn. & Pft.

1st Theme — M131a

2nd Theme — M131b

MARIE, Gabriel, see GABRIEL-MARIE

MARSHNER, Heinrich August (1795-1861)

Hans Heiling
Overture

1st Theme — M132

2nd Theme — M133

3rd Theme — M134

MARTUCCI, Giuseppe (1856-1909)

Notturno, Orch.
Copyright 1922 by G. Ricordi & Co., Inc.

— M135

MASCAGNI, Pietro (1863-1945)

Cavalleria Rusticana,
Opera

Prelude
1st Theme — M136

MASSENET, Jules (1842-1912)

Le Cid, Ballet
By permission of the copyright owner, Heugel Ltd., London.

Les Erinnyes (Incidental Music) Orch.
By permission of the copyright owner, Heugel Ltd., London.

2nd Theme — M156

Meditation from Opera
Thais
By permission of
the copyright owner,
Heugel Ltd., London.
     1st Theme — M157

2nd Theme — M158

Phèdre
Overture
By permission of the
copyright owner,
Heugel Ltd., London.
     1st Theme — M159

2nd Theme — M160

3rd Theme — M161

Le Roi De Lahore
Overture
By permission of the
copyright owner,
Heugel Ltd., London.
     1st Theme — M162

2nd Theme — M163

Scènes Alsaciennes,
Suite No. 7,
By permission of the
copyright owner,
Heugel Ltd., London.
     I--Sunday Morning
1st Theme — M164

2nd Theme — M165

II--Cabaret
1st Theme — M166

2nd Theme — M167

3rd Theme — M168

III--Under the Lindens — M169

IV--Sunday Evening
1st Theme — M170

2nd Theme
Alsatian Folk Tune — M171

3rd Theme
Alsatian Tune — M17

Scènes Pittoresques,
Suite No. 4,
By permission of the
copyright owner,
Heugel Ltd., London.
     I--March
1st Theme — M17

2nd Theme — M17

3rd Theme — M1

4th Theme   M176

II--Air De Ballet
1st Theme   M177

2nd Theme   M178

III--Angelus
1st Theme   M179

2nd Theme   M180

IV--Fête Bohême
1st Theme   M181

2nd Theme   M182

McDONALD, Harl (1899-1955)

Rhumba, from
Symphony No. 2
Permission granted by
Elkan-Vogel Co., Inc.,
Philadelphia, Pa.
Copyright 1936

1st Theme   M183

2nd Theme   M184

3rd Theme   M185

4th Theme   M186

MEDTNER, Nicolas (1880-1951)

Arabesque, "Tragedie-Fragment",
Op. 7, No. 3, Pft.
By permission of International Music Co.   M187

Fairy Tales, Pft.   1st Theme
Op. 14, No. 2
By permission of International Music Co.   M188

2nd Theme   M189

Op. 20, No. 1   M190

Op. 26, No. 3   M191

Op. 34, No. 2   M192

Op. 51, No. 1   M193

Op. 51, No. 2   M194

Novelette, Op. 17, No. 1, Pft.   M195
By permission of International Music Co.

MENDELSSOHN, Felix (1809-1847)

Capriccio Brilliant,   1st Theme   M196
Op. 22, Pft. & Orch.   Intro.

2nd Theme   M197

3rd Theme   M198

4th Theme   M199

Concerto No. 1,   1st Movement   M200
in G Minor, Op. 25,   Intro.
Pft. & Orch.

1st Movement   M201
1st Theme

1st Movement   M202
2nd Theme

1st Movement   M203
3rd Theme

2nd Movement   M204

3rd Movement   M205

Concerto No. 2,   1st Movement   M206
in D Minor, Op. 40,   Intro.
Pft. & Orch.

1st Movement   M207
1st Theme

1st Movement   M208
2nd Theme

2nd Movement   M209

3rd Movement   M210

Concerto in E Minor,   1st Movement   M211
Op. 64, Vn. & Orch.   1st Theme

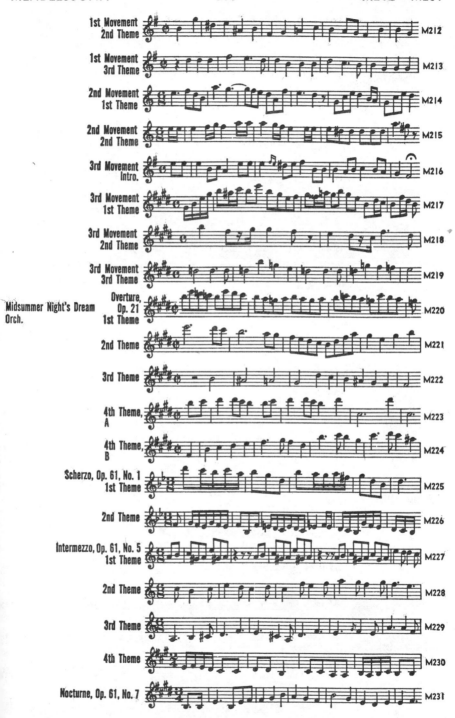

1st Movement
2nd Theme — M212

1st Movement
3rd Theme — M213

2nd Movement
1st Theme — M214

2nd Movement
2nd Theme — M215

3rd Movement
Intro. — M216

3rd Movement
1st Theme — M217

3rd Movement
2nd Theme — M218

3rd Movement
3rd Theme — M219

Midsummer Night's Dream
Orch.

Overture,
Op. 21
1st Theme — M220

2nd Theme — M221

3rd Theme — M222

4th Theme,
A — M223

4th Theme,
B — M224

Scherzo, Op. 61, No. 1
1st Theme — M225

2nd Theme — M226

Intermezzo, Op. 61, No. 5
1st Theme — M227

2nd Theme — M228

3rd Theme — M229

4th Theme — M230

Nocturne, Op. 61, No. 7 — M231

Ruy Blas, Overture, Op. 95 — Intro. — M252

1st Theme — M253

2nd Theme, A — M254

2nd Theme, B — M255

3rd Theme — M256

Quartet No. 1, in E Flat, Op. 12, Str. — 1st Movement Intro. — M257

1st Movement 1st Theme — M258

1st Movement 2nd Theme — M259

1st Movement 3rd Theme — M260

2nd Movement — M261

3rd Movement — M262

4th Movement 1st Theme — M263

4th Movement 2nd Theme — M264

Quartet, No. 3 in D, Op. 44, No. 1, Str. — 1st Movement 1st Theme — M265

1st Movement 2nd Theme — M266

1st Movement 3rd Theme — M267

2nd Movement 1st Theme — M268

2nd Movement 2nd Theme — M269

3rd Movement 1st Theme, A — M270

3rd Movement 1st Theme, B — M271

3rd Movement / 2nd Theme — M272

4th Movement / 1st Theme — M273

4th Movement / 1st Theme — M274

4th Movement / 2nd Theme — M275

Quartet, No. 4, / in E Minor, Op. 44, No. 2, / Str. — 1st Movement / 1st Theme — M276

1st Movement / 2nd Theme — M277

2nd Movement — M278

3rd Movement / 1st Theme — M279

3rd Movement / 2nd Theme — M280

4th Movement / 1st Theme — M281

4th Movement / 2nd Theme — M282

Andante and Rondo / Capriccioso, Op. 14, Pft. — Andante — M283

Rondo / 1st Theme — M284

2nd Theme — M285

Songs Without Words, Pft.

No. 1 in E, Op. 19, No. 1 — M286

No. 3 in A, Op. 19, No. 3, / "Hunting Song" — M287

No. 6 in G Minor, Op. 19, No. 6 / "Venetian Boat Song" No. 1 — M288

No. 9 in E, Op. 30, No. 3 / "Consolation" — M289

No. 10 in B Minor, Op. 30, No. 4 — M290

No. 12 in F Sharp Minor, / Op. 30 No. 6 / "Venetian Boat Song", No. 2 — M291

No.14 in C Minor, Op. 38, No. 2, "Lost Happiness" — M292

No.18 in A Flat, Op. 38, No. 6, "Duet" — M293

No.20 in E Flat, Op. 53, No. 2, "The Fleecy Cloud" — M294

No.22 in F, Op. 53, No. 4, "Sadness of Soul" — M295

No.23 in A, Op. 53, No. 5, "Folk Song" — 1st Theme — M296

2nd Theme — M297

No.25 in G, Op. 62, No. 1, "May Breezes" — M298

No. 27, in E Minor Op. 62, No. 3, "Funeral March" — M299

No. 28, in G Op. 62, No. 4, "Morning Song" — M300

No.29, in A Minor, Op.62, No. 5 "Venetian Boat Song", No. 3 — M301

No. 30, in A, Op.62, No. 6 "Spring Song" — M302

No.34, in C, Op.67, No.4 "Spinning Song" — M303

No.35, in B Minor, Op.67, No. 5 "Song of the Heather" — M304

No.45, in C, "Tarantella" — M305

No.47, in A, Op.102 No. 5 "The Joyous Peasant" — M306

No.48, in C, Op.102, No. 6 "Faith" — M307

No. 49, in A, Op.102, No. 7 "Boat-Song" — M308

Scherzo, Op. 16, No. 2, Pft. — 1st Theme — M309

2nd Theme — M310

Symphony No.3, in A Minor, Op.56 "Scotch" — 1st Movement Intro. — M311

1st Movement 1st Theme — M312

1st Movement 2nd Theme — M313

1st Movement 3rd Theme — M314

1st Movement 4th Theme — M315

2nd Movement 1st Theme — M316

2nd Movement 2nd Theme — M317

3rd Movement 1st Theme — M318

3rd Movement 2nd Theme — M319

4th Movement 1st Theme — M320

4th Movement 2nd Theme — M321

4th Movement 3rd Theme — M322

4th Movement 4th Theme — M323

Symphony No. 4, in A, Op. 90, "Italian"

1st Movement 1st Theme — M324

1st Movement 2nd Theme — M325

1st Movement 3rd Theme — M326

2nd Movement Intro. — M327

2nd Movement 1st Theme — M328

2nd Movement 2nd Theme — M329

2nd Movement 3rd Theme — M330

3rd Movement 1st Theme — M331

3rd Movement 2nd Theme — M332

4th Movement 1st Theme — M333

4th Movement 2nd Theme — M334

4th Movement 3rd Theme — M335

4th Movement 4th Theme — M336

Symphony No. 5, in D, Op. 107, "Reformation"

1st Movement Intro. — M337

1st Movement 1st Theme — M338

1st Movement 2nd Theme — M339

2nd Movement 1st Theme — M340

2nd Movement 2nd Theme — M341

3rd Movement 1st Theme — M342

Chorale, Eine Feste Burg ist unser Gott!

3rd Movement 2nd Theme — M343

3rd Movement 3rd Theme — M344

3rd Movement 4th Theme — M345

3rd Movement 5th Theme — M346

3rd Movement 6th Theme — M347

Trio No. 1, in D Minor, Op. 49, Vn, Cello, Pft.

1st Movement 1st Theme A — M348

1st Movement 1st Theme B — M349

2nd Movement 1st Theme — M350

2nd Movement 2nd Theme — M351

3rd Movement — M352

4th Movement
1st Theme — M353

4th Movement
2nd Theme — M354

Trio No. 2, in C Minor, Op. 66, Vn, Cello, Pft.
1st Movement
1st Theme — M355

1st Movement
2nd Theme — M356

1st Movement
3rd Theme — M357

2nd Movement
1st Theme — M358

2nd Movement
2nd Theme — M359

3rd Movement
1st Theme — M360

3rd Movement
2nd Theme — M361

4th Movement
1st Theme — M362

4th Movement
2nd Theme — M363

Variations Serieuses, Op. 54, Pft.
Theme — M364

MEYERBEER, Giacomo (1791-1864)

Le Prophète Opera
Coronation March
1st Theme — M36

2nd Theme — M36

MIASKOVSKY, Nicolas (1881-1950)

Sinfonietta in B Minor, Op. 32, No. 2, Str. Orch.
1st Movement
1st Theme — M36

1st Movement
2nd Theme — M3

2nd Movement
Theme for Variations — M3

3rd Movement 1st Theme — M370

3rd Movement 2nd Theme — M371

3rd Movement 3rd Theme — M372

Symphony No. 21, in F Sharp Minor, Op. 51

1st Theme — M372a

2nd Theme — M372b

3rd Theme — M372c

4th Theme — M372d

5th Theme — M372e

6th Theme (Variant of 4th Theme Used as Fugue Theme) — M372f

MILHAUD, Darius (1892-1974)

Le Boeuf Sur Le Toit, (The Nothing Doing Bar), Ballet based on South American Tunes
Copyright by Editions Salabert
Editions Salabert, 22 Rue Chaucat, Paris Salabert, Inc., East 57 St., N. Y.

1st Theme Barman Theme — M373

2nd Theme Entry of the Negroes — M374

3rd Theme Entry of the Women, A — M375

3rd Theme, B — M376

4th Theme Entry of the Men — M377

5th Theme Dance of the Bookmakers — M378

6th Theme Tango — M379

7th Theme Dance of the Policemen — M380

8th Theme Dance of the Negro — M381

ncerto, Pft. & Orch.
pyright by Editions
abert Editions Salabert,
Rue Chaucat, Paris
abert, Inc.,
ast 57 St. N Y

1st Movement 1st Theme — M382

Création Du Monde,
Ballet
By permission of
Associated Music
Publishers, Inc.

Pastorale
for Oboe, Cl., Bassoon
By permission of
Associated Music
Publishers, Inc.

Saudades Do Brazil,
Pft.
Copyright by Editions
Salabert Editions Salabert,
22 Rue Chaucat, Paris
Salabert, Inc.,
1 East 57 St., N. Y.

MONIUSZKO, Stanislaw (1819-1872)

Halka
Overture

1st Theme — M402
2nd Theme — M403
3rd Theme — M404
4th Theme — M405

MORGENSTERN, Sam (1907-   )

Toccata Guatemala, Pft.
Copyright 1947 by Carl
Fischer, Inc., N. Y.
Reprinted by permisssion.
1st Theme — M405a
2nd Theme — M405b

MOSZKOWSKI, Moritz (1854-1925)

Caprice Espagnol,
Op. 37, Pft.
1st Theme — M406
2nd Theme — M407
3rd Theme — M408

Étincelles (Sparks),
Op. 36, No. 6, Pft. — M409

Guitarre, Op. 45, No. 2,
Pft.
Copyright 1920 by Carl
Fischer, Inc., N. Y.
1st Theme — M410
2nd Theme — M411

Malagueña, from opera Boabdil,
Op. 49
By Permission of C. F. Peters, Clayton F. Summy Co.,
Chicago, Agents in the U. S.
— M412

Serenata, Op. 15, No. 1, Pft. — M413

Spanish Dances, Pft.
Op. 12, No. 1
1st Theme — M414
2nd Theme — M415
3rd Theme — M416

Op. 12, No. 2
1st Theme — M417

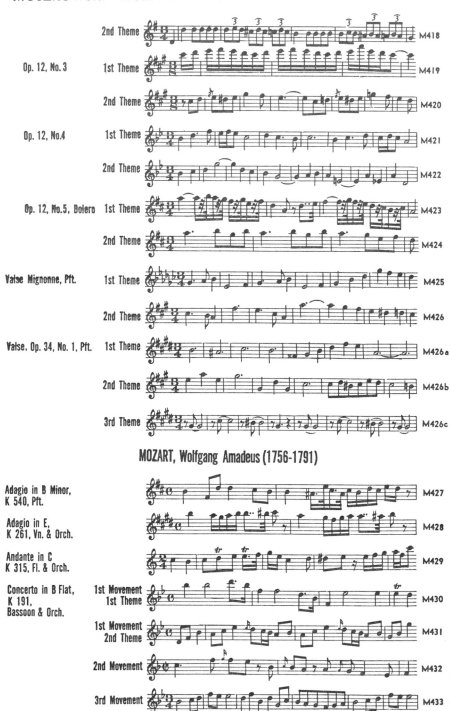

2nd Theme — M418

Op. 12, No. 3   1st Theme — M419

2nd Theme — M420

Op. 12, No.4   1st Theme — M421

2nd Theme — M422

Op. 12, No.5, Bolero   1st Theme — M423

2nd Theme — M424

Valse Mignonne, Pft.   1st Theme — M425

2nd Theme — M426

Valse, Op. 34, No. 1, Pft.   1st Theme — M426a

2nd Theme — M426b

3rd Theme — M426c

MOZART, Wolfgang Amadeus (1756-1791)

Adagio in B Minor, K 540, Pft. — M427

Adagio in E, K 261, Vn. & Orch. — M428

Andante in C K 315, Fl. & Orch. — M429

Concerto in B Flat, K 191, Bassoon & Orch.   1st Movement 1st Theme — M430

1st Movement 2nd Theme — M431

2nd Movement — M432

3rd Movement — M433

Concerto in A, K 414, Pft. & Orch. — 1st Movement 1st Theme — M454

1st Movement 2nd Theme — M455

2nd Movement — M456

3rd Movement 1st Theme — M457

3rd Movement 2nd Theme — M458

Concerto in E Flat, K 449, Pft. & Orch. — 1st Movement — M459

2nd Movement — M460

3rd Movement — M461

Concerto in B Flat K 450, Pft. & Orch. — 1st Movement 1st Theme — M462

1st Movement 2nd Theme — M463

2nd Movement — M464

3rd Movement — M465

Concerto in G K 453, Pft. & Orch. — 1st Movement 1st Theme — M466

1st Movement 2nd Theme — M467

2nd Movement — M468

3rd Movement — M469

Concerto in F K 459, Pft. & Orch. — 1st Movement — M470

2nd Movement — M471

3rd Movement 1st Theme — M472

3rd Movement 2nd Theme — M473

Concerto in D Minor, K 466, Pft. & Orch.
1st Movement 1st Theme — M474
1st Movement 2nd Theme — M475
1st Movement 3rd Theme (Solo Theme) — M476
2nd Movement — M477
3rd Movement 1st Theme — M478
3rd Movement 2nd Theme — M479

Concerto in C K 467, Pft. & Orch.
1st Movement 1st Theme — M480
1st Movement 2nd Theme — M481
2nd Movement — M482
3rd Movement 1st Theme — M483
3rd Movement 2nd Theme — M484

Concerto in E Flat, K 482, Pft. & Orch.
1st Movement 1st Theme — M485
1st Movement 2nd Theme — M486
2nd Movement — M487
3rd Movement 1st Theme — M488
3rd Movement 2nd Theme — M489

Concerto in A, K 488, Pft. & Orch.
1st Movement 1st Theme — M490
1st Movement 2nd Theme — M491
2nd Movement 1st Theme — M492
2nd Movement 2nd Theme — M493

3rd Movement / 1st Theme — M494
3rd Movement / 2nd Theme — M495
Concerto in C Minor, K 491, Pft & Orch. — 1st Movement — M496
2nd Movement — M497
3rd Movement — M498
Concerto in C, K 503, Pft. & Orch. — 1st Movement / 1st Theme — M499
1st Movement / 2nd Theme — M500
2nd Movement — M501
3rd Movement — M502
Concerto in D, K 537, Pft. & Orch. "Coronation" — 1st Movement / 1st Theme — M503
1st Movement / 2nd Theme — M504
2nd Movement — M505
3rd Movement / 1st Theme — M506
3rd Movement / 2nd Theme — M507
Concerto in B Flat, K 595, Pft. & Orch. — 1st Movement — M508
2nd Movement — M509
3rd Movement / 1st Theme — M510
3rd Movement / 2nd Theme — M511
Concerto in G, K 216, Vn. & Orch. — 1st Movement — M512
2nd Movement — M513

3rd Movement / 1st Theme — M514

3rd Movement / 2nd Theme — M515

3rd Movement / 3rd Theme — M516

Concerto in D, K 218, Vn. & Orch.

1st Movement / 1st Theme — M517

1st Movement / 2nd Theme — M518

2nd Movement — M519

3rd Movement / 1st Theme — M520

3rd Movement / 2nd Theme — M521

3rd Movement / 3rd Theme — M522

Concerto in A, K 219, Vn. & Orch. "Turkish"

1st Movement / Intro. — M522 a

1st Movement / 1st Theme — M523

1st Movement / 2nd Theme — M524

2nd Movement — M525

3rd Movement / 1st Theme — M526

3rd Movement / 2nd Theme — M527

3rd Movement / 3rd Theme — M528

Concerto in E Flat, K 268, Vn. & Orch.

1st Movement — M529

2nd Movement — M530

3rd Movement — M531

Deutsche Tänze, Orch. K 509, No. 1 — M532

K 509, No. 2 — M533

K 509, No. 4 — M534

K 509, No. 5 — M535

K 509, No. 6 — M536

K 571, No. 4 — M537

K 571, No. 6 — M538

K 600, No. 1 — M539

K 600, No. 2 — M540

K 600, No. 3 — M541

K 600, No. 4 — M542

K 600, No. 5 — 1st Theme — M543

2nd Theme (Der Kanarienvogel) — M544

K 600, No. 6 — M545

K 602, No. 3 — 1st Theme — M546

2nd Theme (Der Leiermann) — M547

K 605, No. 1 — M548

K 605, No. 2 — M549

K 605, No. 3 — 1st Theme — M550

2nd Theme (Die Schlitten Fahrt) — M551

Divertimento in D, K 136 — 1st Movement — M552
2 Vns., Viola & Bass

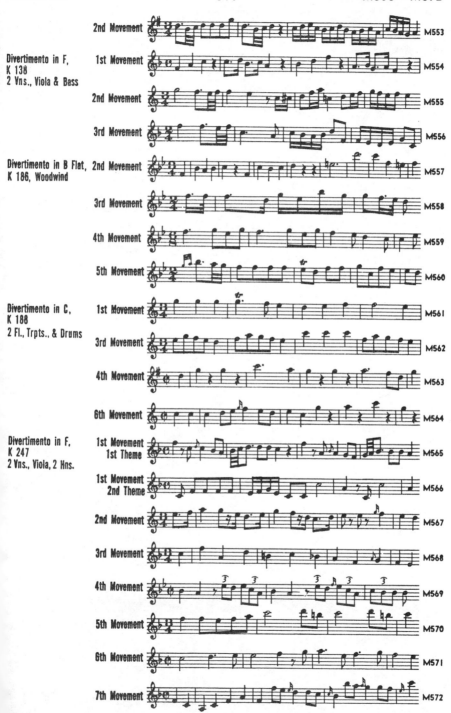

2nd Movement — M553

Divertimento in F,
K 138
2 Vns., Viola & Bass

1st Movement — M554

2nd Movement — M555

3rd Movement — M556

Divertimento in B Flat, 2nd Movement — M557
K 186, Woodwind

3rd Movement — M558

4th Movement — M559

5th Movement — M560

Divertimento in C,
K 188
2 Fl., Trpts., & Drums

1st Movement — M561

3rd Movement — M562

4th Movement — M563

6th Movement — M564

Divertimento in F,
K 247
2 Vns., Viola, 2 Hns.

1st Movement
1st Theme — M565

1st Movement
2nd Theme — M566

2nd Movement — M567

3rd Movement — M568

4th Movement — M569

5th Movement — M570

6th Movement — M571

7th Movement — M572

The Abduction From The Seraglio, Overture, K 384 — 1st Theme — M593

2nd Theme — M594

Bastien et Bastienne, Opera — Intro. — M594a

Cosi Fan Tutte, Overture K 588 — 1st Theme — M595

2nd Theme — M596

3rd Theme — M597

Don Giovanni, Overture K 527 — 1st Theme — M598

2nd Theme — M599

Idomeneo, Overture, K 366 — M600

The Magic Flute, Overture, K 620 — Intro. — M601

Theme — M602

Marriage of Figaro, Overture, K 492 — 1st Theme — M603

2nd Theme — M604

3rd Theme — M605

4th Theme — M606

5th Theme — M607

Il Re Pastore, Overture, K 208 — 1st Theme — M608

2nd Theme — M609

Der Schauspieldirektor, Overture, K 486 — 1st Theme — M610

2nd Theme — M611

Quartet in D,
K 285, Fl. & Str. — 1st Movement — M612

2nd Movement — M613

3rd Movement — M614

Quartet in A,
K 298, Fl. & Str. — 1st Movement — M615

2nd Movement 1st Theme — M616

2nd Movement 2nd Theme — M617

3rd Movement — M618

Quartet in F,
K 370, Oboe & Str. — 1st Movement — M619

2nd Movement — M620

3rd Movement — M621

Quartet in G Minor
K 4, Pft. & Str. — 1st Movement 1st Theme — M622

1st Movement 2nd Theme — M623

2nd Movement — M624

3rd Movement 1st Theme — M625

3rd Movement 2nd Theme — M626

Quartet in E Flat
K 493, Pft. & Str. — 1st Movement 1st Theme — M627

1st Movement 2nd Theme — M628

2nd Movement — M629

3rd Movement — M630

Quartet in G
K 80, Str. — 1st Movement — M631

2nd Movement   M632

3rd Movement
1st Theme   M633

3rd Movement
2nd Theme   M634

4th Movement   M635

Quartet in G
K 387, Str.   1st Movement   M636

2nd Movement
1st Theme   M637

2nd Movement
2nd Theme   M638

3rd Movement   M639

4th Movement   M640

Quartet in D Minor,
K 421, Str.   1st Movement   M641

2nd Movement   M642

3rd Movement
1st Theme   M643

3rd Movement
2nd Theme   M644

4th Movement   M645

Quartet in E Flat,
K 428, Str.   1st Movement   M646

2nd Movement   M647

3rd Movement   M648

4th Movement   M649

Quartet in B Flat,
K 458, Str.
"Hunting"   1st Movement   M650

2nd Movement
1st Theme   M651

2nd Movement / 2nd Theme — M652

3rd Movement — M653

4th Movement — M654

Quartet in A, K 464, Str. — 1st Movement — M655

2nd Movement — M656

3rd Movement — M657

4th Movement — M658

Quartet in C, K 465, Str. "Dissonant" — 1st Movement Intro. — M659

1st Movement — M660

2nd Movement — M661

3rd Movement / 1st Theme — M662

3rd Movement / 2nd Theme — M663

4th Movement — M664

Quartet in D K 499, Str. — 1st Movement — M665

2nd Movement / 1st Theme — M666

2nd Movement / 2nd Theme — M667

3rd Movement — M668

4th Movement — M669

Quartet in D K 575, Str. — 1st Movement — M670

2nd Movement — M671

	3rd Movement	M672
	4th Movement	M673
Quartet in B Flat K 589, Str.	1st Movement	M674
	2nd Movement	M675
	3rd Movement	M676
	4th Movement	M677
Quartet in F K 590, Str.	1st Movement	M678
	2nd Movement	M679
	3rd Movement	M680
	4th Movement	M681
Quintet in A, K 581, Cl. & Str.	1st Movement	M682
	2nd Movement	M683
	3rd Movement 1st Theme	M684
	3rd Movement 2nd Theme	M685
	4th Movement	M686
Quintet in E Flat, K 452, Piano & Woodw.	1st Movement Intro.	M687
	1st Movement	M688
	2nd Movement	M689
	3rd Movement	M690
Quintet in C, K 515, Str.	1st Movement	M691

2nd Movement — M692

3rd Movement — M693

4th Movement — M694

Quintet in G Minor
K 516, Str.   1st Movement — M695

2nd Movement — M696

3rd Movement — M697

4th Movement — M698

5th Movement — M699

Quintet in D,
K 593, Str.   1st Movement
                     1st Theme — M700

1st Movement
2nd Theme — M701

2nd Movement — M702

3rd Movement — M703

4th Movement — M704

Adagio in B Flat,
K 411, WW., Quintet,
2 Cl. & 3 Basset Hns. — M705

Rondo in D, K 485,
Pft. — M706

Rondo in F, K 494,
Pft. — M707

Rondo in A Minor, K 511,
Pft. — M708

Rondo in C. K 373,
Vn. & Orch. — M709

Serenade in D,
K 239, Str. Orch.   1st Movement
Serenata Notturna   1st Theme — M710

1st Movement
2nd Theme — M711

2nd Movement / 1st Theme — M712

2nd Movement / 2nd Theme — M713

3rd Movement / 1st Theme — M714

3rd Movement / 2nd Theme — M715

Serenade in D, K 250, Orch., "Haffner"

1st Movement / 1st Theme — M716

1st Movement / 2nd Theme — M717

1st Movement / 3rd Theme — M718

2nd Movement — M719

3rd Movement / 1st Theme — M720

3rd Movement / 2nd Theme — M721

4th Movement / 1st Theme — M722

4th Movement / 2nd Theme — M723

5th Movement — M724

6th Movement — M725

7th Movement — M726

8th Movement — M727

Serenade in D, K 320, Orch.

1st Movement / 1st Theme — M728

1st Movement / 2nd Theme — M729

2nd Movement — M730

3rd Movement — M731

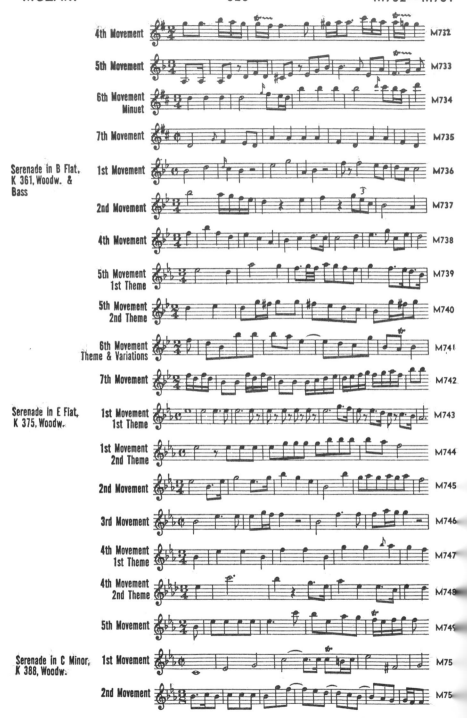

4th Movement   M732

5th Movement   M733

6th Movement
Minuet   M734

7th Movement   M735

**Serenade in B Flat,
K 361, Woodw. &
Bass**

1st Movement   M736

2nd Movement   M737

4th Movement   M738

5th Movement
1st Theme   M739

5th Movement
2nd Theme   M740

6th Movement
Theme & Variations   M741

7th Movement   M742

**Serenade in E Flat,
K 375, Woodw.**

1st Movement
1st Theme   M743

1st Movement
2nd Theme   M744

2nd Movement   M745

3rd Movement   M746

4th Movement
1st Theme   M747

4th Movement
2nd Theme   M748

5th Movement   M749

**Serenade in C Minor,
K 388, Woodw.**

1st Movement   M75

2nd Movement   M75

3rd Movement — M752

4th Movement — M753

Serenade in G,
K 525, Str. Orch.
Eine Kleine Nachtmusik

1st Movement — M754

2nd Movement — M755

3rd Movement
1st Theme
Minuet — M756

3rd Movement
2nd Theme
Trio — M757

4th Movement — M758

Sextet in F, K 522,
2 Vns., Viola, Bass & 2 Horns
Ein Musikalischer Spass

1st Movement — M759

2nd Movement — M760

3rd Movement — M761

4th Movement — M762

Sonata in E Flat
K 282, Pft.

1st Movement — M763

2nd Movement
1st Theme — M764

2nd Movement
2nd Theme — M765

3rd Movement — M766

Sonata in G
K 283, Pft.

1st Movement — M767

2nd Movement — M768

3rd Movement
1st Theme — M769

3rd Movement
2nd Theme — M770

Sonata in C
K 309, Pft.

1st Movement — M771

2nd Movement — M772

3rd Movement — M773

Sonata in A Minor
K 310, Pft.

1st Movement — M774

2nd Movement — M775

3rd Movement — M776

Sonata in D
K 311, Pft.

1st Movement
1st Theme — M777

1st Movement
2nd Theme — M778

2nd Movement — M779

3rd Movement — M780

Sonata in C
K 330, Pft.

1st Movement — M781

2nd Movement
1st Theme — M782

2nd Movement
2nd Theme — M783

3rd Movement — M784

Sonata in A
K 331, Pft.

1st Movement — M785

2nd Movement — M786

3rd Movement
1st Theme — M787

3rd Movement
2nd Theme — M788

Sonata in F
K 332, Pft.

1st Movement
1st Theme — M789

1st Movement
2nd Theme — M790

1st Movement
3rd Theme — M791

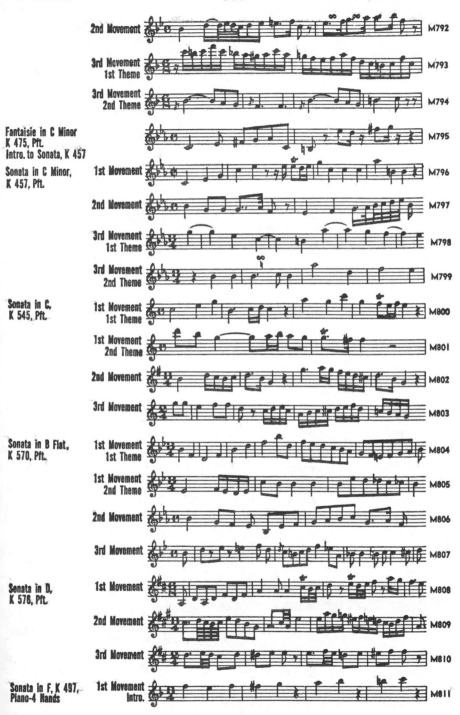

1st Movement — M812

2nd Movement — M813

3rd Movement — M814

Sonata in D, K 448, 2 Pianos — 1st Movement 1st Theme — M815

1st Movement 2nd Theme — M816

2nd Movement — M817

3rd Movement 1st Theme — M818

3rd Movement 2nd Theme — M819

Sonata in C, K 329, Organ & Orch. (In One Movement) — M820

Sonata in E Flat, K 67, Organ & Str. (In One Movement) — M821

Sonata in F, K 745, Organ & Str. (In One Movement) — M822

Sonata in C, K 336, Organ & Str. (In One Movement) — M823

Sonata in C, K 296, Vn. & Pft. — 1st Movement — M824

2nd Movement — M825

3rd Movement — M826

Sonata in G, K 301, Vn. & Pft. — 1st Movement 1st Theme — M827

1st Movement 2nd Theme — M828

2nd Movement — M829

Sonata in E Minor, K 304, Vn. & Pft. — 1st Movement — M830

2nd Movement 1st Theme — M831

2nd Movement / 2nd Theme — M832

Sonata in F, K 376, Vn. & Pft.
1st Movement / 1st Theme — M833
1st Movement / 2nd Theme — M834
2nd Movement — M835
3rd Movement — M836

Sonata in F, K 377, Vn. & Pft.
1st Movement — M837
2nd Movement — M838
3rd Movement — M839

Sonata in B Flat, K 378, Vn. & Pft.
1st Movement — M840
2nd Movement — M841
3rd Movement — M842

Sonata in G K 379, Vn. & Pft.
1st Movement / 1st Theme — M843
1st Movement / 2nd Theme — M844
2nd Movement — M845

Sonata in E Flat, K 380, Vn. & Pft.
1st Movement — M846
2nd Movement — M847
3rd Movement — M848

Sonata in C, K 404, Vn. & Pft.
1st Movement — M849
2nd Movement — M850

Sonata in E Flat, K 481, Vn. & Pft.
1st Movement / 1st Theme — M851

1st Movement / 2nd Theme M852

2nd Movement M853

3rd Movement M854

Sonata in A, K 526, Vn. & Pft. 1st Movement / 1st Theme M855

1st Movement / 2nd Theme M856

3rd Movement M857

Symphony No. 1, in E Flat, K 16 1st Movement / 1st Theme M858

1st Movement / 2nd Theme M859

2nd Movement M860

3rd Movement / 1st Theme M861

3rd Movement / 2nd Theme M862

Symphony No. 12 in G, K 110 1st Movement / 1st Theme M863

1st Movement / 2nd Theme M864

2nd Movement / 1st Theme M865

2nd Movement / 2nd Theme M866

3rd Movement / 1st Theme M867

3rd Movement / 2nd Theme M868

4th Movement / 1st Theme M869

4th Movement / 2nd Theme M870

Symphony No. 13 in F, K 112 1st Movement / 1st Theme M871

4th Movement 1st Theme — M892
4th Movement 2nd Theme — M893

Symphony No. 29 in A, K 201

1st Movement 1st Theme — M894
1st Movement 2nd Theme — M895
1st Movement 3rd Theme — M896
2nd Movement 1st Theme — M897
2nd Movement 2nd Theme — M898
3rd Movement 1st Theme — M899
3rd Movement 2nd Theme — M900
4th Movement 1st Theme — M901
4th Movement 2nd Theme — M902

Symphony No. 31 in D, K 297, "Paris"

1st Movement 1st Theme — M903
1st Movement 2nd Theme — M904
2nd Movement 1st Theme — M905
2nd Movement 2nd Theme — M906
3rd Movement 1st Theme — M907
3rd Movement 2nd Theme — M908

Symphony No. 32 in G, K 318, (In One Movement)

1st Theme — M909
2nd Theme — M910
3rd Theme — M911

Symphony No. 33 in B Flat, K 319

1st Movement 1st Theme  M912

1st Movement 2nd Theme, A — M913

1st Movement 2nd Theme, B — M914

2nd Movement 1st Theme — M915

2nd Movement 2nd Theme — M916

3rd Movement 1st Theme — M917

3rd Movement 2nd Theme — M918

4th Movement 1st Theme — M919

4th Movement 2nd Theme — M920

4th Movement 3rd Theme — M921

Symphony No. 34, in C, K 338

1st Movement 1st Theme — M922

1st Movement 2nd Theme — M923

2nd Movement 1st Theme — M924

2nd Movement 2nd Theme — M925

3rd Movement 1st Theme — M926

3rd Movement 2nd Theme — M927

Symphony No. 35, in D, K 385, "Haffner"

1st Movement 1st Theme — M928

1st Movement 2nd Theme — M929

2nd Movement 1st Theme — M930

2nd Movement 2nd Theme — M931

3rd Movement / 1st Theme — M932
3rd Movement / 2nd Theme — M933
4th Movement / 1st Theme — M934
4th Movement / 2nd Theme — M935

Symphony No. 36, in C, K 425 "Linz"

1st Movement / Intro. — M936
1st Movement / 1st Theme — M937
1st Movement / 2nd Theme — M938
1st Movement / 3rd Theme — M939
2nd Movement / 1st Theme — M940
2nd Movement / 2nd Theme — M941
3rd Movement / 1st Theme — M942
3rd Movement / 2nd Theme — M943
4th Movement / 1st Theme — M944
4th Movement / 2nd Theme — M945
4th Movement / 3rd Theme — M946

Symphony No. 37 in G, K 444

1st Movement / Intro. — M947
1st Movement / 1st Theme — M948
1st Movement / 2nd Theme — M949
2nd Movement / 1st Theme — M950
2nd Movement / 2nd Theme — M951

Symphony No. 40 in G Minor, K 550

1st Movement / 1st Theme   M972

1st Movement / 2nd Theme   M973

2nd Movement / 1st Theme   M974

2nd Movement / 2nd Theme   M975

2nd Movement / 3rd Theme   M976

3rd Movement / 1st Theme   M977

3rd Movement / 2nd Theme   M978

4th Movement / 1st Theme   M979

4th Movement / 2nd Theme   M980

Symphony No. 41, in C K 551, "Jupiter"

1st Movement / 1st Theme   M981

1st Movement / 2nd Theme   M982

1st Movement / 3rd Theme   M983

2nd Movement / 1st Theme   M984

2nd Movement / 2nd Theme   M985

3rd Movement / 1st Theme   M986

3rd Movement / 2nd Theme   M987

4th Movement / 1st Theme   M988

4th Movement / 2nd Theme   M989

4th Movement / 3rd Theme   M990

Symphonie Concertante in E Flat, K 364, Vn., Viola & Orch.

1st Movement / 1st Theme   M991

1st Movement 2nd Theme — M992

2nd Movement — M993

3rd Movement 1st Theme — M994

3rd Movement 2nd Theme — M995

Trio in B Flat, K 502, Pft., Vn. & Cello — 1st Movement — M996

2nd Movement — M997

3rd Movement — M998

Trio in E, K 542, Pft., Vn. & Cello — 1st Movement — M999

2nd Movement — M1000

3rd Movement — M1001

Trio in C, K 548, Pft., Vn. & Cello — 1st Movement — M1002

2nd Movement — M1003

3rd Movement — M1004

Trio in G, K 564, Pft., Vn. & Cello — 1st Movement — M1005

2nd Movement — M1006

3rd Movement — M1007

Variations in C, K 265, Pft. Theme: "Ah, Vous Dirai-Je, Maman" — M1008

Variations, K 455, Pft., (Theme of Gluck) — M1009

Variations on an Allegretto, in B Flat, K 500, Pft. — M1010

Variations, K 573, Pft., (Theme of Duport) — M1011

MUSSORGSKY, Modest Petrovich (1839-1881)

Boris Godunov Opera	Prelude	M1012
	Coronation Scene 1st Theme	M1013
	2nd Theme	M1014
The Fair at Sorochinsk Opera	Hopak	M1015
Khovantstchina Opera	I Prelude 1st Theme	M1016
	2nd Theme	M1017
	II Persian Dance 1st Theme	M1018
	2nd Theme	M1019
A Night on Bald Mountain, Orch.	1st Theme	M1020
	2nd Theme	M1021
	3rd Theme	M1022
	4th Theme	M1023
	5th Theme	M1024
Pictures From an Exposition, Pft. or Orch.	Intro. Promenade	M1025
	I The Gnome 1st Theme	M1026
	2nd Theme	M1027
	3rd Theme	M1028
	II The Old Castle	M1029
	III Tuileries, (Children Quarreling at Play)	M1030

IV Bydlo — M1031

V Ballet of Unhatched Chickens — M1032

VI Samuel Goldenberg and Schmuyle 1st Theme — M1033

2nd Theme — M1034

VII The Market Place at Limoges — M1035

VIII Con mortuis in lingua mortua — M1036

IX The Hut of Baba Yaga — M1037

X The Great Gate at Kiev — M1038

NARDINI, Pietro (1722-1793)

Sonata No. 2 in D, Vn. & Pft.

1st Movement — N1

2nd Movement 1st Theme — N2

2nd Movement 2nd Theme — N3

3rd Movement (Larghetto from another Sonata) — N4

4th Movement — N5

Sonata No. 7 in B Flat, Vn. & Pft.

1st Movement — N6

2nd Movement — N7

3rd Movement — N8

NARVAEZ, Luis de (16th Century)

Tema y Variaciones, Guitar — N9

NEVIN, Ethelbert (1862-1901)

Barchetta, Op. 21, No. 3, Pft.
By permission of The Boston Music Co., copyright owner.

A Day in Venice, Op. 25, Pft.
Published and copyrighted (1898) by The John Church Co. Used by permission.

1st Movement Dawn Intro.

Theme

2nd Movement Gondolieri

3rd Movement Venetian Love Song 1st Theme

2nd Theme

4th Movement Good Night

Lullaby, Op. 16, No. 3, Pft.
By permission of The Boston Music Co., copyright owner.

Narcissus, Op. 13, No. 4, Pft. 1st Theme
By permission of The Boston Music Co., copyright owner.

2nd Theme

A Shepherd's Tale, Op. 16, No. 1, Pft.
By permission of The Boston Music Co., copyright owner.

NICOLAI, Otto (1810-1849)

The Merry Wives of Windsor, Overture

Intro.

1st Theme

2nd Theme

3rd Theme, A

3rd Theme, B

4th Theme

N10
N11
N12
N13
N14
N15
N16
N17
N18
N19
N20
N21
N22
N23
N24
N25
N26

NIN, Joaquín (1879-1949)

Vals-Serenata from Chaine de Valses, Pft.
By permission of Associated Music Publishers, Inc.

Danse Ibérienne, Pft. 1st Theme
By permission of Associated Music Publishers, Inc.

2nd Theme

3rd Theme

"1830" Variations sur un Theme Frivole
By permission of Associated Music Publishers, Inc.

Suite Espagnole, Vcl. & Pft. 1st Movement Old Castile
By permission of Associated Music Publishers, Inc.

2nd Movement 1st Theme Murciana A'

2nd Movement 1st Theme, B

3rd Movement Asturiana

4th Movement Andaluza

NIN-KOCHANSKI

Granadina, Vn. & Pft.
By permission of Associated Music Publishers, Inc.

Saeta, Vn. & Pft.
By permission of Associated Music Publishers, Inc.

OFFENBACH, Jacques (1819-1880)

La Belle Hélène, Opera Overture 1st Theme

2nd Theme

Act II Entr'acte

Act III Entr'acte

La Grande Duchesse de Gerolstein, Opera Overture 1st Theme

2nd Theme — O6

3rd Theme — O7

Act III Entr'acte
1st Theme — O8

2nd Theme — O9

Galop — O10

Orpheus in Hades,
Opera

Overture
1st Theme — O11

2nd Theme — O12

Act I Duo — O13

Galop
1st Theme,
A — O14

1st Theme,
B — O15

2nd Theme — O16

La Perichole, Overture

1st Theme — O17

2nd Theme — O18

Le Roi Carrotte, Waltz,
"Apache Dance"

1st Theme — O19

2nd Theme — O20

Tales of Hoffman,
Opera

Act II Entr'acte — O21

Act II Intermezzo
(Barcarolle) — O22

La Vie Parisienne,
Opera

Overture
1st Theme — O23

2nd Theme — O24

Act II Entr'acte
1st Theme — O25

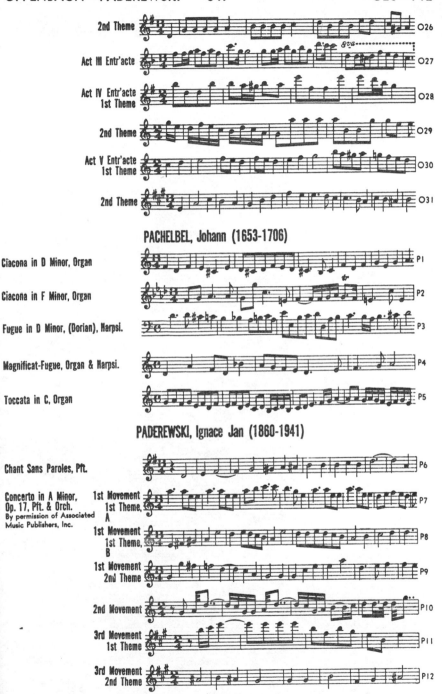

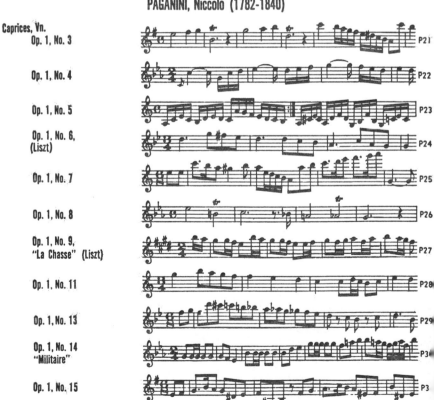

Cracovienne Fantastique, Op. 14, No. 6, Pft.
By permission of Associated Music Publishers, Inc.

1st Theme   P13

2nd Theme   P14

Mélodie, Op. 16, No. 2, Pft.
By permission of Associated Music Publishers, Inc.   P15

Minuet, Op. 14, No. 1, Pft.
Copyright 1899 by G. Schirmer, Inc.

1st Theme, A   P16

1st Theme, B   P17

2nd Theme   P18

3rd Theme   P19

Nocturne, Op. 16, No. 4, Pft.
Copyright 1892 by G. Schirmer, Inc.   P20

PAGANINI, Niccolo (1782-1840)

Caprices, Vn.

Op. 1, No. 3   P21

Op. 1, No. 4   P22

Op. 1, No. 5   P23

Op. 1, No. 6, (Liszt)   P24

Op. 1, No. 7   P25

Op. 1, No. 8   P26

Op. 1, No. 9, "La Chasse" (Liszt)   P27

Op. 1, No. 11   P28

Op. 1, No. 13   P29

Op. 1, No. 14 "Militaire"   P30

Op. 1, No. 15   P31

Op. 1, No. 17, (Liszt) — P32

Op. 1, No. 18 — P33

Op. 1, No. 20 — P34

Op. 1, No. 21 — P35

Op. 1, No. 22 — P36

Op. 1, No. 24, (Liszt, Brahms, Rachmaninoff) — P37

Concerto No. 1, in D Op. 6, Vn. & Orch.
1st Movement 1st Theme, A — P38
1st Movement 1st Theme B — P39
1st Movement 2nd Theme — P40
2nd Movement — P41
3rd Movement 1st Theme — P42
3rd Movement 2nd Theme — P43

Concerto No. 2, in B Minor, Op. 7, Vn. & Orch.
1st Movement 1st Theme — P44
1st Movement 2nd Theme — P45
2nd Movement — P46

Rondo (La Campanella)
3rd Movement 1st Theme, A — P47
3rd Movement 1st Theme, B — P48
3rd Movement 2nd Theme — P49

Moto Perpetuo, Op. 11, Vn. — P50

I Palpiti, Op. 13, Vn. & Orch. Intro. — P51

Theme P52

Le Streghe, Op. 8, Vn. & Pft.   Intro. P53

Theme P54

Sonata No. 11, Op. 3,
No. 5, Vn. & Guitar   1st Movement P55

2nd Movement P56

Sonata No. 12, Op. 3,
No. 6, Vn. & Guitar   1st Movement P57

2nd Movement P58

PAISIELLO, Giovanni (1740-1816)

Il Barbiere Di Siviglia,
Overture   1st Theme P59

2nd Theme P60

PALMGREN, Selim (1878-1951)

Finnish Romance, Op. 78, No. 5,
Vn. & Pft. P61

May Night, Pft.
By permission of The Boston Music Co.,
copyright owner. P61a

PARADIES, Pietro Domenico (1707-1791)

Sonata in A,
Pft. or Harpsi.   1st Movement P62

2nd Movement
Toccata P63

Sonata in D,
Pft. or Harpsi.   1st Movement
Napolitano P64

2nd Movement P65

PARADIS, Marie Therese von (1759-1824)

Sicilienne, Vn. & Pft. P66

PASQUINI, Bernardo (1637-1710)

Aria, Harpsi.   P67

Aria, Harpsi.   P68

Aria, Harpsi.   P69

Toccata Con Lo Scherzo Del Cuccò
Harpsi.   P70

PERGOLESI, Giovanni (1710-1736)

Concertino in F Minor,
Str. Orch.   1st Movement   P71

2nd Movement   P72

3rd Movement   P73

4th Movement   P74

PESCETTI, Giovanni (1704-1766)

Sonata in C Minor,
Harpsi.   1st Movement   P75

2nd Movement   P76

3rd Movement   P77

PFITZNER, Hans Eric (1869-1949)

Palestrina, Musical Legend
Prelude to Act I
By permission of Associated
Music Publishers, Inc.   1st Theme   P78

2nd Theme   P79

3rd Theme   P80

Prelude to Act II   1st Theme   P81

2nd Theme   P82

Prelude to Act III — 1st Theme — P83

2nd Theme — P84

PHILIPS, Peter (1560-1633)

Galliardo, Harpsi. — P85

PICK-MANGIAGALLI, Riccardo (1882-1949)

Il Carillon Magico, (Ballet)
Copyright 1920 by
G. Ricordi & Co., Inc. — Intermezzo delle Rose — P86

La Danse d'Olaf,
Op. 33, No. 2
Orch. or Pft.
Copyright 1916 by
G. Ricordi & Co., Inc. — 1st Theme — P87

2nd Theme — P88

Notturno, Op. 28, No. 1,
Orch.
Copyright 1923 by
G. Ricordi & Co., Inc. — 1st Theme — P89

2nd Theme — P90

I Piccoli Soldati, Orch.
Copyright by G. Ricordi
& Co., Inc. — 1st Theme — P91

2nd Theme — P92

Rondo Fantastico, Op. 28,
No. 2, Orch.
Copyright by G. Ricordi
& Co., Inc. — 1st Theme — P93

2nd Theme — P94

3rd Theme — P95

PIERNÉ, Gabriel (1863-1937)

Cydalise et le Chèvre-pied,
Ballet Suite, Orch.
By permission of the
copyright owner,
Heugel Ltd., London. — March of the Little Fauns 1st Theme. A — P96

1st Theme. B — P97

Dance Lesson in the Hypo-Lydian Mode — P98

Finale — P99

Impressions de Music Hall, Ballet, Op. 47
Chorus Girls 1st Theme — P100
2nd Theme — P101

L'excentrique
1st Theme — P102
2nd Theme — P103

Spanish Routine
1st Theme — P104
2nd Theme — P105

Musical Clowns (The Fratellinis)
1st Theme — P106
2nd Theme — P107

Sonata da Camera, Op. 48, Fl., Vcl. & Pft.
Permission for reprint granted by Durand & Cie, Paris. Elkan-Vogel Co., Philadelphia, Copyright Owners, Inc.
Prelude 1st Theme — P108
2nd Theme — P109

Sarabande 1st Theme — P110
2nd Theme — P111

Finale 1st Theme — P112
2nd Theme — P113

PISTON, Walter (1894-)

Concertino Pft. & Orch.
Copyright 1938, by Arrow Music Press, Inc., N. Y.
1st Theme — P113a
2nd Theme — P113b
3rd Theme — P113c

The Incredible Flutist, Suite from Ballet
Copyright by Arrow Music Press, Inc., N. Y.
Intro. — P114
1st Theme — P115

2nd Theme — P116
3rd Theme — P117
4th Theme — P118
5th Theme — P119
6th Theme — P120
7th Theme — P121
8th Theme — P122
9th Theme — P123
10th Theme — P124

Quartet No. 1, Str.
Copyright Cos Cob Press, Inc.

1st Movement 1st Theme, A — P125
1st Movement 1st Theme, B — P126
1st Movement 2nd Theme, A — P127
1st Movement 2nd Theme, B — P128
2nd Movement 1st Theme, A — P129
2nd Movement 1st Theme, B — P130
3rd Movement 1st Theme — P131
3rd Movement 2nd Theme — P132

Suite for Oboe and Pft.
Copyright 1934 by E. C. Schirmer, Boston.

1st Movement Prelude — P133
2nd Movement Sarabande — P134
3rd Movement Minuet — P135

4th Movement Nocturne — P136

5th Movement Gigue — P137

PIZZETTI, Ildebrando (1880-1968)

Sonata in A, Vn. & Pft.
By permission of the copyright holders, J. & W. Chester, Ltd., 11 Great Marlborough Street, London, W. I.

1st Movement 1st Theme. A — P138

1st Movement 1st Theme. B — P139

1st Movement 2nd Theme — P140

2nd Movement Prayer for the Innocent — P141

3rd Movement 1st Theme — P142

3rd Movement 2nd Theme — P143

Tre Canti (Three Songs), Vn. & Pft.
Copyright 1925 by G. Ricordi & Co., Inc.

No. 1 — P144

No. 2 — P145

No. 3 — P146

PLATTI, Giovanni (1690-1762)

Sonata No. 1 in E Minor, Fl. or Vn. & Pft. — **1st Movement** — P147

2nd Movement — P148

3rd Movement Minuet 1st Theme — P149

3rd Movement 2nd Theme — P150

4th Movement Gigue — P151

POLDINI, Eduard (1869-1957)

Poupée Valsante (Dancing Doll), Pft. — **1st Theme** — P152

2nd Theme P153

PONCHIELLI, Amilcare (1834-1886)

La Gioconda
Opera
Dance of the Hours
1st Theme P154

2nd Theme P155

3rd Theme P156

4th Theme P157

I Promessi Sposi, Overture 1st Theme P158

2nd Theme P159

3rd Theme P160

POPPER, David (1843-1913)

Gavotte No. 2, Op. 23,
Vcl. & Pft.
1st Theme P161

2nd Theme P162

Mazurka, Op. 11, No. 3,
Vcl. & Pft.
1st Theme P163

2nd Theme P164

PORPORA, Niccolo (1686-1766 or '67)

Sonata in G,
Vn. & Pft.
1st Movement P165

2nd Movement
Fugue P166

3rd Movement
Aria P167

4th Movement P168

POULENC, Francis (1899-1963)

Mouvements Perpétuels, Pft.
By permission of the copyright holders, J. & W. Chester, Ltd., 11 Great Marlborough Street, London, W. 1.

No. 1  P169

No. 2  P170

No. 3
1st Theme  P171

2nd Theme  P172

Novelette No. 1, Pft.
By permission of the copyright holders, J. & W. Chester, Ltd., 11 Great Marlborough Street, London, W. 1.

1st Theme P173

2nd Theme 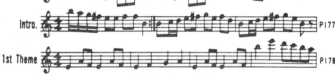 P174

Novelette No. 2, Pft.
By permission of the copyright holders, J. & W. Chester, Ltd., 11 Great Marlborough Street, London, W. 1.

1st Theme P175

2nd Theme P176

Toccato, Pft.
By permission of the copyright owner, Heugel Ltd., London.

Intro. P177

1st Theme P178

PROKOFIEFF, Serge (1891-1953)

Alexander Nevsky, Cantata for Solo, Chorus and Orch., Op. 78
Copyright 1945 by Leeds Music Corp., N. Y. Reprinted here by permission of the copyright owner.

1st Movement P179

2nd Movement
1st Theme P180

2nd Movement
2nd Theme P181

3rd Movement
1st Theme P182

3rd Movement
2nd Theme P183

4th Movement
1st Theme P184

4th Movement
2nd Theme P185

4th Movement
3rd Theme P186

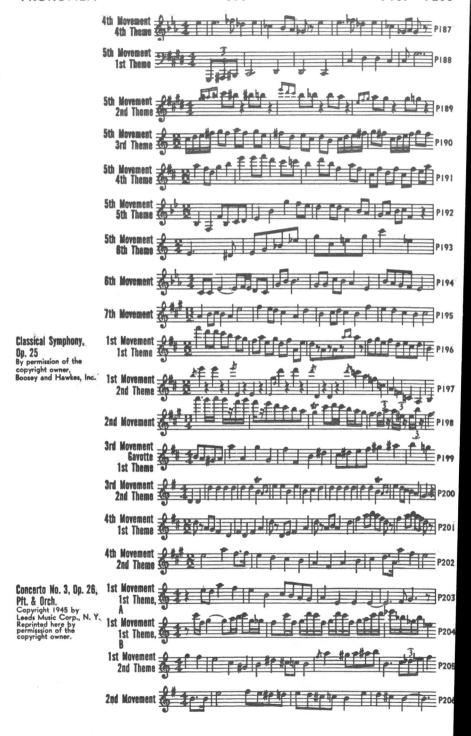

PROKOFIEFF

4th Movement / 4th Theme — P187

5th Movement / 1st Theme — P188

5th Movement / 2nd Theme — P189

5th Movement / 3rd Theme — P190

5th Movement / 4th Theme — P191

5th Movement / 5th Theme — P192

5th Movement / 6th Theme — P193

6th Movement — P194

7th Movement — P195

Classical Symphony, Op. 25
By permission of the copyright owner, Boosey and Hawkes, Inc.

1st Movement / 1st Theme — P196

1st Movement / 2nd Theme — P197

2nd Movement — P198

3rd Movement / Gavotte / 1st Theme — P199

3rd Movement / 2nd Theme — P200

4th Movement / 1st Theme — P201

4th Movement / 2nd Theme — P202

Concerto No. 3, Op. 26, Pft. & Orch.
Copyright 1945 by Leeds Music Corp., N. Y. Reprinted here by permission of the copyright owner.

1st Movement / 1st Theme, A — P203

1st Movement / 1st Theme, B — P204

1st Movement / 2nd Theme — P205

2nd Movement — P206

3rd Movement / 1st Theme — P207

3rd Movement / 2nd Theme — P208

Concerto No. 1, Op. 19, Vn. & Orch.
By permission of the copyright owner, Boosey and Hawkes, Inc.

1st Movement — P209

2nd Movement / 1st Theme — P210

2nd Movement / 2nd Theme — P211

3rd Movement / 1st Theme — P212

3rd Movement / 2nd Theme — P213

Concerto No. 2, Op. 63, Vn. & Orch.
By permission of International Music Co.

1st Movement / 1st Theme — P214

1st Movement / 2nd Theme — P215

2nd Movement / 1st Theme — P216

2nd Movement / 2nd Theme — P217

3rd Movement / 1st Theme — P218

3rd Movement / 2nd Theme — P219

3rd Movement / 3rd Theme — P220

Contes de la Vieille Grand'mère, Pft. Op. 31, No. 2
By permission of the copyright owner, Boosey and Hawkes, Inc. — P221

Op. 31, No. 3 — P222

Gavotte, Op. 12, No. 2, Pft. — P223

Gavotte, Op. 32, No. 3, Pft.
By permission of the copyright owner, Boosey and Hawkes, Inc. — P224

Lieutenant Kije, Op. 60, Orch.
By permission of Broude Brothers

1st Movement / Birth of Kije / 1st Theme — P225

1st Movement / 2nd Theme — P226

1st Movement
3rd Theme   P227

2nd Movement
Romance
1st Theme   P228

2nd Movement
2nd Theme   P229

2nd Movement
3rd Theme   P230

3rd Movement
Kije's Wedding
1st Theme   P231

3rd Movement
2nd Theme   P232

4th Movement
Troika   P233

Love of Three Oranges, Op. 33   March   P234
Opera
By permission of the
copyright owner,
Boosey and Hawkes, Inc.   Scherzo   P235

March, Op. 12, No. 1, Pft.   P236

Music for Children, Op. 65, Pft.   March   P237
Copyright 1946 by Leeds
Music Corp., N. Y.
Reprinted here by permission
of the copyright owner.   Waltz   P238

Overture on Hebrew Themes,
Op. 34, Cl., Pft. &   1st Theme   P239
Str. Quartet
By permission of the
copyright owner,
Boosey and Hawkes, Inc.   2nd Theme   P240

Peter and the Wolf,   1st Theme
Op. 67, Orch.   Peter   P241
Copyright 1946 by
Leeds Music Corp., N. Y.   2nd Theme
Reprinted here by   The Bird   P242
permission of the
copyright owner.   3rd Theme
The Duck   P243

4th Theme
The Cat   P244

5th Theme
The Grandfather   P245

6th Theme
The Wolf   P246

7th Theme
March of the Hunters · P247

Quartet, Op. 50
Str.
By permission of
International Music Co.

1st Movement
1st Theme · P248

1st Movement
2nd Theme · P249

2nd Movement
1st Theme · P250

2nd Movement
2nd Theme · P251

2nd Movement
3rd Theme · P252

2nd Movement
4th Theme · P253

3rd Movement · P254

Romeo and Juliet,
Op. 64, Suite No. 1,
Orch.
Copyright 1946 by
Leeds Music Corp., N. Y.
Reprinted here by
permission of the
copyright owner.

1st Movement
Folk Dance
1st Theme · P255

1st Movement
2nd Theme · P256

2nd Movement
A Scene
1st Theme,
A · P257

2nd Movement
1st Theme,
B · P258

3rd Movement
Madrigal
1st Theme · P259

3rd Movement
2nd Theme · P260

4th Movement
Minuet
1st Theme · P261

4th Movement
2nd Theme · P262

5th Movement
Masks · P263

6th Movement
Romeo and Juliet · P264

7th Movement
Death of Tybalt
1st Theme · P265

7th Movement
2nd Theme · P266

Romeo and Juliet, The Montagues and Op. 64, Suite No. 2, Orch.

Sonata No. 6, Op. 82, Pft.

7th Movement 3rd Theme — P267

1st Movement the Capulets 1st Theme — P268

1st Movement 2nd Theme — P269

1st Movement 3rd Theme — P270

2nd Movement Juliet—The Little Girl 1st Theme — P271

2nd Movement 2nd Theme — P272

2nd Movement 3rd Theme, A — P273

2nd Movement 3rd Theme, B — P274

3rd Movement Friar Lawrence 1st Theme — P275

3rd Movement 2nd Theme — P276

4th Movement Dance — P277

5th Movement Romeo and Juliet Before Parting 1st Theme — P278

5th Movement 2nd Theme — P279

5th Movement 3rd Theme — P280

6th Movement Dance of the Maids From the Antilles — P281

7th Movement Romeo at Juliet's Grave — P282

1st Movement 1st Theme — P283

1st Movement 2nd Theme — P284

2nd Movement 1st Theme — P285

2nd Movement 2nd Theme — P286

3rd Movement 1st Theme — P287

3rd Movement 2nd Theme — P288

4th Movement 1st Theme — P289

4th Movement 2nd Theme — P290

4th Movement 3rd Theme — P291

Sonata No. 7, Op. 83 Pft.
Copyright 1945 by Leeds Music Corp., N. Y. Reprinted here by permission of the copyright owner.

1st Movement 1st Theme — P292

1st Movement 2nd Theme — P293

2nd Movement — P294

3rd Movement — P295

Sonata in D, Op. 94, Vn. & Pft.
Copyright 1946 by Leeds Music Corp., N. Y. Reprinted here by permission of the copyright owner.

1st Movement 1st Theme — P296

1st Movement 2nd Theme — P297

2nd Movement 1st Theme — P298

2nd Movement 2nd Theme — P299

2nd Movement 3rd Theme — P300

3rd Movement — P301

4th Movement 1st Theme — P302

4th Movement 2nd Theme — P303

4th Movement 3rd Theme — P304

4th Movement 4th Theme — P305

Suggestion Diabolique, Op. 4, No. 4, Pft. — P306

Symphony No. 5 in B Flat, Op. 100

1st Movement / 1st Theme — P307
1st Movement / 2nd Theme — P308
1st Movement / 3rd Theme — P309
1st Movement / 4th Theme — P310
2nd Movement / 1st Theme — P311
2nd Movement / 2nd Theme — P312
2nd Movement / 3rd Theme — P313
3rd Movement / 1st Theme — P314
3rd Movement / 2nd Theme A — P315
3rd Movement / 2nd Theme B — P316
3rd Movement — P317
4th Movement / 1st Theme — P318
4th Movement / 2nd Theme — P319
4th Movement / 3rd Theme — P320

PUGNANI, Gaetano (1731-1798)

Sonata in E, No. 1, Vn. & Pft.

1st Movement — P321
2nd Movement — P322
3rd Movement — P323

PURCELL, Henry (c. 1659-1695)

Bonduca, or The British Heroine Opera

Air No. 1 — P324

Hornpipe — P325
Air No. 2 — P326

Dido and Aeneas
Opera

Overture 1st Theme — P327
2nd Theme — P328
The Triumphing Dance — P329
Sailor's Dance — P330

Fairy Queen
Opera

Hornpipe — P331
Rondeau — P332
Jig — P333
The Monkey's Dance — P334

Three-Part Fantasia, No. 3, Str. — P335
Four-Part Fantasia, No. 1, Str. — P336
Four-Part Fantasia, No. 4, Str. — P337
Four-Part Fantasia, No. 9, Str. — P338
A New Irish Tune (Lillibullero), Harpsi. — P339

Sonata No. 3, in A Minor, 2 Vns. & Harpsi.

1st Movement — P340
2nd Movement — P341
3rd Movement — P342
4th Movement — P343
5th Movement — P344

Sonata No. 6, in G Minor (also known as Chacony) 2 Vns. & Harpsi. — P345

Ground Bass — P346

Sonata No. 9, in F, "Golden Sonata", 2 Vns. & Harpsi. 1st Movement — P347

2nd Movement — P348

3rd Movement — P349

4th Movement — P350

5th Movement — P351

Suite No. 1 in G, Harpsi. Prelude — P352

Almand — P353

Courant — P354

Minuet — P355

Suite No. 2 in G Minor, Harpsi. Prelude — P356

Almand — P357

Courant — P358

Saraband — P359

Suite No. 7 in B Minor, Harpsi. Almand — P360

Courant — P361

Hornpipe — P362

Suite in G Minor, Harpsi. Overture — P363

Air — P364

Jig P365

QUANTZ, Johann (1697-1773)

Concerto in G, Fl. & Str.

1st Movement
1st Theme, A Q1

1st Movement
1st Theme, B Q2

2nd Movement
Arioso Q3

3rd Movement Q4

QUILTER, Roger (1877-1953)

A Children's Overture, Orch.

1st Theme
Girls & Boys, Come Out to Play Q5

2nd Theme
Upon Paul's Steeple Stands a Tree Q6

3rd Theme
Dance, Get Up and Bake Your Pies Q7

4th Theme
I Saw Three Ships Go Sailing By Q8

5th Theme
Sing a Song of Sixpence Q9

6th Theme
There Was a Lady Loved a Swine Q10

7th Theme
Over the Hills and Far Away Q11

8th Theme
The Frog and the Crow Q12

9th Theme
A Frog He Would A-Wooing Go Q13

10th Theme
Baa, Baa, Black Sheep Q14

11th Theme
Here We Go Round the Mulberry Bush Q15

12th Theme
Oranges and Lemons Q16

RACHMANINOFF, Sergei (1873-1943)

Concerto No. 1, in
F Sharp Minor, Op. 1,
Pft. & Orch.
By permission of the
copyright owner,
Boosey and Hawkes, Inc.

1st Movement
1st Theme — R1

1st Movement
2nd Theme — R2

2nd Movement — R3

3rd Movement
1st Theme — R4

3rd Movement
2nd Theme — R5

3rd Movement
3rd Theme — R6

Concerto No. 2, in
C Minor, Op. 18,
Pft. & Orch.

1st Movement
1st Theme — R7

1st Movement
2nd Theme — R8

2nd Movement
1st Theme,
A — R9

2nd Movement
1st Theme,
B — R10

3rd Movement
1st Theme — R11

3rd Movement
2nd Theme — R12

Concerto No. 3, Op. 30,
Pft. & Orch.
By permission of the
copyright owner,
Boosey and Hawkes, Inc.

1st Movement
1st Theme — R13

1st Movement
2nd Theme — R14

2nd Movement
1st Theme — R15

2nd Movement
2nd Theme — R16

3rd Movement
1st Theme — R17

3rd Movement
2nd Theme — R18

3rd Movement
3rd Theme — R19

Elégie, Op. 3, No. 1, Pft.   1st Theme   R20

2nd Theme   R21

Etude Tableau, Op. 33, No. 1, Pft.
By permission of
International Music Co.   R22

Etude Tableau, Op. 33, No. 2, Pft.
By permission of
International Music Co.   R23

Fantasy, Suite No. 1,
Op. 5, 2 Pfts., 4 Hands
By permission of the
copyright owner,
Boosey and Hawkes, Inc.   1st Movement Barcarolle 1st Theme   R24

1st Movement 2nd Theme   R25

2nd Movement A Night for Love   R26

3rd Movement Tears   R27

4th Movement A Russian Easter 1st Theme   R28

4th Movement 2nd Theme   R29

The Isle of the Dead,
Op. 29, Orch.
By permission of
International Music Co.   1st Theme   R30

2nd Theme   R31

Mélodie, Op. 3, No. 3, Pft.
Copyright by
Charles Foley,
New York   R32

Moment Musical, Op. 16, No. 2, Pft.
Copyright by
Charles Foley,
New York   R33

Polichinelle, Op. 3,
No. 4, Pft.
By permission of the
copyright owner,
Boosey and Hawkes, Inc.   1st Theme   R34

2nd Theme   R35

Preludes, Pft.
Op. 3, No. 2,
(Famous C Sharp Minor)
Copyright renewal assigned
1925 to G. Schirmer, Inc.   1st Theme   R36

2nd Theme   R37

Op. 23, No. 1
Copyright renewal assigned
1925 to G. Schirmer, Inc.   R38

No. 2   R39

4th Movement
2nd Theme — R60

Suite No. 2, Op. 17,
2 Pfts., 4 Hands
By permission of
International Music Co.

1st Movement
Intro. — R61

2nd Movement
Valse
1st Theme — R62

2nd Movement
2nd Theme — R63

2nd Movement
3rd Theme — R64

3rd Movement
Romance — R65

4th Movement
Tarantelle (Italian Folksong) — R66

Symphony No. 2 in
E Minor, Op. 27
By permission of the
copyright owner,
Boosey and Hawkes, Inc.

1st Movement
1st Theme — R67

1st Movement
2nd Theme — R68

2nd Movement
1st Theme — R69

2nd Movement
2nd Theme — R70

3rd Movement
Intro. — R71

3rd Movement
1st Theme — R72

3rd Movement
2nd Theme — R73

4th Movement
1st Theme — R74

4th Movement
2nd Theme — R75

Waltz, Op. 10, No. 2, Pft.
By permission of the
copyright owner,
Boosey and Hawkes, Inc.
— R76

RAFF, Joseph Joachim (1822-1882)

Cavatina, Op. 85, No. 3, Vn. & Pft. — R77

La Fileuse, Op. 157, No. 2, Pft. — R78

RAMEAU, Jean Philippe (1683-1764)

Castor et Pollux, Opera	Gavotte No. 1 — R79
	Gavotte No. 2 — R80
	Minuet No. 1 — R81
	Minuet No. 2 — R82
	Passepied No. 1 — R83
	Passepied No. 2 — R84
Dardanus, Opera	Rigaudon No. 1 — R85
	Air en Rondeau — R86
	Rigaudon No. 2 — R87
Les Fêtes de Hébé Opera	Tambourin — R88
	Musette — R89
La Follette, Harpsi.	R90
Gavotte Variée, Harpsi.	R91
L'Indifferente, Harpsi.	R92
La Joyeuse, Harpsi.	1st Theme — R93
	1st Theme — R94
Minuet No. 1, Harpsi.	R95
Minuet No. 2, Harpsi.	R96
Pièces de Clavecin en Concert, No. 3, Fl., Vn. & Harpsi.	La Timide — R97

Tambourin No. 1 — R98

Tambourin No. 2 — R99

No. 4 — La Pantomime — R100

L'Indiscrète — R101

No. 5 — La Forqueray — R102

La Cupis — R103

La Marais — R104

Platée, Opera — Minuet No. 1 — R105

Minuet No. 2 — R106

La Poule, Harpsi. — R107

Les Sauvages, Harpsi. — R108

Suite in E Minor, Harpsi. — Allemande — R109

Gigue en Rondeau No. 1 — R110

Gigue en Rondeau No. 2 — R111

Le Rappel des Oiseaux — R112

Rigaudon No. 1 — R113

Rigaudon No. 2 — R114

Musette en Rondeau — R115

Tambourin — R116

La Villageoise — R117

Les Tendres Plaintes, Harpsi.   R118

Les Tourbillons, Harpsi.   R119

Les Tricotets, Harpsi.   R120

Les Triolets, Harpsi.   R121

La Triompante, Harpsi.   R122

RAVEL, Maurice (1875-1937)

Alborada Del Graciosa (Miroirs No. 4), Pft.
By permission of Associated Music Publishers, Inc.
Theme, A   R123
Theme, B   R124

Bolero, Orch.
Permission for reprint granted by Durand & Cie, Paris. Elkan-Vogel Co., Inc. Philadelphia, Copyright Owners.
Theme, A   R125
Theme, B   R126

Concerto, Pft. & Orch.
Permission for reprint granted by Durand & Cie, Paris. Elkan-Vogel Co., Inc. Philadelphia, Copyright Owners.
1st Movement 1st Theme   R127
1st Movement 2nd Theme   R128
2nd Movement   R129
3rd Movement 1st Theme   R130
3rd Movement 2nd Theme   R131

Concerto for the Left Hand, Pft. & Orch.
Permission for reprint granted by Durand & Cie, Paris. Elkan-Vogel Co., Inc. Philadelphia, Copyright Owners.
1st Theme, A   R132
1st Theme, B   R133
2nd Theme   R134

Daphnis et Chloe, Ballet Suite No. 1, Orch.
Permission for reprint granted by Durand & Cie, Paris. Elkan-Vogel Co., Inc. Philadelphia, Copyright Owners.
1st Theme   R135
2nd Theme   R136

3rd Theme — R137

4th Theme — R138

5th Theme — R139

Daphnis et Chloe, Ballet Suite No. 2, Orch.
Permission for reprint granted by Durand & Cie, Paris. Elkan-Vogel Co., Inc., Philadelphia, Copyright Owners,

1st Theme, A — R140

1st Theme, B — R141

2nd Theme — R142

3rd Theme — R143

4th Theme — R144

5th Theme — R145

6th Theme — R146

Gaspard de la Nuit, Pft.
Permission for reprint granted by Durand & Cie, Paris. Elkan-Vogel Co., Inc., Philadelphia, Copyright Owners,

No. 1 Ondine — R147

No. 2 La Gibet — R148

No. 3 Scarbo — R149

Introduction and Allegro, Harp, Str. Quart., Fl. & Cl.
Permission for reprint granted by Durand & Cie, Paris. Elkan-Vogel Co., Inc., Philadelphia, Copyright Owners.

Intro. 1st Theme, A — R150

1st Theme, B — R151

2nd Theme — R152

Allegro 1st Theme — R153

2nd Theme — R154

Jeux D'Eau, Pft.
Copyright 1930 by Edward B. Marks Music Co. Copyright Assigned 1932 to Edward B. Marks Music Corp. Used by Permission

1st Theme — R155

2nd Theme — R156

Ma Mère L'Oye,
(Mother Goose Suite)
Orch.
Permission for reprint granted by Durand & Cie, Paris. Elkan-Vogel Co., Inc., Philadelphia, Copyright Owners.

Pavane of the Sleeping Beauty (Pavane de la Belle au Bois Dormant) — R157

Hop O' My Thumb (Petit Poucet) — R158

Empress of the Pagodas (Laideronnette, Impératrice des Pagodes) — R159

Beauty and the Beast (Les Entretiens de la Belle et de la Bête) — R160

The Enchanted Garden (La Jardin Féerique) — R161

Pavane for a Dead Infanta,
Small Orch. or Pft.
By permission of Associated Music Publishers, Inc. — R162

Quartet in F,
Str.
By permission of International Music Co.

1st Movement 1st Theme — R163

1st Movement 2nd Theme — R164

2nd Movement Intro. — R165

2nd Movement 1st Theme — R166

2nd Movement 2nd Theme — R167

3rd Movement 1st Theme — R168

3rd Movement 2nd Theme — R169

4th Movement — R170

Rapsodie Espagnole,
Orch.
Permission for reprint granted by Durand & Cie, Paris. Elkan-Vogel Co., Inc. Philadelphia, Copyright Owners.

1st Movement Prélude à la Nuit — R171

2nd Movement Malagueña Intro. — R172

2nd Movement 1st Theme — R173

2nd Movement 2nd Theme — R174

3rd Movement Habañera 1st Theme — R175

3rd Movement 2nd Theme — R176

3rd Movement
3rd Theme   R177

4th Movement
Feria
1st Theme   R178

4th Movement
2nd Theme,
A   R179

4th Movement
2nd Theme,
B   R180

4th Movement
3rd Theme   R181

Sonatine, Pft.
Permission for reprint
granted by Durand &
Cie, Paris. Elkan-Vogel
Co., Inc. Philadelphia,
Copyright Owners.

1st Movement
1st Theme   R182

1st Movement
2nd Theme   R183

2nd Movement   R184

3rd Movement
1st Theme   R185

3rd Movement
2nd Theme   R186

**Le Tombeau de Couperin,
Pft. or Orch.**
Permission for reprint
granted by Durand &
Cie, Paris. Elkan-Vogel
Co., Inc. Philadelphia,
Copyright Owners.

Prelude   R187

Fugue   R188

Forlane
1st Theme   R189

2nd Theme   R190

Rigaudon
1st Theme   R191

2nd Theme   R192

Minuet
1st Theme   R193

2nd Theme   R194

Toccata
1st Theme   R195

2nd Theme   R196

Tzigane, Vn. & Orch.
Permission for reprint granted
by Durand & Cie, Paris.
Elkan-Vogel Co.,Inc.
Philadelphia, Copyright
Owners.

La Valse, Orch.
Permission for reprint granted
by Durand & Cie, Paris.
Elkan-Vogel Co.,Inc.
Philadelphia, Copyright
Owners.

**Valses Nobles et
Sentimentales
Pft. or Orch.**
Permission for reprint granted
by Durand & Cie, Paris.
Elkan-Vogel Co., Inc.
Philadelphia, Copyright
Owners.

Intro. Cadenza — R197
1st Theme — R198
1st Theme — R199
2nd Theme — R200
3rd Theme — R201
1st Theme — R202
2nd Theme — R203
3rd Theme — R204
4th Theme — R205
5th Theme — R206
6th Theme — R207
7th Theme — R208
8th Theme — R209
No. 1 — R210
No. 2 — R211
No. 3 — R212
No. 4 — R213
No. 5 — R21
No. 6 — R21
No. 7 — R21

No. 8   R217

REBIKOFF, Vladimir (1866-1920)

The Christmas Tree, Opera   Dance of the Dolls 1st Theme   R218

2nd Theme   R219

March of the Gnomes 1st Theme   R220

2nd Theme   R221

Dance of the Chinese Dolls   R222

REGER, Max (1873-1916)

Balletmusik, Op. 130
By Permission of C. F. Peters, Clayton F. Summy Co., Chicago,   Waltz   R223

Finale   R224

Gavotte, Op. 82, No 5, Pft.
By permission of Associated Music Publishers, Inc.   R225

Konzert im Alten Stil, Op. 123, Orch.
By permission of Associated Music Publishers, Inc.   1st Movement   R226

2nd Movement   R227

3rd Movement   R228

Quintet, in A, Op. 146, Cl. & Str. Quart.
By permission of Associated Music Publishers, Inc.   1st Movement 1st Theme   R229

1st Movement 2nd Theme   R230

2nd Movement 1st Theme   R231

2nd Movement 2nd Theme   R232

3rd Movement   R233

4th Movement   R234

Romance, Op. 87, No. 2, Vn. & Pft.   R235

Serenade, Op. 77a, Fl., Vn. & Vla.   1st Movement   R236

2nd Movement   R237

3rd Movement 1st Theme   R238

3rd Movement 2nd Theme   R239

Suite in A Minor, Op. 103a, Vn. & Pft. By permission of Associated Music Publishers, Inc.   1st Movement Präludium   R240

2nd Movement Gavotte 1st Theme   R241

2nd Movement 2nd Theme   R242

3rd Movement Aria   R243

4th Movement Burleske   R244

5th Movement Minuet 1st Theme   R245

5th Movement 2nd Theme   R246

6th Movement Gigue   R247

RESPIGHI, Ottorino (1879-1936)

Adagio con Variazioni, Vcl. & Pft.   R248

Antiche Danze Ed Arie Per Liuto. Copyright 1920 by G. Ricordi & Co., Inc. Suite No 1, Orch.   1st Movement Balletto "Il Conte Orlando"(After Simone Molinaro)   R249

2nd Movement Gagliarda (After Vincenzo Galilei) 1st Theme   R250

2nd Movement 2nd Theme   R251

3rd Movement Villanella (After Ignoto) 1st Theme   R252

3rd Movement 2nd Theme   R253

4th Movement
Passo Mezzo e Mascherada (Ignoto)
1st Theme — R254

4th Movement
2nd Theme — R255

4th Movement
3rd Theme — R256

4th Movement
4th Theme — R257

Suite No. 2, Orch.
Copyright 1924 by
G. Ricordi & Co.,
Inc.
1st Movement
Laura Soave
(After Carosio)
1st Theme — R258

1st Movement
2nd Theme — R259

1st Movement
3rd Theme — R260

2nd Movement
Danza Rustica (After Besardo) — R261

3rd Movement
1st Theme
Campanae Parisienses (Author Unknown) — R262

3rd Movement
2nd Theme
Aria (After Mersenne Marin) — R263

4th Movement
Bergamasca (After Bernardo Gianoncelli) — R264

Suite No. 3, Orch.
Copyright 1932
by G. Ricordi
& Co., Inc.
1st Movement
Italiana (After Ignoto) — R265

2nd Movement
Arie di Corte (After Besardo)
1st Theme — R266

2nd Movement
2nd Theme — R267

3rd Movement
Siciliano (After Ignoto) — R268

4th Movement
Passacaglia (After Roncalli) — R269

Fountains of Rome, Orch.
Copyright 1918 by G. Ricordi & Co., Inc.
The Fountain of Valle Giulia at Dawn
1st Theme — R270

2nd Theme — R271

The Triton Fountain at Morning — R272

The Fountains of Trevi at Mid-day — R273

The Villa Medici Fountain at Sunset
1st Theme — R274

2nd Theme — R275

Notturne, Pft. — R276

Pines of Rome, Orch.
Copyright 1925 by G. Ricordi & Co., Inc.
The Pines of the Villa Borghese
1st Theme — R277

2nd Theme — R278

3rd Theme — R279

Pines Near a Catacomb — R280

Pines of the Gianicolo
1st Theme — R281

2nd Theme — R282

Pines of the Appian Way
1st Theme — R283

2nd Theme — R284

Rossiniana,
Suite for Orch.
1st Movement
Capri and Taormina
(Barcarola & Siciliana)
1st Theme — R285

1st Movement
2nd Theme — R286

2nd Movement
Lament
1st Theme — R287

2nd Movement
2nd Theme — R288

3rd Movement
Intermezzo
1st Theme — R289

3rd Movement
2nd Theme — R290

4th Movement
Tarantella & Procession
1st Theme — R291

4th Movement
2nd Theme — R292

Trittico Botticelliano,
Chamber Orch.
Copyright 1928 by G.
Ricordi & Co., Inc.
1st Movement
La Primavera
1st Theme — R293

REYER, Ernest (1823-1909)

Sigurd, Overture
By permission of
the copyright owner,
Heugel & Cie, Paris.

REZNIČEK, Emil Nikolaus von (1860-1945)

Donna Diana, Overture
By permission of Associated
Music Publishers, Inc.

RIEGGER, Wallingford (1885-1961)

New Dance, 2 Pfts.
Copyright 1940 by Arrow
Music Press, Inc., N. Y.

RIMSKY-KORSAKOFF, Nicolas (1844-1908)

Antar Symphony, Op. 9

1st Movement 2nd Theme — R307

1st Movement 3rd Theme — R308

2nd Movement 1st Theme — R309

2nd Movement 2nd Theme — R310

3rd Movement 1st Theme — R311

3rd Movement 2nd Theme — R312

4th Movement — R313

Capriccio Espagnol, Op. 34, Orch.
By permission of Associated Music Publishers, Inc.

Intro. and Alborada — R314

Variations — R315

Scene and Gypsy Song 1st Theme — R316

2nd Theme — R317

Fandango Asturiano — R318

Le Coq D'Or, Suite Orch.
By permission of Associated Music Publishers, Inc.

1st Movement 1st Theme — R319

1st Movement 2nd Theme — R320

1st Movement 3rd Theme — R321

2nd Movement — R322

3rd Movement 1st Theme — R323

3rd Movement 2nd Theme — R324

3rd Movement 3rd Theme — R325

3rd Movement 4th Theme — R326

La Grande Paque Russe, Overture, Op. 36
By permission of Associated Music Publishers, Inc.
- 1st Theme — R327
- 2nd Theme — R328
- 3rd Theme — R329
- 4th Theme — R330
- 5th Theme — R331

May Night, Overture
By permission of Associated Music Publishers, Inc.
- 1st Theme — R332
- 2nd Theme — R333
- 3rd Theme — R334

Mlada, Ballet
By permission of Associated Music Publishers, Inc.
- 1st Theme — Cortège des Nobles — R335
- 2nd Theme — R336

Scheherezade, Op. 35, Orch.
By permission of Associated Music Publishers, Inc.
- 1st Movement — The Sea & Sinbad's Ship — Intro. A — R337
- 1st Movement — Intro. B — R338
- 1st Movement — 1st Theme — R339
- 1st Movement — 2nd Theme — R340
- 1st Movement — 3rd Theme — R341
- 2nd Movement — The Story of the Kalander Prince — 1st Theme, A — R342
- 2nd Movement — 1st Theme, B — R343
- 2nd Movement — 2nd Theme — R344
- 3rd Movement — The Young Prince & the Young Princess — 1st Theme — R345
- 3rd Movement — 2nd Theme — R346

4th Movement
Festival at Bagdad — R347

Snow Maiden, (Snegourotchka), Opera
Dance of the Buffoons
1st Theme — R348

2nd Theme — R349

3rd Theme — R350

Tale of the Invisible City of Kitezh, Opera
Battle of Kershenetz
1st Theme — R351

2nd Theme — R352

Tsar Saltan, Opera
Flight of the Bumble Bee
1st Theme — R353

2nd Theme — R354

The Tsar's Bride, Overture
By permission of Associated Music Publishers, Inc.
1st Theme — R355

2nd Theme — R356

3rd Theme — R357

ROSAS, J. (1868-1894)

Over the Waves, Waltzes
1st Theme — R358

2nd Theme — R359

ROSSINI, Gioacchino Antonio (1792-1868)

The Barber of Seville, Overture
Intro. — R360

1st Theme — R361

2nd Theme — R362

3rd Theme — R363

La Boutique Fantasque, Ballet
1st Movement Overture
1st Theme — R364

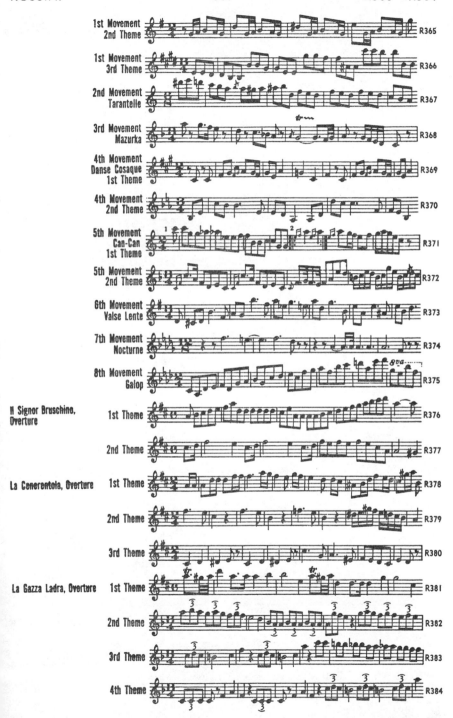

1st Movement 2nd Theme   R365
1st Movement 3rd Theme   R366
2nd Movement Tarantelle   R367
3rd Movement Mazurka   R368
4th Movement Danse Cosaque 1st Theme   R369
4th Movement 2nd Theme   R370
5th Movement Can-Can 1st Theme   R371
5th Movement 2nd Theme   R372
6th Movement Valse Lente   R373
7th Movement Nocturne   R374
8th Movement Galop   R375
Il Signor Bruschino, Overture   1st Theme   R376
2nd Theme   R377
La Cenerentola, Overture   1st Theme   R378
2nd Theme   R379
3rd Theme   R380
La Gazza Ladra, Overture   1st Theme   R381
2nd Theme   R382
3rd Theme   R383
4th Theme   R384

L'Italiana In Algeri, Overture 1st Theme — R385

2nd Theme — R386

Semiramide, Overture 1st Theme — R387

2nd Theme — R388

3rd Theme — R389

Tancredi, Overture 1st Theme — R390

2nd Theme — R391

William Tell
Opera — Overture 1st Theme — R392

2nd Theme — R393

Act 3
Soldier's Ballet 1st Theme — R394

2nd Theme — R395

ROUSSEL, Albert (1869-1937)

Le Festin de L'Araignée,
Ballet, Op. 17
Permission for reprint
granted by Durand & Cie,
Paris. Elkan-Vogel Co., Inc.
Philadelphia, Copyright
Owners. — Prelude 1st Theme — R396

2nd Theme — R397

Entrée des Fourmis — R398

Danse du Papillon — R399

Danse de l'Éphémère 1st Theme — R400

2nd Theme — R401

Funerailles de l'Éphémère — R402

La Naissance de la
Lyre, Op. 24, Orch.
Permission for reprint granted
by Durand & Cie, Paris.
Elkan-Vogel Co., Inc.
Philadelphia, Copyright Owners. — Danse des Nymphes 1st Theme — R403

2nd Theme — R404

Sinfonietta, Op. 52, Str. Orch.
Permission for reprint granted by Durand & Cie, Paris. Elkan-Vogel Co., Inc. Philadelphia, Copyright Owners.

1st Movement / 1st Theme — R405

1st Movement / 2nd Theme — R406

2nd Movement — R407

3rd Movement / 1st Theme — R408

3rd Movement / 2nd Theme — R409

Symphony No. 3 in G Minor, Op. 42
Permission for reprint granted by Durand & Cie, Paris. Elkan-Vogel Co., Inc. Philadelphia, Copyright Owners.

1st Movement / 1st Theme — R410

1st Movement / 2nd Theme — R411

2nd Movement / 1st Theme — R412

2nd Movement / 2nd Theme — R413

3rd Movement / 1st Theme — R414

3rd Movement / 2nd Theme — R415

4th Movement / 1st Theme — R416

4th Movement / 2nd Theme — R417

Symphony No. 4, Op. 53
Permission for reprint granted by Durand & Cie, Paris. Elkan-Vogel Co., Inc. Philadelphia, Copyright Owners.

1st Movement / 1st Theme — R418

1st Movement / 2nd Theme — R419

2nd Movement — R420

3rd Movement / 1st Theme — R421

3rd Movement / 2nd Theme — R422

4th Movement / 1st Theme — R423

RUBINSTEIN, Anton (1829-1894)

Barcarolle, Op. 30,
No. 1, Pft.
By permission of Associated
Music Publishers, Inc.
— 1st Theme — R424

2nd Theme — R425

Concerto No. 4 in
D Minor, Op. 70,
Pft. & Orch.
By permission of
Associated Music
Publishers, Inc.
— 1st Movement 1st Theme, A — R426

1st Movement 1st Theme, B — R427

1st Movement 2nd Theme — R428

2nd Movement — R429

3rd Movement 1st Theme — R430

3rd Movement 2nd Theme — R431

Cracovienne, Op. 5,
No. 3, Pft.
— 1st Theme — R432

2nd Theme — R433

Etude, Op. 23, No. 2, Pft.
"Staccato"
— 1st Theme — R434

2nd Theme — R435

Feramors (Lalla Rookh)
Opera
By permission of Associated
Music Publishers, Inc.
— Bridal March 1st Theme — R436

2nd Theme — R437

Kamennoi-Ostrow, Op. 10,
No. 22, Pft.
— 1st Theme — R438

2nd Theme — R439

Melody in F, Op. 3,
No. 1, Pft.
— 1st Theme — R440

2nd Theme — R441

Romance, Op. 44, No. 1, Pft. 1st Theme — R442

2nd Theme — R443

Toreador et Andalouse, Op. 103, No. 7, from Bal Costumé, Pft., 4 Hands
By permission of Associated Music Publishers, Inc.

1st Theme — R444
2nd Theme — R445

Valse in F, Pft.
By permission of Associated Music Publishers, Inc. — R446

Valse Caprice, Pft.
By permission of Associated Music Publishers, Inc.

1st Theme — R447
2nd Theme — R448
3rd Theme — R449

SACCHINI, Antonio (1730-1786)

Sonata in F
Harpsi.

1st Movement — S1
2nd Movement 1st Theme — S2
2nd Movement 2nd Theme — S3

SAINT-SAËNS, Camille (1835-1921)

Caprice Arabe, Op. 96, 2 Pfts.
Permission for reprint granted by Durand & Cie, Paris. Elkan-Vogel Co., Inc. Philadelphia, Copyright Owners.

1st Theme — S4
2nd Theme — S5
3rd Theme — S6

Carnaval des Animaux, Orch. & 2 Pfts.
Permission for reprint granted by Durand & Cie, Paris. Elkan-Vogel Co., Inc. Philadelphia, Copyright Owners.

Marche Royale du Lion — S7
Poules et Coqs — S8
Tortues (Theme from Orpheus in Hades — Offenbach) — S9
L'Éléphant — S10
Kangorous — S11

2nd Movement / 1st Theme — S32

2nd Movement / 2nd Theme — S33

3rd Movement — S34

No. 3 in B Minor, Op. 61, Vn. & Orch.
Copyright 1905 by Carl Fischer, Inc., N. Y.

1st Movement / 1st Theme — S35

1st Movement / 2nd Theme — S36

2nd Movement / 1st Theme — S37

2nd Movement / 2nd Theme — S38

3rd Movement / 1st Theme, A — S39

3rd Movement / 1st Theme, B — S40

3rd Movement / 2nd Theme — S41

3rd Movement / 3rd Theme — S42

Concertstück, Op. 20, Vn. & Orch.
By permission of J. Hamelle Music Publishers, Paris.

Intro. — S43

1st Theme — S44

2nd Theme — S45

3rd Theme — S46

Danse Macabre, Op. 40, Orch. or 2 Pfts.
Permission for reprint granted by Durand & Cie, Paris. Elkan-Vogel Co., Inc. Philadelphia, Copyright Owners.

1st Theme — S47

2nd Theme — S48

Elégie, Op. 143, Vn. & Pft.
Permission for reprint granted by Durand & Cie, Paris. Elkan-Vogel Co., Inc. Philadelphia, Copyright Owners.

1st Theme — S49

2nd Theme — S50

Havanaise, Op. 83, Vn. & Orch.
Permission for reprint granted by Durand & Cie, Paris. Elkan-Vogel Co., Inc. Philadelphia, Copyright Owners.

1st Theme — S51

2nd Theme — S72
3rd Theme — S73

Phaëton, Op. 39, Orch.
Permission for reprint granted
by Durand & Cie, Paris.
Elkan-Vogel Co., Inc.
Philadelphia, Copyright
Owners.

1st Theme — S74
2nd Theme — S75
3rd Theme — S76

Romance, Op. 36, Fr. Horn & Orch.
Permission for reprint granted
by Durand & Cie, Paris. Elkan-Vogel
Co., Inc. Philadelphia, Copyright
Owners. — S77

**Le Rouet d'Omphale,
Op. 31, Orch.**
Permission for reprint granted
by Durand & Cie, Paris.
Elkan-Vogel Co., Inc.
Philadelphia, Copyright
Owners.

1st Theme — S78
2nd Thème — S79

**Samson et Dalila,
Opera, Op. 47**
Copyright 1892
by G. Schirmer, Inc.

Bacchanale
1st Theme — S80
2nd Theme, A — S81
2nd Theme, B — S82
3rd Theme — S83
4th Theme — S84

Scherzo, Op. 87, 2 Pfts.
By permission of
International Music Co.

Intro. — S85
1st Theme — S86
2nd Theme — S87
3rd Theme — S88

**Septet, Op. 65, Tpt.,
Str. Quin. & Pft.**
Permission for reprint
granted by Durand &
Cie. Paris. Elkan-Vogel
Co., Inc. Philadelphia,
Copyright Owners,

1st Movement
Préambule — S89
2nd Movement
Minuet
1st Theme — S90
2nd Movement
2nd Theme — S91

3rd Movement Intermède — S92

4th Movement Gavotte & Finale — S93

Sonatas
No. 1 in C Minor, Op. 32, Vcl. & Pft.
Permission for reprint granted by Durand & Cie, Paris. Elkan-Vogel Co., Inc. Philadelphia, Copyright Owners.

1st Movement Intro. — S94

1st Movement 1st Theme — S95

1st Movement 2nd Theme — S96

2nd Movement — S97

3rd Movement 1st Theme — S98

3rd Movement 2nd Theme — S99

No. 2 in F, Op. 123, Vcl. & Pft.
Permission for reprint granted by Durand & Cie, Paris. Elkan-Vogel Co., Inc. Philadelphia, Copyright Owners.

1st Movement Intro. — S100

1st Movement 1st Theme — S101

1st Movement 2nd Theme — S102

2nd Movement Scherzo con Variazione — S103

3rd Movement Romance — S104

4th Movement 1st Theme — S105

4th Movement 2nd Theme — S106

No. 1, Op. 75, Vn. & Pft.
Permission for reprint granted by Durand & Cie, Paris. Elkan-Vogel Co., Inc. Philadelphia, Copyright Owners.

1st Movement 1st Theme — S107

1st Movement 2nd Theme — S108

1st Movement 3rd Theme — S109

2nd Movement 1st Theme — S110

2nd Movement 2nd Theme — S111

SAINT-SAENS

3rd Movement 1st Theme — S112

3rd Movement 2nd Theme — S113

3rd Movement 3rd Theme — S114

Song Without Words, Pft. — S115

Suite Algérienne, Op. 60, Orch.
Permission for reprint granted by Durand & Cie, Paris. Elkan-Vogel Co., Inc. Philadelphia, Copyright Owners.

1st Movement Prélude, en Vue d'Alger 1st Theme — S116

1st Movement 2nd Theme — S117

2nd Movement Rapsodie Mauresque 1st Theme, A — S118

2nd Movement 1st Theme, B — S119

2nd Movement 2nd Theme, A — S120

2nd Movement 2nd Theme, B — S121

2nd Movement 3rd Theme — S122

3rd Movement Rêverie du Soir Intro. — S123

3rd Movement Theme — S124

4th Movement Marche Militaire Française 1st Theme — S125

4th Movement 2nd Theme — S126

Symphony No. 3, in C Minor, Op. 78, Orch., Organ & Pft.
Published and Copyrighted (1930) by Oliver Ditson Co.

1st Movement 1st Theme — S127

1st Movement 2nd Theme — S128

1st Movement 3rd Theme — S129

1st Movement 4th Theme — S130

2nd Movement 1st Theme — S131

2nd Movement 2nd Theme — S132

3rd Movement 1st Theme — S133

3rd Movement 2nd Theme — S134

Tarantelle, Op. 6, Fl., Cl. & Orch.
Permission for reprint granted by Durand & Cie, Paris. Elkan-Vogel Co., Inc. Philadelphia, Copyright Owners.

1st Theme — S135

2nd Theme — S136

3rd Theme — S137

Wedding Cake, (Valse Caprice), Op. 76, Pft. & Str.
Permission for reprint granted by Durand & Cie, Paris. Elkan-Vogel Co., Inc. Philadelphia, Copyright Owners.

1st Theme — S138

2nd Theme — S139

3rd Theme — S140

SAMMARTINI, Giovanni (1698-1775)

Sonata in G, Vcl. & Pft. 1st Movement — S141

2nd Movement — S142

3rd Movement — S143

SAMMARTINI, Giuseppe (1693-1750)

Canto Amoroso, Vn. & Pft. (Arr. by Elman) — S144

SARASATE, Pablo (1844-1908)

Caprice Basque, Op. 24, Vn. & Pft.
By permission of Associated Music Publishers, Inc.

1st Theme — S145

2nd Theme — S146

3rd Theme — S147

Danses Espagnoles
By permission of Associated Music Publishers, Inc.
Op. 21, No. 1, Vn. & Pft.

Malagueña 1st Theme — S148

4th Theme   S169

5th Theme   S170

6th Theme   S171

SATIE, Erik (1866-1925)

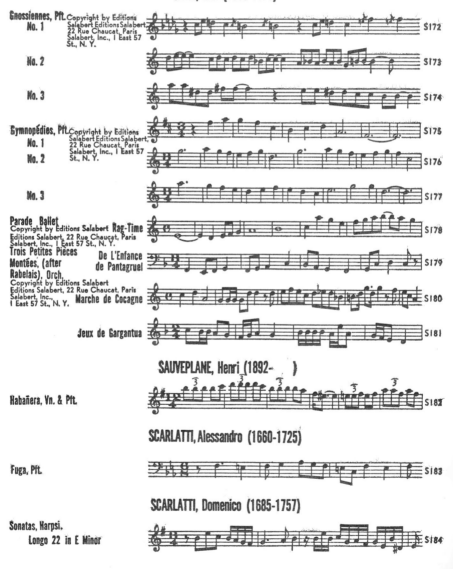

Gnossiennes, Pft.
No. 1   S172

No. 2   S173

No. 3   S174

Gymnopédies, Pft.
No. 1   S175

No. 2   S176

No. 3   S177

Parade Ballet **Rag-Time**   S178

Trois Petites Pièces   De L'Enfance
Montées, (after   de Pantagruel
Rabelais), Orch. **Marche de Cocagne**   S179 / S180

Jeux de Gargantua   S181

SAUVEPLANE, Henri (1892-)

Habañera, Vn. & Pft.   S182

SCARLATTI, Alessandro (1660-1725)

Fuga, Pft.   S183

SCARLATTI, Domenico (1685-1757)

Sonatas, Harpsi.
   Longo 22 in E Minor   S184

Longo 23 in E   S185

Longo 33 in B Minor   S186

Longo 58 in D Minor "Gavotte"   S187

Longo 104 in C   S188

Longo 107 in D   S189

Longo 108 in D Minor   S190

Longo 129 in G   S191

Longo 142 in E Flat   S192

Longo 152 in A   S193

Longo 205 in C   S194

Longo 208 in D   S195

Longo 232 in G   S196

Longo 239 in A Minor   S197

Longo 243 in A Minor, "Pastorale"   S198

Longo 256 in C Sharp Minor   S199

Longo 257 in E   S200

Longo 261 in D   S201

Longo 263 in B Minor   S202

Longo 294 in F Sharp Minor   S203

Longo 338 in G Minor "Burlesca"   S204

Longo 345 in A — S205
Longo 352 in C Minor — S206
Longo 375 in E, — S207
Longo 382 in F Minor — S208
Longo 384 in F — S209
Longo 387 in G — S210
Longo 395 in A — S211
Longo 407 in C Minor — S212
Longo 411 in D — S213
Longo 413 in D Minor "Pastorale" — S214
Longo 422 in D Minor "Toccata" — S215
Longo 429 in A Minor — S216
Longo 434 in B Flat — S217
Longo 438 in F Minor — S218
Longo 449 in B Minor — S219
Longo 463 in D "Tempo di Ballo" — S220
Longo 465 in D — S221
Longo 474 in F — S222
Longo 475 in F Minor — S223
Longo 479 in F — S224

Longo 486 in G — S225

Longo 487 in G — S226

Longo 488 in G Minor "Sarabande" — S227

Longo 490 in G — S228

Longo 499 in G Minor "Cat Fugue" — S229

Longo Supplement 27 in G — S230

The Good-Humored Ladies Ballet-Suite, Orch.

1st Movement Sonata Longo 388 — S231

2nd Movement Sonata Longo 361 — S232

3rd Movement Sonata Longo 33 — S233

4th Movement Sonata Longo 463 — S234

5th Movement Sonata Longo 385 — S235

SCHARWENKA, Franz (1850-1924)

Polish Dance, Op. 3, No. 1, Pft.

1st Theme — S236

2nd Theme — S237

SCHEIN, Johann (1586-1630)

Banchetto Musicale, Suite No. 1, Str. Quint.

1st Movement Padouna — S238

2nd Movement Galliarde — S239

3rd Movement Courente — S240

4th Movement Allemande — S241

5th Movement Tripla — S242

SCHELLING, Ernest (1876-1939)

Impressions from an Artist's
Life (Variations), Orch. & Pft.
By permission of Associated
Music Publishers, Inc.

A Victory Ball, Orch.
By permission of Associated
Music Publishers, Inc.

SCHMITT, Florent (1870-1958)

Rapsodie Viennoise,
Op. 53, No. 3, Orch.
Permission for reprint granted
by Durand & Cie, Paris.
Elkan-Vogel Co., Inc.
Philadelphia, Copyright
Owners.

Reflets d'Allemagne,
Orch.

SCHOBERT, Johann (c. 1720-1767)

Sonata in F,
Op. 8, Pft.

1st Movement — S261

2nd Movement — S262

3rd Movement
Polonaise — S263

4th Movement
1st Theme — S264

4th Movement
2nd Theme — S265

SCHÖNBERG, Arnold (1874-1951)

Six Little Piano Pieces,
Op. 19
By permission of Associated
Music Publishers, Inc.

No. 1 — S266

No. 2 — S267

No. 3 — S268

No. 4 — S269

No. 5 — S270

Verklärte Nacht, Op. 4,
Str. Sextet

1st Theme — S271

2nd Theme — S272

3rd Theme — S273

4th Theme — S274

5th Theme — S275

SCHREKER, Franz (1878-1934)

Birthday of the Infanta, 1st Movement
Orch.   "Reigen" (Rounds)
By permission of   1st Theme
Associated Music
Publishers, Inc. — S276

1st Movement
2nd Theme — S277

2nd Movement
Marionetten — S278

3rd Movement
Minuet der Tanzknaben (Dancing Boys)
1st Theme — S279

3rd Movement
2nd Theme — S280

4th Movement
Tänze des Zwerges
(Dances of the Dwarf) — S281

4th Movement
2nd Theme — S282

4th Movement
3rd Theme — S283

Kleine Suite,
Chamber Orch.
By permission of
Associated Music
Publishers, Inc.

1st Movement
Präludium — S284

2nd Movement
Marcia — S285

3rd Movement
Canon — S286

4th Movement
Fughette — S287

5th Movement
Intermezzo — S288

6th Movement
Capriccio — S289

SCHUBERT, Franz (1797-1828)

Allegretto in C Minor, Pft. — S290

Deutsche Tänze, Pft.
Op. 33, No. 2 — S291

Op. 33, No. 6 — S292

Op. 33, No. 7 — S293

Fantaisie in C, "Wanderer"
Op. 15, Pft.
1st Theme — S294

2nd Theme — S295

3rd Theme — S296

4th Theme — S297

Impromptus, Pft.
Op. 90, No. 1 in C Minor — S298

Op. 90, No. 2, in E Flat — 1st Theme — S299

2nd Theme — S300

Op. 90, No. 3, in G Flat — S301

Op. 90, No. 4, in A Flat — 1st Theme — S302

2nd Theme — S303

Op. 142, No. 1, in F Minor — S304

Op. 142, No. 2, in A Flat — S305

Op. 142, No. 3 in B Flat, (Theme & Variations) — S306

Op. 142, No. 4, in F Minor — S307

March, Op. 40, No. 2, Pft., — 1st Theme — S308

2nd Theme — S309

Military Marches, Pft. 4 Hands Op. 51, No. 1 — 1st Theme — S310

2nd Theme — S311

3rd Theme — S312

Op. 51, No. 2 — S313

Op. 51, No. 3 — 1st Theme — S314

2nd Theme — S315

Moments Musicals Op. 94, Pft. No. 1, in C — S316

No. 2, in A Flat — 1st Theme — S317

2nd Theme — S318

No. 3, in F Minor — S319

No. 4, in C Sharp Minor — 1st Theme — S320

2nd Theme — S321

No. 5, in F Minor — S322

No. 6, in A Flat — 1st Theme — S323

2nd Theme — S324

Nocturne in E Flat, Op. 148, Pft., Vn. & Vcl. — 1st Theme — S325

2nd Theme — S326

Octet in F, Op. 166, Str. Quint., Fg., Cl. & Hn. — 1st Movement 1st Theme — S327

1st Movement 2nd Theme — S328

2nd Movement 1st Theme — S329

2nd Movement 2nd Theme — S330

3rd Movement 1st Theme — S331

3rd Movement 2nd Theme — S332

4th Movement Theme & Variations — S333

5th Movement 1st Theme — S334

5th Movement 2nd Theme — S335

6th Movement — S336

Adagio & Rondo Concertante in F, Pft. & Str.

1st Movement   S337

2nd Movement   S338

Quartets
No. 4, in C, Str.

1st Movement   S339

2nd Movement   S340

3rd Movement   S341

4th Movement   S342

No. 6, in D, Str.   1st Movement   S343

2nd Movement   S344

3rd Movement   S345

4th Movement   S346

No. 8, in B Flat, Op. 168, Str.   1st Movement   S347

2nd Movement 1st Theme   S348

2nd Movement 2nd Theme   S349

3rd Movement 1st Theme   S350

3rd Movement 2nd Theme   S351

4th Movement   S352

No. 9, in G Minor, Str.   1st Movement   S353

2nd Movement   S354

3rd Movement   S355

4th Movement   S356

No. 10, in E Flat,
Op. 125, No. 1, Str.   1st Movement / 1st Theme   S357

1st Movement / 2nd Theme   S358

2nd Movement   S359

3rd Movement   S360

4th Movement   S361

No. 12, in C Minor,
Str. (One Movement)   1st Theme   S362

2nd Theme   S363

No. 13, in A Minor,   1st Movement / 1st Theme   S364
Op. 29, Str.

1st Movement / 2nd Theme   S365

2nd Movement   S366

3rd Movement   S367

4th Movement / 1st Theme   S368

4th Movement / 2nd Theme   S369

No. 14, in D
Minor, Str.
"Der Tod und das
Mädchen"   1st Movement / 1st Theme   S370

1st Movement / 2nd Theme   S371

2nd Movement   S372

3rd Movement / 1st Theme   S373

3rd Movement / 2nd Theme   S374

4th Movement / 1st Theme   S375

4th Movement / 2nd Theme   S376

No. 15, in G
Op. 161, Str.

1st Movement — S377

2nd Movement — S378

3rd Movement
1st Theme — S379

3rd Movement
2nd Theme — S380

4th Movement — S381

Quintet, in A, Op. 114,
Pft. & Str., "Forellen"

1st Movement
1st Theme — S382

1st Movement
2nd Theme — S383

2nd Movement — S384

3rd Movement
1st Theme — S385

3rd Movement
2nd Theme — S386

4th Movement
(Theme & Variation on "Die Forelle") — S387

5th Movement
Finale — S388

Quintet in C,
Op. 163, Str.

1st Movement
1st Theme — S389

1st Movement
2nd Theme — S390

2nd Movement — S391

3rd Movement
1st Theme — S392

3rd Movement
2nd Theme — S393

4th Movement
1st Theme — S394

4th Movement
2nd Theme — S395

Rondo in B Minor, Op. 70
Vn. & Pft.

1st Theme — S396

2nd Theme — S397

Rondo in A, Vn. & Str. Orch. 1st Theme — S398

2nd Theme — S399

Rosamunde,
Alfonso & Estrella, Overture — S400

Rosamunde, Overture, Op. 26   Intro. — S401

•1st Theme — S402

2nd Theme — S403

3rd Theme — S404

Entr'Acte
(Same as Slow Movement, A Min. Qt.) — S405

Ballet No. 1   1st Theme — S406

2nd Theme — S407

Ballet No. 2 — S408

Scherzo in B Flat, Pft. — S409

Sonata in A Minor,
Op. 42, Pft.   1st Movement — S410

2nd Movement — S411

3rd Movement — S412

Sonata in G, Op. 78,
Pft.   1st Movement — S413

2nd Movement
1st Theme — S414

2nd Movement
2nd Theme — S415

3rd Movement
1st Theme — S416

3rd Movement
2nd Theme — S417

4th Movement — S418

Sonata in A, Op. 120, Pft.

1st Movement
1st Theme — S419

1st Movement
2nd Theme — S420

2nd Movement — S421

3rd Movement
1st Theme — S422

3rd Movement
2nd Theme — S423

Sonata in A Minor, Op. 143, Pft.

1st Movement — S424

2nd Movement — S425

3rd Movement
1st Theme — S426

3rd Movement
2nd Theme — S427

Sonata in B, Op. 147, Pft.

1st Movement
1st Theme — S428

1st Movement
2nd Theme — S429

1st Movement
3rd Theme — S430

2nd Movement — S431

3rd Movement — S432

4th Movement
1st Theme — S433

4th Movement
2nd Theme — S434

Sonata in B Flat, Pft. (Posth.)

1st Movement
1st Theme — S435

1st Movement
2nd Theme — S436

2nd Movement — S437

3rd Movement — S438

4th Movement — S439

Sonata in A Minor, Pft. & Vcl.,(Arpeggione) 1st Movement — S440

2nd Movement — S441

3rd Movement 1st Theme — S442

3rd Movement 2nd Theme, A — S443

3rd Movement 2nd Theme, B — S444

Sonatina in D, Op.137, No. 1, Vn. & Pft. 1st Movement — S445

2nd Movement — S446

3rd Movement — S447

Sonatina in G Minor, Op. 137, No. 3, Vn. & Pft. 1st Movement — S448

2nd Movement — S449

3rd Movement 1st Theme — S450

3rd Movement 2nd Theme — S451

4th Movement 1st Theme — S452

4th Movement 2nd Theme — S453

Sonata in A, Op. 162, Vn. & Pft. 1st Movement — S454

2nd Movement — S455

3rd Movement — S456

Symphony No. 3 in D

Symphony No. 4 in C Minor, "Tragic"

4th Movement 2nd Theme S497

4th Movement 3rd Theme S498

Symphony No. 5 in B Flat

1st Movement Intro. S499

1st Movement 1st Theme S500

1st Movement 2nd Theme S501

2nd Movement 1st Theme S502

2nd Movement 2nd Theme S503

3rd Movement 1st Theme S504

3rd Movement 2nd Theme S505

4th Movement 1st Theme S506

4th Movement 2nd Theme S507

Symphony No. 6 in C

1st Movement Intro. S508

1st Movement 1st Theme S509

1st Movement 2nd Theme S510

2nd Movement 1st Theme S511

2nd Movement 2nd Theme S512

3rd Movement 1st Theme S513

3rd Movement 2nd Theme S514

4th Movement 1st Theme S515

4th Movement 2nd Theme S516

4th Movement / 3rd Theme — S517

Symphony No. 7 in C, "Great"
1st Movement / Intro. — S518
1st Movement / 1st Theme — S519
1st Movement / 2nd Theme — S520
1st Movement / 3rd Theme — S521
2nd Movement / 1st Theme — S522
2nd Movement / 2nd Theme — S523
2nd Movement / 3rd Theme — S524
2nd Movement / 4th Theme — S525
3rd Movement / 1st Theme — S526
3rd Movement / 2nd Theme — S527
3rd Movement / 3rd Theme — S528
3rd Movement / 4th Theme — S529
4th Movement / Intro. — S530
4th Movement / 1st Theme — S531
4th Movement / 2nd Theme — S532

Symphony No. 8 in B Minor, "Unfinished"
1st Movement / Intro. — S533
1st Movement / 1st Theme — S534
1st Movement / 2nd Theme — S535
2nd Movement / (Intro-motive) — S536

Trio in B Flat, Vn., Vla. & Vcl. (One Movement) — S557

Waltzes, Pft.
Op. 9, No. 1 — S558

Op. 9, No. 2 — S559

Op. 9, No. 12 — S560

Op. 50, No. 13 — S561

Op. 77, No. 9 — S562

Op. 77, No. 10 — S563

SCHUMAN, William (1910-)

American Festival Overture, Orch.
Copyright 1941 by G. Schirmer, Inc.
1st Theme, A — S564

1st Theme, B — S565

2nd Theme Fugue Theme — S566

3rd Theme Counter Theme — S567

4th Theme — S568

Symphony for Strings
Copyright 1943 by G. Schirmer, Inc.
1st Movement 1st Theme, A — S569

1st Movement 1st Theme, B — S570

1st Movement 2nd Theme, A — S571

1st Movement 2nd Theme, B — S572

2nd Movement Intro. — S573

2nd Movement 1st Theme — S574

2nd Movement 2nd Theme — S575

3rd Movement 1st Theme — S576

3rd Movement 2nd Theme — S577

Symphony No. 3
Part I
Passacaglia & Fugue
Copyright 1942 by
G. Schirmer, Inc.

1st Theme Passacaglia — S578

2nd Theme Fugue — S579

Part II
Chorale & Toccata

1st Theme Chorale — S580

2nd Theme Toccata — S581

SCHUMANN, Robert (1810-1856)

Abegg Variations, Op. 1, Pft. — S582

Abendlied (Evening Song),
Op. 85, No. 12, Pft., 4 Hands — S583

Des Abends, Op. 12, No. 1, Pft. — S584

Album for the Young,
Op. 68, Pft.

Soldiers' March — S584a

The Wild Horseman — S584b

Folk Song — S584c

The Happy Farmer — S584d

Sicilienne — S584e

Little Romance — S584f

The Strange Man — S584g

Italian Sailors' Song — S584h

Arabeske, Op. 18, Pft.

1st Theme — S585

2nd Theme — S586

3rd Theme — S587

Aufschwung (Soaring), Op. 12, No. 2, Pft.
1st Theme — S588
2nd Theme — S589

Carnaval, Op. 9, Pft.
Préambule — S590
Pierrot — S591
Arlequin — S592
Valse Noble — S593
Eusebius — S594
Florestan — S595
Lettres Dansantes — S596
Chopin — S597
Estrella — S598
Reconnaissance — S599
March of the Davidsbündler — S600

Concerto in A Minor, Op. 129, Vcl. & Orch.
1st Movement 1st Theme — S601
1st Movement 2nd Theme — S602
1st Movement 3rd Theme — S603
2nd Movement — S604
3rd Movement 1st Theme — S605
3rd Movement 2nd Theme — S606

3rd Movement / 3rd Theme — S607

Concerto in A Minor, Op. 54, Pft. & Orch.
1st Movement / 1st Theme — S608
1st Movement / 2nd Theme, A — S609
1st Movement / 2nd Theme, B — S610
1st Movement / 3rd Theme — S611
1st Movement / Coda — S612
2nd Movement / Intermezzo / 1st Theme — S613
2nd Movement / 2nd Theme — S614
3rd Movement / 1st Theme — S615
3rd Movement / 2nd Theme — S616
3rd Movement / 3rd Theme — S617

Concerto in D Minor, Vn. & Orch.
1st Movement / 1st Theme — S618
1st Movement / 2nd Theme — S619
2nd Movement — S620
3rd Movement / 1st Theme — S621
3rd Movement / 2nd Theme — S622

Davidsbündler, Op. 6, Pft.
No. 1 — S623
No. 2 — S624
No. 5 — S625
No. 9 — S626

No. 13 — S627
No. 16 — S628
Faschingsschwank Aus Wien, Op. 26, Pft. — 1st Movement 1st Theme — S629
1st Movement 2nd Theme — S630
1st Movement 3rd Theme — S631
2nd Movement Romance — S632
3rd Movement Scherzino — S633
4th Movement Intermezzo — S634
Grillen, (Whims), from Fantasicstücke, Op. 12, No. 4, Pft. — S635
Kreisleriana, Op. 16, Pft. — No. 2 — S636
No. 8 — S637
Nachtstück, Op. 23, No. 4, Pft. — S638
Novelette, Op. 21, No. 1, Pft. 1st Theme — S639
2nd Theme — S640
Novelette, Op. 21, No. 6, Pft. — S641
Novelette, Op. 99, No. 9, Pft. — 1st Theme — S642
2nd Theme — S643
Papillons, Op. 2, Pft. — No. 1 — S644
No. 2 — S645
No. 3 — S646

2nd Movement / 1st Theme / Scherzo — S667

2nd Movement / 2nd Theme / Intermezzo — S668

3rd Movement — S669

4th Movement — S670

Quartet in F, Op. 41, No. 2, Str.

1st Movement / 1st Theme — S671

1st Movement / 2nd Theme — S672

2nd Movement — S673

3rd Movement / 1st Theme — S674

3rd Movement / 2nd Theme — S675

4th Movement / 1st Theme — S676

4th Movement / 2nd Theme, A — S677

4th Movement / 2nd Theme, B — S678

Quartet in A, Op. 41, No. 3, Str.

1st Movement / 1st Theme — S679

1st Movement / 2nd Theme — S680

2nd Movement / 1st Theme — S681

2nd Movement / 2nd Theme — S682

2nd Movement / 3rd Theme — S683

3rd Movement / 1st Theme — S684

3rd Movement / 2nd Theme — S685

4th Movement / 1st Theme — S686

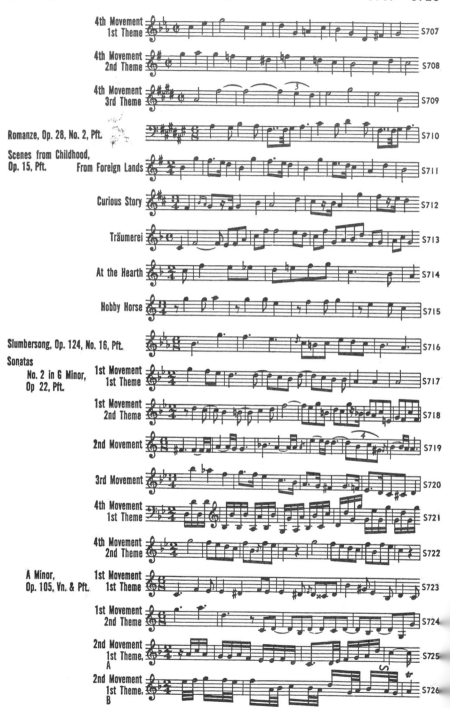

4th Movement, 1st Theme — S707

4th Movement, 2nd Theme — S708

4th Movement, 3rd Theme — S709

Romanze, Op. 28, No. 2, Pft. — S710

Scenes from Childhood, Op. 15, Pft. — From Foreign Lands — S711

Curious Story — S712

Träumerei — S713

At the Hearth — S714

Hobby Horse — S715

Slumbersong, Op. 124, No. 16, Pft. — S716

Sonatas, No. 2 in G Minor, Op 22, Pft. — 1st Movement, 1st Theme — S717

1st Movement, 2nd Theme — S718

2nd Movement — S719

3rd Movement — S720

4th Movement, 1st Theme — S721

4th Movement, 2nd Theme — S722

A Minor, Op. 105, Vn. & Pft. — 1st Movement, 1st Theme — S723

1st Movement, 2nd Theme — S724

2nd Movement, 1st Theme, A — S725

2nd Movement, 1st Theme, B — S726

2nd Movement 2nd Theme — S727
3rd Movement 1st Theme — S728
3rd Movement 2nd Theme — S729
3rd Movement 3rd Theme — S730

D Minor, Op. 121, Vn. & Pft.

1st Movement Intro. — S731
1st Movement 1st Theme — S732
1st Movement 2nd Theme — S733
2nd Movement 1st Theme — S734
2nd Movement 2nd Theme — S735
2nd Movement 3rd Theme — S736
3rd Movement 1st Theme — S737
3rd Movement 2nd Theme — S738
4th Movement 1st Theme — S739
4th Movement 2nd Theme — S740

Symphonic Etudes, in C Sharp Minor, Op. 13, Pft.

Theme — S741
Etude I — S742
Etude II — S743
Etude III — S744
Etude VI — S745
Finale 1st Theme — S746

1st Movement 1st Theme — S767

1st Movement 2nd Theme — S768

1st Movement 3rd Theme — S769

2nd Movement 1st Theme — S770

2nd Movement 2nd Theme — S771

2nd Movement 3rd Theme — S772

2nd Movement 4th Theme — S773

3rd Movement 1st Theme — S774

3rd Movement 2nd Theme — S775

4th Movement Intro. — S776

4th Movement 1st Theme — S777

4th Movement 2nd Theme — S778

4th Movement 3rd Theme — S779

Symphony No. 3 in E Flat, Op. 97, "Rhenish" 1st Movement 1st Theme — S780

1st Movement 2nd Theme — S781

2nd Movement 1st Theme — S782

2nd Movement 2nd Theme — S783

3rd Movement 1st Theme — S784

3rd Movement 2nd Theme — S785

4th Movement — S786

5th Movement 1st Theme   S787

5th Movement 2nd Theme   S788

5th Movement 3rd Theme   S789

5th Movement 4th Theme   S790

Symphony No. 4 in D Minor, Op. 120   1st Movement Intro.   S791

1st Movement 1st Theme   S792

1st Movement 2nd Theme   S793

2nd Movement   S794

2nd Movement 2nd Theme   S795

3rd Movement 1st Theme   S796

3rd Movement 2nd Theme   S797

4th Movement 1st Theme   S798

4th Movement 2nd Theme   S799

4th Movement 3rd Theme   S800

4th Movement 4th Theme   S801

Three Romances, Op. 94, Oboe & Pft.   No. 1   S802

No. 2   S803

No. 3 1st Theme   S804

No. 3 2nd Theme   S805

Toccata, Op. 7, Pft.   Intro.   S806

1st Theme — S807

2nd Theme — S808

Vogel Als Prophet,
(Bird as Prophet),
Op. 82, No. 7, Pft.

1st Theme — S809

2nd Theme — S810

Warum? (Why?), Op. 12, No. 3, Pft. — S811

SCOTT, Cyril (1879-1970)

Danse Nègre, Op. 58, No. 5, Pft.
Copyright 1911 by
Elkin & Co., Ltd.
By permission of Galaxy
Music Corporation, N. Y.

S812

Lotus Land, Op. 47,
No. 1, Pft.
Copyright 1905 by
Elkin & Co., Ltd.
By permission of Galaxy
Music Corporation, N. Y.

1st Theme — S813

2nd Theme — S814

A Song from the East,
Op. 54, No. 2, Pft.
Copyright 1907
by Elkin & Co., Ltd.
By permission of Galaxy
Music Corporation, N. Y.

S815

SCRIABIN, Alexander (1872-1915)

Etudes
By permission of The Boston Music Co.,
Op. 2, No. 1, Pft. copyright owner.

S816

Op. 8, No. 10, Pft.
By permission of Associated
Music Publishers, Inc.

S817

Op. 8, No. 12, Pft.
By permission of Associated
Music Publishers, Inc.

S818

Fantaisie, Op. 28, Pft.   1st Theme
By permission of Associated
Music Publishers, Inc.

S819

2nd Theme — S820

Mazurka, Op. 25, No. 3, Pft.
By permission of Associated
Music Publishers, Inc.

S821

Nocturne, Pft. (For Left Hand Alone)
By permission of Associated
Music Publishers, Inc.

S822

Poème, Op. 32, No. 1, Pft.
By permission of Associated
Music Publishers, Inc.

S823

Poème, Op. 32, No. 2, Pft.
By permission of Associated
Music Publishers, Inc.

S824

Poème D'Extase, Op. 34, Orch. By permission of Associated Music Publishers, Inc. — 1st Theme — S825

2nd Theme — S826

3rd Theme — S827

Preludes
Op. 9, No. 1, Pft. (For Left Hand Alone) By permission of Associated Music Publishers, Inc. — S828

Op. 11, No. 2, Pft. By permission of Associated Music Publishers, Inc. — S829

No. 9, Pft. — S830

No. 10, Pft. — S831

Sonata, No. 4, Op. 30, Pft. By permission of International Music Co. — 1st Movement — S832

2nd Movement — S833

Symphony No. 3, Op. 43 "Le Divin Poème" By permission of Associated Music Publishers, Inc. — Intro. — S834

1st Movement Luttes 1st Theme — S835

1st Movement 2nd Theme — S836

2nd Movement Voluptés — S837

3rd Movement Jeu Divin 1st Theme — S838

3rd Movement 2nd Theme — S839

Waltz, Op. 38, Pft. By permission of Associated Music Publishers, Inc. — S840

SGAMBATI, Giovanni (1841-1914)

Serenata Napoletana, Op. 24, No. 2, Vn. & Pft. — 1st Theme, A — S841

1st Theme, B — S842

2nd Theme — S843

Vecchio Minuetto, Op. 18, Pft. S844

SHOSTAKOVICH, Dmitri (1906-1975)

Concerto, Op. 35,
Pft. & Orch.
By permission of
Broude Brothers

1st Movement
1st Theme S845

1st Movement
2nd Theme S846

2nd Movement S847

3rd Movement
Finale
1st Theme S848

3rd Movement
2nd Theme S849

3rd Movement
3rd Theme S850

The Golden Age, Op. 22,
Ballet
Copyright 1941 by Leeds
Music Corp., N. Y.
Reprinted here by permission
of the copyright owner.

1st Theme
Polka S851

2nd Theme S852

3rd Theme S853

Quartet, Op. 49, Str.
By permission of
International Music Co.

1st Movement
1st Theme S854

1st Movement
2nd Theme S855

2nd Movement S856

3rd Movement
1st Theme S857

3rd Movement
2nd Theme S858

4th Movement
1st Theme S859

4th Movement
2nd Theme S860

Quintet, Op. 57,
Pft. & Str.

1st Movement
Prelude
1st Theme S861

1st Movement
2nd Theme S862

Symphony No. 6, Op. 53

Symphony No. 7, Op. 60

Symphony No. 9, Op. 70

1st Movement 1st Theme — S896
1st Movement 2nd Theme — S897
2nd Movement 1st Theme — S898
2nd Movement 2nd Theme — S899
3rd Movement 1st Theme — S900
3rd Movement 2nd Theme — S901
3rd Movement 3rd Theme — S902
1st Movement 1st Theme — S903
1st Movement 2nd Theme — S904
1st Movement 3rd Theme — S905
2nd Movement 1st Theme — S906
2nd Movement 2nd Theme — S907
2nd Movement 3rd Theme — S908
3rd Movement 1st Theme — S909
3rd Movement 2nd Theme — S910
3rd Movement 3rd Theme — S911
4th Movement 1st Theme — S912
4th Movement 2nd Theme — S913
1st Movement 1st Theme — S914
1st Movement 2nd Theme — S915

2nd Movement
1st Theme — S916

2nd Movement
2nd Theme — S917

3rd Movement
1st Theme — S918

3rd Movement
2nd Theme — S919

4th Movement — S920

5th Movement
1st Theme — S921

5th Movement
2nd Theme — S922

Three Fantastic Dances,
Op. 1, Pft.
Copyright 1944 and 1945 by
Leeds Music Corp., N. Y.
Reprinted here by permission
of the copyright owner.

No. 1 — S923

No. 2 — S924

No. 3 — S925

Two Pieces for String
Octet, Op. 11
Copyright 1946 by Leeds
Music Corp., N. Y.
Reprinted here by permission
of the copyright owner.

No. 1
Prelude
1st Theme — S925a

2nd Theme — S925b

No. 2
Scherzo
1st Theme — S925c

2nd Theme — S925d

SIBELIUS, Jean (1865-1957)

The Bard, Op. 64, Orch.
By permission of Associated
Music Publishers, Inc.

1st Theme — S926

2nd Theme — S927

Concerto, Op. 47,
Vn. & Orch.
By permission of
International Music Co.

1st Movement
1st Theme — S928

1st Movement
2nd Theme,
A — S929

1st Movement
2nd Theme,
B — S930

2nd Movement Intro. — S931

2nd Movement — S932

3rd Movement 1st Theme — S933

3rd Movement 2nd Theme — S934

En Saga, Op. 9, Orch.
By permission of Associated
Music Publishers, Inc.

1st Theme — S935

2nd Theme — S936

3rd Theme — S937

4th Theme — S938

5th Theme — S939

6th Theme — S940

Finlandia, Op. 26,
No. 7, Orch.
By permission of Associated
Music Publishers, Inc.

1st Theme — S941

2nd Theme — S942

3rd Theme — S943

In Memoriam, Op. 59
(Funeral March), Orch.
By permission of Associated
Music Publishers, Inc.

— S944

Karelia, Op. 11,
Suite for Orch.
By permission of Associated
Music Publishers, Inc.

1st Movement Intermezzo — S945

2nd Movement Ballade — S946

3rd Movement Alla Marcia 1st Theme — S947

3rd Movement 2nd Theme — S948

King Christian II, Op. 27,
Suite for Orch.
By permission of Associated
Music Publishers, Inc.

Nocturne 1st Theme — S949

2nd Theme — S950

Elégie and Musette
1st Theme
Elégie — S951

2nd Theme
Musette — S952

Serenade
1st Theme — S953

2nd Theme — S954

Ballade
1st Theme — S955

2nd Theme — S956

Lemminkäinen's Homeward
Journey, Op. 22, No. 4
Orch.
By permission of Associated
Music Publishers, Inc.
1st Theme — S957

2nd Theme — S958

3rd Theme — S959

Nightride and Sunrise,
Op. 55, Orch.
1st Theme — S960

2nd Theme — S961

3rd Theme — S962

The Oceanides,
Op. 73, Orch.
By permission of Associated
Music Publishers, Inc.
1st Theme — S963

2nd Theme — S964

Pelléas et Mélisande,
(Incidental Music)
Op. 46, Orch.
Mélisande — S965

A Spring in the Park — S966

Pastorale — S967

Entr'acte — S968

Death of Mélisande — S969

Pohjola's Daughter,
Op. 49, Orch.
Copyright by Lienau,
Licensed by SESAC, Inc., N. Y.
1st Theme
A — S970

1st Theme, B — S971

2nd Theme — S972

3rd Theme — S973

4th Theme — S974

4th Theme — S975

5th Theme — S976

Quartet, Op. 56, Str. "Voces Intimae" By permission of Associated Music Publishers, Inc.

1st Movement 1st Theme, A — S977

1st Movement 1st Theme, B — S978

1st Movement 2nd Theme — S979

2nd Movement 1st Theme — S980

2nd Movement 2nd Theme — S981

3rd Movement 1st Theme, A — S982

3rd Movement 1st Theme, B — S983

4th Movement 1st Theme — S984

4th Movement 2nd Theme — S985

4th Movement 3rd Theme — S986

5th Movement 1st Theme — S987

5th Movement 2nd Theme — S988

5th Movement 3rd Theme — S989

Rakastava, (The Lover), Op. 14, Suite for Orch. By permission of Associated Music Publishers, Inc.

1st Movement — S990

2nd Movement — S991

3rd Movement — S992

Romance, Op. 24, No. 9, Pft. 1st Theme — S993

2nd Theme — S994

The Swan of Tuonela,
(from Kalevala)
Op. 22, No. 3
Orch.
By permission of Associated
Music Publishers, Inc.

1st Theme, A — S995

1st Theme, B — S996

1st Theme, C — S997

2nd Theme — S998

Symphony No. 1
in E Minor, Op. 39
By permission of Associated
Music Publishers, Inc.

1st Movement Intro. — S999

1st Movement 1st Theme — S1000

1st Movement 2nd Theme — S1001

1st Movement 3rd Theme — S1002

2nd Movement 1st Theme, A — S1003

2nd Movement 1st Theme, B — S1004

2nd Movement 2nd Theme — S1005

3rd Movement 1st Theme — S1006

3rd Movement 2nd Theme — S1007

4th Movement 1st Theme — S1008

4th Movement 2nd Theme — S1009

4th Movement 3rd Theme — S1010

**Symphony No. 2
in D, Op. 43**
By permission of Associated
Music Publishers, Inc.

1st Movement
1st Theme — S1011

1st Movement
2nd Theme — S1012

1st Movement
3rd Theme — S1013

2nd Movement
Intro. — S1014

2nd Movement
1st Theme — S1015

2nd Movement
2nd Theme — S1016

3rd Movement
1st Theme — S1017

3rd Movement
2nd Theme — S1018

3rd Movement
3rd Theme — S1019

4th Movement
1st Theme — S1020

4th Movement
2nd Theme — S1021

4th Movement
3rd Theme — S1022

4th Movement
4th Theme — S1023

**Symphony No. 3
in C, Op. 52**
Copyright by Lienau,
Licensed by SESAC
Inc., N. Y.

1st Movement
1st Theme — S1024

1st Movement
2nd Theme — S1025

1st Movement
3rd Theme — S1026

2nd Movement — S1027

3rd Movement
1st Theme — S1028

3rd Movement
2nd Theme — S1029

3rd Movement
3rd Theme — S1030

Symphony No. 4 in A Minor, Op. 63
By permission of Associated Music Publishers, Inc.

1st Movement 1st Theme — S1031
1st Movement 2nd Theme — S1032
1st Movement 3rd Theme — S1033
2nd Movement 1st Theme — S1034
2nd Movement 2nd Theme — S1035
2nd Movement 3rd Theme — S1036
2nd Movement 4th Theme — S1037
2nd Movement 5th Theme — S1038
3rd Movement 1st Theme — S1039
3rd Movement 2nd Theme — S1040
4th Movement 1st Theme — S1041
4th Movement 2nd Theme — S1042
4th Movement 3rd Theme — S1043
4th Movement 4th Theme — S1044
4th Movement 5th Theme — S1045

Symphony No. 5 in E Flat, Op. 82
By permission of Associated Music Publishers, Inc.

1st Movement 1st Theme — S1046
1st Movement 2nd Theme — S1047
1st Movement 3rd Theme — S1048
1st Movement 4th Theme — S1049
1st Movement 5th Theme — S1050

2nd Movement Intro. — S1051
2nd Movement 1st Theme — S1052
2nd Movement 2nd Theme — S1053
3rd Movement 1st Theme — S1054
3rd Movement 2nd Theme — S1055
3rd Movement 3rd Theme — S1056

Symphony No. 6
in D Minor, Op. 104
By permission of Associated
Music Publishers, Inc.

1st Movement 1st Theme — S1057
1st Movement 2nd Theme — S1058
1st Movement 3rd Theme — S1059
1st Movement 4th Theme — S1060
1st Movement 5th Theme — S1061
1st Movement 6th Theme — S1062
2nd Movement 1st Theme — S1063
2nd Movement 2nd Theme — S1064
2nd Movement 3rd Theme — S1065
3rd Movement 1st Theme — S1066
3rd Movement 2nd Theme — S1067
3rd Movement 3rd Theme — S1068
3rd Movement 4th Theme — S1069
4th Movement 1st Theme — S1070

4th Movement 2nd Theme — S1071

4th Movement 3rd Theme — S1072

4th Movement 4th Theme — S1073

Symphony No. 7 in C, Op. 105
By permission of Associated Music Publishers, Inc.

1st Theme — S1074

2nd Theme — S1075

3rd Theme A — S1076

3rd Theme B — S1077

4th Theme — S1078

5th Theme — S1079

6th Theme — S1080

7th Theme — S1081

8th Theme — S1082

9th Theme — S1083

10th Theme — S1084

11th Theme — S1085

Tapiola, Op. 112, Orch.
By permission of Associated Music Publishers, Inc.

1st Theme — S1086

2nd Theme — S1087

3rd Theme — S1088

Valse Triste (from Kuolema), Op. 44 Orch.
Copyright 1926 by G. Schirmer, Inc.

1st Theme — S1089

2nd Theme — S1090

3rd Theme  S1091

4th Theme S1092

SINDING, Christian (1856-1941)

Marche Grotesque, Op. 32, No. 1, Pft. S1093

Rustle of Spring
(Frühlingsrauschen),
Op. 32, No. 3, Pft.
A
1st Theme
A
 S1094

Copyright renewal assigned
1931 to G. Schirmer, Inc.

1st Theme
B
S1095

SMETANA, Bedřich (1824-1884)

Aus Meinem Leben,
Quartet No. 1
in E Minor, Str.
1st Movement
1st Theme
 S1096

1st Movement
2nd Theme
S1097

2nd Movement
1st Theme
S1098

2nd Movement
2nd Theme
S1099

3rd Movement
S1100

4th Movement
1st Theme
S1101

4th Movement
2nd Theme
S1102

The Bartered Bride,
Opera
Overture
Intro.
S1103

1st Theme
S1104

2nd Theme
S1105

Act I
Polka
1st Theme
S1106

2nd Theme,
A
S1107

2nd Theme,
B
S1108

2nd Movement 2nd Theme — S1129

2nd Movement 3rd Theme — S1130

3rd Movement 1st Theme — S1131

3rd Movement 2nd Theme — S1132

SOLER, Padre Antonio (1729-1783)

Sonatas
F, Harpsi. — S1133

A Minor, Harpsi. — S1134

D, Harpsi. — S1135

SOUSA, John Philip (1854-1932)

El Capitan, March
© Church — 1st Theme — S1136

2nd Theme — S1137

3rd Theme — S1138

4th Theme — S1139

Hail to the Spirit of Liberty, March
© Church — 1st Theme — S1140

2nd Theme — S1141

3rd Theme — S1142

The High School Cadets, March — 1st Theme — S1143

2nd Theme — S1144

3rd Theme — S1145

4th Theme — S1146

King Cotton, March
Published and copyrighted
(renewal 1923) by The John
Church Co. Used by
permission.

The Liberty Bell, March
© Church

Manhattan Beach, March
© Church

Semper Fidelis, March

Stars and Stripes Forever, March
Published and copyrighted
(renewal 1925) by The John
Church Co. Used by
permission.

The Thunderer, March

3rd Theme — S1167

4th Theme — S1168

The Washington Post, March

1st Theme — S1169

2nd Theme — S1170

3rd Theme — S1171

SOWERBY, Leo (1895-1968)

Comes Autumn Time, Overture, Orch.
By permission of The Boston Music Co., copyright owner.

1st Theme — S1172

2nd Theme — S1173

SPOHR, Ludwig (1784-1859)

Concerto No. 8 in A Minor, Op. 47, Vn. & Orch.

1st Movement — S1174

2nd Movement — S1175

3rd Movement 1st Theme — S1176

3rd Movement 2nd Theme — S1177

SPONTINI, Gasparo (1774-1851)

La Vestale, Overture

1st Theme — S1178

2nd Theme — S1179

3rd Theme — S1180

STAMITZ, Karl (1746-1801)

Concerto in B Flat, Vn. & Pft.

1st Movement 1st Theme — S1181

1st Movement 2nd Theme — S1182

2nd Movement — S1183

3rd Movement
1st Theme — S1184

3rd Movement
2nd Theme — S1185

Orchestra-Quartet in F,
Op. 4, No. 4

1st Movement
1st Theme — S1186

1st Movement
2nd Theme — S1187

2nd Movement
1st Theme — S1188

2nd Movement
2nd Theme — S1189

3rd Movement
1st Theme — S1190

3rd Movement
2nd Theme — S1191

Sonata in D, Viola
d'Amore & Harpsi.

1st Movement — S1192

2nd Movement — S1193

3rd Movement — S1194

4th Movement — S1195

STILL, William Grant (1895-   )

Afro-American Symphony
Copyright 1935 by
J. Fischer & Bro., N. Y.
Used by permission.

1st Movement
1st Theme,
A — S1196

1st Movement
1st Theme,
B — S1197

1st Movement
2nd Theme — S1198

2nd Movement
Intro. — S1199

2nd Movement — S1200

3rd Movement
1st Theme — S1201

3rd Movement
2nd Theme — S1202

4th Movement
1st Theme — S1203

4th Movement
2nd Theme — S1204

STOJOWSKI, Sigismond (1869-1946)

Chant d'Amour, Op. 26, No. 3, Pft.
Copyright renewal assigned 1939
to G. Schirmer, Inc. — S1205

Melodie, Op. 26, No. 1, Pft.
By Permission of C. F. Peters, Clayton
F. Summy Co., Chicago, Agents in the U. S. — S1206

Thème Cracovien Varié,
Op. 26, No. 4, Pft.
By Permission of C. F. Peters, Clayton
F. Summy Co., Chicago, Agents in the U. S. — S1207

STRAUSS, Eduard (1835-1916)

Doctrinen Waltzes,
Op. 79, Orch.

No. 1
1st Theme — S1208

2nd Theme — S1209

No. 2
1st Theme — S1210

2nd Theme — S1211

No. 3 — S1212

No. 4 — S1213

No. 5 — S1214

STRAUSS, Johann, Jr. (1825-1899)

Perpetuum Mobile,
Op. 257, Orch.

Theme — S1215

Variation — S1216

Variation — S1217

Die Fledermaus, Overture　1st Theme — S1218

2nd Theme — S1219
3rd Theme — S1220
4th Theme — S1221
5th Theme — S1222

Eine Nacht in Venedig, Overture
1st Theme — S1223
2nd Theme — S1224
3rd Theme — S1225
4th Theme — S1226
5th Theme — S1227

Der Zigeunerbaron, Overture
1st Theme — S1228
2nd Theme — S1229
3rd Theme — S1230
4th Theme — S1231

An Der Schönen Blauen Donau (On the Beautiful Blue Danube), Op. 317 Waltzes, Orch.
No. 1 1st Theme — S1232
2nd Theme — S1233
No. 2 1st Theme — S1234
2nd Theme — S1235
No. 3 1st Theme — S1236
2nd Theme — S1237
No. 4 1st Theme — S1238

2nd Theme — S1239

No. 5 1st Theme — S1240

2nd Theme — S1241

Du Und Du, Waltzes from Die Fledermaus, Op. 367, Orch.

No. 1 1st Theme — S1242

2nd Theme — S1243

No. 2 1st Theme — S1244

2nd Theme — S1245

No. 3 1st Theme — S1246

2nd Theme — S1247

Frühlingsstimmen (Voices of Spring), Op. 410 Waltz, Orch.

1st Theme — S1248

2nd Theme — S1249

3rd Theme — S1250

4th Theme — S1251

5th Theme — S1252

6th Theme — S1253

G'schichten Aus Dem Wienerwald (Tales of the Vienna Woods), Op. 325 Waltzes, Orch.

No. 1 1st Theme — S1254

2nd Theme — S1255

No. 2 1st Theme — S1256

2nd Theme — S1257

No. 3 — S1258

No. 4 1st Theme — S1259

2nd Theme — S1260

No. 5 1st Theme — S1261

2nd Theme — S1262

Kaiser-Waltzer (Emperor-Waltzes), Op. 437 Orch.

No. 1 1st Theme — S1263

2nd Theme — S1264

No. 2 — S1265

No. 3 1st Theme — S1266

2nd Theme — S1267

No. 4 1st Theme — S1268

2nd Theme — S1269

Künstlerleben (Artist's Life), Op. 316 Waltzes, Orch.

No. 1 1st Theme — S1270

2nd Theme — S1271

No. 2 1st Theme — S1272

2nd Theme — S1273

No. 3 — S1274

No. 4 1st Theme — S1275

2nd Theme — S1276

No. 5 1st Theme — S1277

2nd Theme — S1278

Kuss (Kiss) Waltz from Der Lustige Krieg , Op. 400, Orch.

1st Theme — S1279

2nd Theme — S1280

3rd Theme — S1281

4th Theme — S1282

Lagunen-Waltzes, from Eine Nacht in Venedig (Same as Artist's Life), Orch.

1st Theme — S1283

2nd Theme — S1284

3rd Theme — S1285

4th Theme — S1286

5th Theme — S1287

Morgenblätter Waltz, Op. 279, Orch.

1st Theme — S1288

2nd Theme — S1289

3rd Theme — S1290

4th Theme — S1291

5th Theme — S1292

O Schöner Mai, Waltzes, Op. 375, Orch.

No. 1 — S1293

No. 2 1st Theme — S1294

2nd Theme — S1295

No. 3 — S1296

Roses From the South Waltzes, (from Queen's Lace Handkerchief), Op. 388, Orch.

No. 1 1st Theme — S1297

2nd Theme — S1298

No. 2 — S1299
No. 3 1st Theme — S1300
2nd Theme — S1301
No. 4 1st Theme — S1302
2nd Theme — S1303

Schatz Waltzer,
(Treasure Waltzes),
Op. 418, Orch.

No. 1 — S1304
No. 2 — S1305
No. 3 — S1306
No. 4 1st Theme — S1307
2nd Theme — S1308

Thousand and One
Nights, Op. 346
Waltzes, Orch.

No. 1 1st Theme — S1309
2nd Theme — S1310
3rd Theme — S1311
No. 2 — S1312
No. 3 — S1313

Wein, Weib und Gesang
(Wine, Women and Song),
Op. 333, Waltzes, Orch.

No. 1 1st Theme — S1314
2nd Theme — S1315
No. 2 1st Theme — S1316
2nd Theme — S1317
No. 3 — S1318

STRAUSS, Joseph (1827-1870)

2nd Theme — S1337
No. 2 — S1338
No. 3 — S1339
No. 4 — S1340
No. 5 — S1341

Sphärenklange, Op. 235
Waltzes, Orch.
No. 1
1st Theme — S1342
2nd Theme — S1343
No. 2 — S1344
No. 3 — S1345
No. 4 — S1346
No. 5 — S1347

Wiener Kinder, Op. 61
Waltzes, Orch.
No. 1 — S1348
No. 2 — S1349
No. 3 — S1350
No. 4 — S1351
No. 5 — S1352

STRAUSS, Richard (1864-1949)

Alpensinfonie, Op. 64
Orch.
By permission of Associated
Music Publishers, Inc.
1st Theme — S1353
2nd Theme — S1354
3rd Theme — S1355

4th Theme — S1356
5th Theme — S1357
6th Theme — S1358
7th Theme — S1359
8th Theme — S1360
9th Theme — S1361
10th Theme — S1362
11th Theme — S1363
12th Theme — S1364

Also Sprach Zarathustra
(Thus Spake Zarathustra),
Op. 30, Orch.

Intro. — S1365
1st Theme — S1366
2nd Theme — S1367
3rd Theme, A — S1368
3rd Theme, B — S1369
4th Theme — S1370
5th Theme, A — S1371
5th Theme, B — S1372
6th Theme — S1373
7th Theme, A — S1374
7th Theme, B — S1375

Aus Italien, Symphonic Fantasy, Op. 16
In the Campagna (Auf der Campagna) 1st Theme — S1376
2nd Theme — S1377
3rd Theme — S1378

In the Roman Ruins (In Roms Ruinen) 1st Theme — S1379
2nd Theme — S1380
3rd Theme — S1381
4th Theme — S1382
5th Theme — S1383

The Beach at Sorrento (Am Strande von Sorrent) 1st Theme — S1384
2nd Theme — S1385
3rd Theme — S1386
4th Theme — S1387

Neapolitan Folk Life (Neapolitanisches Volksleben) 1st Theme A — S1388
1st Theme B — S1389
2nd Theme — S1390
3rd Theme — S1391
4th Theme — S1392

Der Bürger Als Edelmann, Op. 60, Orch.
By permission of the copyright owner, Boosey and Hawkes, Inc.
Overture 1st Theme — S1393
2nd Theme — S1394
Minuet — S1395

3rd Theme — S1416

4th Theme — S1417

5th Theme — S1418

Don Juan, Op. 20, Orch.　1st Theme — S1419

2nd Theme — S1420

3rd Theme — S1421

4th Theme — S1422

5th Theme — S1423

6th Theme — S1424

Don Quixote, Op. 35, Orch.　1st Theme — S1425

2nd Theme — S1426

3rd Theme — S1427

4th Theme — S1428

5th Theme, A — S1429

5th Theme, B — S1430

Ein Heldenleben, Op. 40, Orch.
By permission of Associated Music Publishers, Inc.　1st Theme — S1431

2nd Theme, A — S1432

2nd Theme, B — S1433

2nd Theme, C — S1434

3rd Theme — S1435

4th Theme — S1436
5th Theme — S1437
6th Theme — S1438
7th Theme — S1439
8th Theme — S1440
9th Theme — S1441

Rêverie, Op. 9, No. 4,
Pft. or Pft. & Vn. — S1442

Der Rosenkavalier, Waltz Themes,
Op. 59.
By permission of the copyright
owner, Boosey and Hawkes, Inc. — S1443

S1444
S1445
S1446
S1447

Salome, Opera,
Op. 54
By permission of the
copyright owner,
Boosey and Hawkes, Inc.

Dance of the
Seven Veils
1st Theme — S1448

2nd Theme — S1449

3rd Theme — S1450

4th Theme — S1451

5th Theme — S1452

Sonata in E Flat,
Op. 18, Vn. & Pft.

1st Movement
1st Theme
A — S1453

1st Movement
1st Theme
B — S1454

1st Movement
2nd Theme — S1455

STRAUSS

1st Movement
3rd Theme — S1456

2nd Movement
Improvisation — S1457

3rd Movement
Finale
1st Theme — S1458

3rd Movement
2nd Theme — S1459

3rd Movement
3rd Theme — S1460

Sinfonia Domestica,
Op. 53
By permission of Associated
Music Publishers, Inc.

1st Movement
1st Theme,
A — S1461

1st Theme,
B — S1462

2nd Theme,
A — S1463

2nd Theme,
B — S1464

3rd Theme — S1465

4th Theme
Cradle Song — S1466

5th Theme — S1467

Till Eulenspiegels Lustige
Streiche, Op. 28, Orch.

1st Theme — S1468

2nd Theme — S1469

3rd Theme
(Variant of First Theme) — S1470

4th Theme — S1471

5th Theme — S1472

6th Theme — S1473

7th Theme — S1474

Tod Und Verklärung
(Death and Transfiguration),
Op. 24, Orch

1st Theme — S1475

2nd Theme	S1476
3rd Theme	S1477
4th Theme	S1478
5th Theme	S1479

STRAVINSKY, Igor (1882-1971)

Apollon Musagètes, Ballet
By permission of the copyright owner, Boosey and Hawkes, Inc.

Birth of Apollo, Prologue 1st Theme, A	S1480
1st Theme, B	S1481
2nd Theme	S1482
Variation of Apollo	S1483
Pas d'Action 1st Theme	S1484
2nd Theme	S1485
Variation of Calliope	S1486
Variation of Polymnie	S1487
Variation of Terpsichore	S1488
Pas de Deux	S1489
Coda	S1490
Apotheosis	S1491

Le Baiser de la Fée, Ballet on Tschaikovsky Themes
By permission of the copyright owner, Boosey and Hawkes, Inc.

1st Movement Berceuse de la Tempête 1st Theme	S1492
1st Movement 2nd Theme	S1493
2nd Movement Fête au Village 1st Theme	S1494

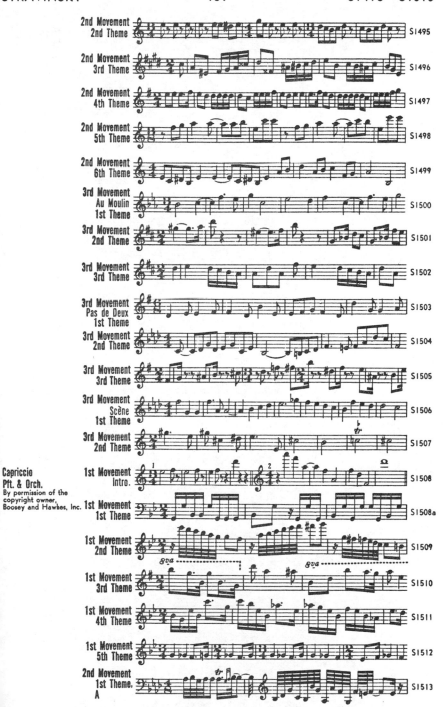

2nd Movement 1st Theme, B — S1514
2nd Movement 2nd Theme — S1515
2nd Movement 3rd Theme — S1516
3rd Movement 1st Theme — S1517
3rd Movement 2nd Theme — S1518
3rd Movement 3rd Theme, A — S1519
3rd Movement 3rd Theme, B — S1520
3rd Movement Coda — S1521

Chant du Rossignol
Poème Symphonique, Orch.
By permission of the copyright owner, Boosey and Hawkes, Inc.

1st Movement 1st Theme — S1521a
1st Movement 2nd Theme — S1521b
2nd Movement Marche Chinoise 1st Theme — S1521c
2nd Movement 2nd Theme — S1521d
Jeu du Rossignol Mécanique 3rd Movement 1st Theme — S1521e
3rd Movement 2nd Theme — S1521f

Concerto, Pft. & Orch.
By permission of the copyright owner, Boosey and Hawkes, Inc.

1st Movement — S1522
2nd Movement 1st Theme — S1523
2nd Movement 2nd Theme — S1524
3rd Movement 1st Theme — S1525
3rd Movement 2nd Theme — S1526
3rd Movement 3rd Theme — S1527

Concerto in D, Vn. & Orch.
By permission of Associated Music Publishers, Inc.

1st Movement 1st Theme — S1528

1st Movement 2nd Theme, A — S1529

1st Movement 2nd Theme, B — S1530

2nd Movement Aria, A — S1531

3rd Movement Aria, B — S1532

4th Movement Intro. — S1533

4th Movement Theme — S1534

Dumbarton Oaks Concerto, Chamber Orch.
By permission of Associated Music Publishers, Inc.

1st Movement 1st Theme — S1534a

1st Movement 2nd Theme — S1534b

1st Movement 3rd Theme — S1534c

2nd Movement — S1534d

3rd Movement 1st Theme — S1534e

3rd Movement 1st Theme — S1534f

3rd Movement 2nd Theme — S1534g

The Fire Bird Ballet Suite, Orch.
By permission of the copyright holders, J. & W. Chester, Ltd., 11 Great Marlborough Street, London, W. 1.

Intro. — S1535

Ronde des Princesses 1st Theme — S1536

2nd Theme — S1537

Dance of Kastchei — S1538

Berceuse — S1539

Finale — S1540

**Octet for Fl., Cl.,
2 Fg., 2 Trpts.,
2 Tromb.**
By permission of the
copyright owner,
Boosey and Hawkes, Inc

1st Movement
Intro.   S1541

1st Movement
1st Theme   S1542

1st Movement
2nd Theme   S1543

2nd Movement
Theme & Variations   S1544

3rd Movement
Finale   S1545

**Pastorale
Vn. & Pft.**
By permission of the copyright
owner, Boosey and Hawkes, Inc.

Intro.   S1546

Theme   S1547

**Petrouchka, Suite
Ballet, Orch.**
By permission of the
copyright owner,
Boosey and Hawkes, Inc.

Tableau 1
1st Theme   S1548

2nd Theme   S1549

3rd Theme   S1550

4th Theme   S1551

Le Tour de Passe-passe   S1552

Danse Russe
1st Theme   S1553

2nd Theme   S1554

3rd Theme   S1555

Tableau 2
Chez Petrouchka
1st Theme   S1556

2nd Theme,
A   S1557

2nd Theme,
B   S1558

Tableau 3
Chez le Maure   S1559

Danse de la Ballerina   S1560

Waltz
La Ballerina et le Maure
1st Theme — S1561

2nd Theme, A — S1562

2nd Theme, B — S1563

Tableau 4
Fête De Grand Semaine — S1564
Dance of the Nurses
1st Theme

2nd Theme — S1565

The Peasant and the Bear — S1566

The Merchant — S1567

Dance of the Gypsies — S1568

Dance of the Coachmen — S1569

Dance of the Maskers — S1570

General Dance — S1571

Pulcinella
Ballet after Pergolesi, Orch.   Overture — S1572
By permission of the
copyright owner,
Boosey and Hawkes, Inc.

Larghetto — S1573

Gavotte — S1574

Finale — S1575

Le Sacre du Printemps   Part I,
(Rite of Spring), Orch.   Adoration of
By permission of the copyright   the Earth — S1576
owner, Boosey and Hawkes, Inc.   Intro.
Dance of the Adolescents
1st Theme — S1577

2nd Theme — S1578

3rd Theme — S1579

Rounds of Spring — S1580

Games of the Rival Cities, 1st Theme — S1581

2nd Theme — S1582

Procession of the Wise Men — S1583

Dance of the Earth — S1584

Part II, The Sacrifice, Intro. — S1585

Mysterious Circles of the Adolescents — S1586

Evocation of the Ancestors — S1587

Ritual of the Ancestors — S1588

Sacrificial Dance, Motive A — S1589

Motives B & C — S1590

Suite No. 1, Small Orch.
By permission of the copyright holders, J. & W. Chester, Ltd., 11 Great Marlborough Street, London, W. 1.

1st Movement, Andante — S1591

2nd Movement, Napolitana — S1592

3rd Movement, Española — S1593

4th Movement, Balalaika — S1594

Suite No. 2, Small Orch.
By permission of the copyright holders, J. & W. Chester, Ltd., 11 Great Marlborough Street, London, W. 1.

1st Movement, March — S1595

2nd Movement, Waltz — S1596

3rd Movement, Polka — S1597

4th Movement, Galop — S1598

Symphony in Three Movements
By permission of Associated Music Publishers, Inc.

1st Movement, 1st Theme — S1599

1st Movement, 2nd Theme — S1600

1st Movement / 3rd Theme — S1601
1st Movement / 4th Theme — S1602
2nd Movement / 1st Theme — S1603
2nd Movement / 2nd Theme — S1604
2nd Movement / 3rd Theme — S1605
3rd Movement / 1st Theme — S1606
3rd Movement / 2nd Theme — S1607
3rd Movement / 3rd Theme — S1608

SUK, Joseph (1874-1935)

Serenade, Op. 6
Str. Orch.
By permission of
Associated Music
Publishers, Inc.

1st Movement / 1st Theme — S1609
1st Movement / 2nd Theme — S1610
2nd Movement / 1st Theme — S1611
2nd Movement / 2nd Theme — S1612
3rd Movement / 1st Theme — S1613
3rd Movement / 2nd Theme — S1614
4th Movement — S1615

SUPPÉ, Franz von (1819-1895)

Banditenstreiche,
Overture

1st Theme — S1616
2nd Theme — S1617
3rd Theme — S1618

4th Theme — S1619

Boccaccio, Overture — 1st Theme — S1620

2nd Theme — S1621

3rd Theme — S1622

4th Theme — S1623

Flotte Bursche, Overture — 1st Theme, A — S1624

1st Theme, B — S1625

2nd Theme — S1626

3rd Theme "Gaudeamus Igitur" — S1627

4th Theme — S1628

5th Theme — S1629

Light Cavalry, Overture — 1st Theme — S1629a

2nd Theme — S1629b

3rd Theme, A — S1629c

3rd Theme, B — S1629d

4th Theme — S1629e

Morning, Noon, and Night in Vienna, Overture — 1st Theme — S1630

2nd Theme — S1631

3rd Theme — S1632

4th Theme — S1633

5th Theme — S1634

Pique Dame, Overture
1st Theme — S1635
2nd Theme — S1636
3rd Theme — S1637
4th Theme — S1638

Poet and Peasant, Overture
Intro. — S1639
1st Theme, A — S1640
1st Theme, B — S1641
2nd Theme, A — S1642
2nd Theme, B — S1643
3rd Theme — S1644
4th Theme — S1645

Die Schöne Galathe, Overture
1st Theme — S1646
2nd Theme — S1647
2nd Theme — S1648
3rd Theme — S1649

SVENDSEN, Johan Severin (1840-1911)

Carnival in Paris, Op. 9, Orch.
1st Theme — S1650
2nd Theme — S1651
3rd Theme — S1652

Festival Polonaise, Op. 12, Orch.
By permission of Associated Music Publishers, Inc.
1st Theme — S1653
2nd Theme — S1654
3rd Theme — S1655

Norwegian Artists' Carnival, Op. 14, Orch.
1st Theme — S1656
2nd Theme, Italian Folk Song — S1657
3rd Theme, Norwegian Dance Tune — S1658

Romance, Op. 26, Vn. & Pft.
1st Theme — S1659
2nd Theme — S1660

SZYMANOWSKI, Karol (1883-1937)

The Fountain of Arethusa, Op. 30, No. 1, Vn. & Pft.
By permission of Associated Music Publishers, Inc.
1st Theme — S1661
2nd Theme — S1662

Mazurkas, Pft.
By permission of Associated Music Publishers, Inc.
Op. 50, No. 1
1st Theme — S1663
2nd Theme — S1664

Op. 50, No. 2
1st Theme — S1665
2nd Theme — S1666

Notturno, Op. 28, No. 1, Vn. & Pft.
By permission of Associated Music Publishers, Inc.
1st Theme — S1667
2nd Theme — S1668

Romance, Op. 23, Vn. & Pft.
By permission of Associated Music Publishers, Inc.
1st Theme — S1669
2nd Theme — S1670

Tarantella, Op. 28, No. 2, Vn. & Pft.
By permission of Associated Music Publishers, Inc.
1st Theme — S1671

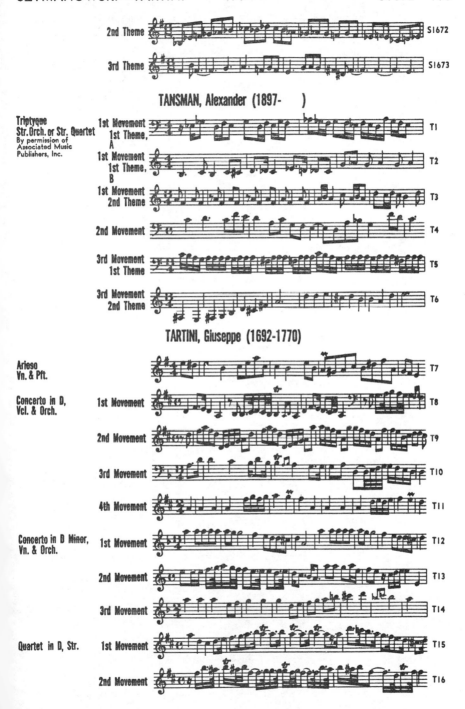

2nd Theme ... S1672

3rd Theme ... S1673

TANSMAN, Alexander (1897-)

Triptyque
Str. Orch. or Str. Quartet
By permission of
Associated Music
Publishers, Inc.

1st Movement
1st Theme, A ... T1

1st Movement
1st Theme, B ... T2

1st Movement
2nd Theme ... T3

2nd Movement ... T4

3rd Movement
1st Theme ... T5

3rd Movement
2nd Theme ... T6

TARTINI, Giuseppe (1692-1770)

Arieso
Vn. & Pft. ... T7

Concerto in D,
Vcl. & Orch.

1st Movement ... T8

2nd Movement ... T9

3rd Movement ... T10

4th Movement ... T11

Concerto in D Minor,
Vn. & Orch.

1st Movement ... T12

2nd Movement ... T13

3rd Movement ... T14

Quartet in D, Str.

1st Movement ... T15

2nd Movement ... T16

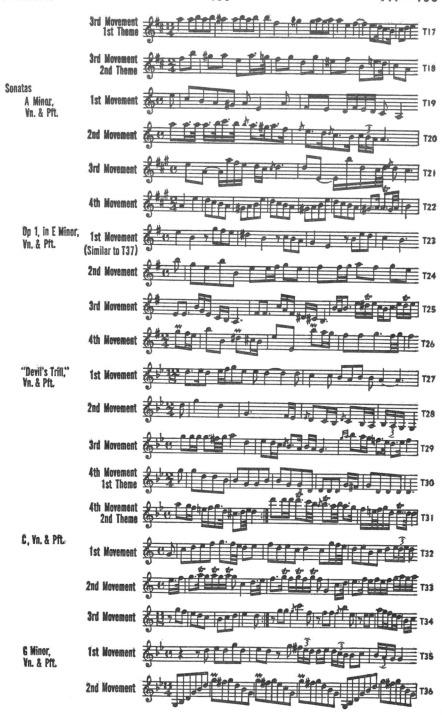

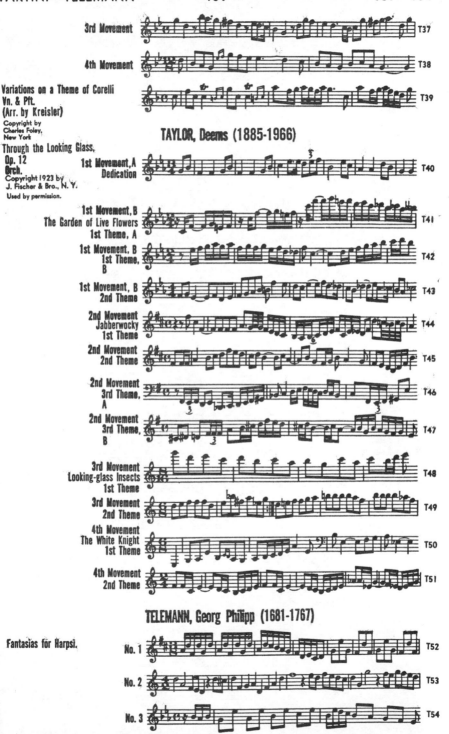

3rd Movement — T37

4th Movement — T38

Variations on a Theme of Corelli
Vn. & Pft.
(Arr. by Kreisler)
Copyright by
Charles Foley,
New York — T39

Through the Looking Glass,
Op. 12
Orch.
Copyright 1923 by
J. Fischer & Bro., N. Y.
Used by permission.

TAYLOR, Deems (1885-1966)

1st Movement, A
Dedication — T40

1st Movement, B
The Garden of Live Flowers
1st Theme, A — T41

1st Movement, B
1st Theme,
B — T42

1st Movement, B
2nd Theme — T43

2nd Movement
Jabberwocky
1st Theme — T44

2nd Movement
2nd Theme — T45

2nd Movement
3rd Theme,
A — T46

2nd Movement
3rd Theme,
B — T47

3rd Movement
Looking-glass Insects
1st Theme — T48

3rd Movement
2nd Theme — T49

4th Movement
The White Knight
1st Theme — T50

4th Movement
2nd Theme — T51

TELEMANN, Georg Philipp (1681-1767)

Fantasias for Harpsi.

No. 1 — T52

No. 2 — T53

No. 3 — T54

No. 4 — T55

No. 5 — T56

Fantasia, Harpsi. — T57

Quartet in E Minor, Fl, Vn., Vcl. & Harpsi.

1st Movement Prelude — T58

2nd Movement 1st Theme — T59

2nd Movement 2nd Theme — T60

3rd Movement 1st Theme — T61

3rd Movement 2nd Theme — T62

4th Movement — T63

5th Movement — T64

6th Movement — T65

7th Movement — T66

Quartet in B Minor, Fl, Vn., Vcl. & Harpsi.

1st Movement — T67

2nd Movement — T68

3rd Movement — T69

4th Movement 1st Theme — T70

4th Movement 2nd Theme — T71

5th Movement — T72

6th Movement — T73

7th Movement — T74

Suite in A Minor, Str. & Pft.
Overture 1st Theme — T75
2nd Theme — T76
Rondo — T77
Gavotte — T78
Courante — T79
Rigaudon — T80
Forlane — T81
Minuet 1st Theme — T82
2nd Theme — T83

Tafelmusik Chamber Orch.
Bergerie — T84
Allegresse — T85

Trio Sonata in E Min., 2 Vns. & Vcl.
1st Movement — T86
2nd Movement — T87

THOMAS, Ambroise (1811-1896)

Le Caïd, Overture
1st Theme — T88
2nd Theme — T89
3rd Theme — T90

Hamlet, Ballet-Act IV
Dance Villageoise — T91
Pas de Chasseurs 1st Theme, A — T92
1st Theme, B — T93

2nd Theme — T94
Pantomime — T95
Valse—Mazurka 1st Theme — T96
2nd Theme — T97
La Freya 1st Theme — T98
2nd Theme — T99
3rd Theme — T100

Mignon, Opera

Overture 1st Theme — T101
2nd Theme — T102
3rd Theme — T103
4th Theme — T104
Act II Intermezzo (Gavotte) — T105

Raymond, Overture

Intro. — T106
1st Theme, A — T107
1st Theme, B — T108
2nd Theme — T109
3rd Theme — T110

THOMÉ, Francis (1850-1909)

Simple Confession (Simple Aveu)

TIII

THOMSON, Virgil (1896-)

Filling Station,
Ballet
Copyright by Arrow
Music Press, Inc., N. Y.

No. 1
Intro.
1st Theme — TIIIa

2nd Theme — TIIIb

No. 2
Mac's Dance — TIIIc

No. 3
Motorist and Mac — TIIId

No. 4
Truck Drivers' Dance — TIIIe

2nd Theme — TIIIf

No. 7
Tango — TIIIg

No. 8
Waltz
1st Theme — TIIIh

2nd Theme — TIIIi

No. 9
The Big Apple — TIIIj

No. 11
The Chase — TIIIk

The Plow That
Broke the Plains
(Suite from film score)
Orch.
By permission of
Music Press, Inc.

1st Movement
Prelude
1st Theme — TII2

1st Movement
2nd Theme — TII3

2nd Movement
Pastorale
(Grass) — TII4

3rd Movement
Cattle — TII5

4th Movement
Blues (Speculation)
1st Theme — TII6

4th Movement
2nd Theme — TII7

5th Movement
Drought
(6th Movement repeats
previous Themes) — TII8

Quartet, No. 2
Str.
Copyright by Arrow
Music Press, Inc., N. Y

1st Movement
1st Theme — TII8a

1st Movement 2nd Theme — T118b

2nd Movement 1st Theme — T118c

2nd Movement 2nd Theme — T118d

3rd Movement — T118e

4th Movement 1st Theme — T118f

4th Movement 2nd Theme — T118g

The River
Film Suite
Small Orch.
By permission of the Composer

1st Movement The Old South 1st Theme — T118h

1st Movement 2nd Theme — T118i

1st Movement 3rd Theme — T118j

1st Movement 4th Theme — T118k

Intro.
2nd Movement
Industrial Expansion
in the Mississippi Valley — T118l

2nd Movement 1st Theme (Hot Time in the Old Town Tonight) — T118m

2nd Movement 2nd Theme (Oh, My Name is Samuel Hall) — T118n

3rd Movement Soil Erosion & Floods — T118o

4th Movement Finale 1st Theme — T118p

4th Movement 2nd Theme — T118q

4th Movement 3rd Theme — T118r

TOCH, Ernst (1887-1964)

The Chinese Flute,
Op. 29, Chamber Orch.
(2nd & 4th Movements
are Vocal)
By permission of Associated
Music Publishers, Inc.

1st Movement — T119

3rd Movement 1st Theme — T120

3rd Movement / 2nd Theme   T121

5th Movement   T122

Pinocchio
Overture
By permission of Associated
Music Publishers, Inc.

1st Theme   T122a

2nd Theme   T122b

3rd Theme   T122c

TSCHAIKOVSKY, Peter Ilyich (1840-1893)

Capriccio Italien, Op. 45
Orch.   1st Theme   T123

2nd Theme   T124

3rd Theme   T125

4th Theme   T126

Chanson Triste,
Op. 40, No. 2, Pft.   T127

Chant Sans Paroles
Op. 2, No. 3, Pft.   T128

Chant Sans Paroles
Op. 40, No. 6, Pft.   T129

Concerto No. 1, in B Flat 1st Movement
Minor, Op. 23, 1st Theme   T130
Pft. & Orch.

1st Movement / 2nd Theme   T131

1st Movement / 3rd Theme   T132

2nd Movement / 1st Theme   T133

2nd Movement / 2nd Theme   T134

3rd Movement / 1st Theme   T135

3rd Movement / 2nd Theme   T136

Concerto No. 2 in G Op. 44, Pft. & Orch.	1st Movement 1st Theme	T136a
	1st Movement 2nd Theme, A	T136b
	1st Movement 2nd Theme, B	T136c
	2nd Movement 1st Theme, A	T136d
	2nd Movement 1st Theme, B	T136e
	3rd Movement 1st Theme	T136f
	3rd Movement 2nd Theme	T136g
Concerto in D, Op. 35, Vn. & Orch.	1st Movement 1st Theme	T137
	1st Movement 2nd Theme	T138
	1st Movement 3rd Theme	T139
	2nd Movement 1st Theme	T140
	2nd Movement 2nd Theme	T141
	3rd Movement 1st Theme	T142
	3rd Movement 2nd Theme	T143
Dolly's Funeral, from Children's Album, Op. 39, No. 7, Pft.		T144
Francesca da Rimini, Op. 32, Orch.	1st Theme	T145
	2nd Theme	T146
	3rd Theme	T147
Humoresque, Op. 10, No. 2, Pft.	1st Theme	T148
	2nd Theme	T149

Marche Slave, Op. 31, Orch. — 1st Theme — T150

2nd Theme — T151

3rd Theme — T152

4th Theme — T153
*

Soldiers' March Op. 39, No 5, from Children's Album, Pft. — T154

Waltz from Eugen Onegin, 2nd Act — T155

Polonaise from Eugen Onegin, 3rd Act — T156

Hamlet, Fantasy Overture, Op. 67 — 1st Theme — T157

2nd Theme — T158

3rd Theme — T159

Romeo and Juliet, Fantasy Overture — 1st Theme — T160

2nd Theme — T161

3rd Theme — T162

4th Theme — T163

1812, Festival Overture, Op. 49 — 1st Theme — T164

2nd Theme — T165

3rd Theme — T166

4th Theme — T167

Quartet in D, Op. 11, Str. — 1st Movement — T168

2nd Movement 1st Theme — T169

*For Melodie, T153a, see page xiv.

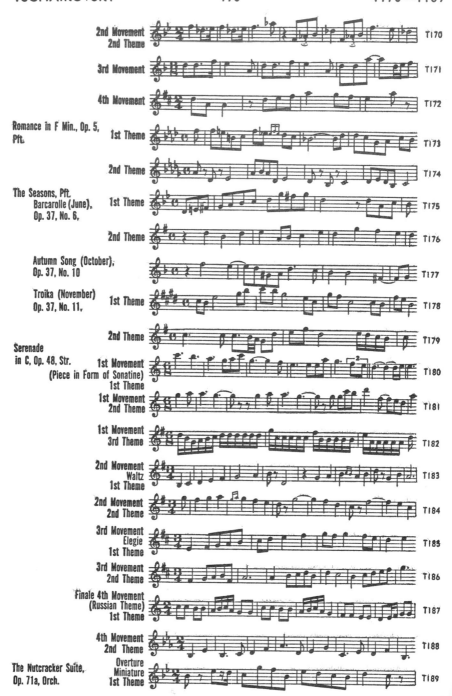

2nd Movement 2nd Theme — T170

3rd Movement — T171

4th Movement — T172

Romance in F Min., Op. 5, Pft. 1st Theme — T173

2nd Theme — T174

The Seasons, Pft. Barcarolle (June), Op. 37, No. 6, 1st Theme — T175

2nd Theme — T176

Autumn Song (October), Op. 37, No. 10 — T177

Troika (November) Op. 37, No. 11, 1st Theme — T178

2nd Theme — T179

Serenade in C, Op. 48, Str. 1st Movement (Piece in Form of Sonatine) 1st Theme — T180

1st Movement 2nd Theme — T181

1st Movement 3rd Theme — T182

2nd Movement Waltz 1st Theme — T183

2nd Movement 2nd Theme — T184

3rd Movement Elegie 1st Theme — T185

3rd Movement 2nd Theme — T186

Finale 4th Movement (Russian Theme) 1st Theme — T187

4th Movement 2nd Theme — T188

The Nutcracker Suite, Op. 71a, Orch. Overture Miniature 1st Theme — T189

5th Movement
Waltz — T210

Swan Lake,
Suite from the
Ballet, Op. 20a, Orch.

1st Movement
Intro. — T211

2nd Movement
Waltz — T212

3rd Movement
Dance of the Swans — T213

4th Movement
Hungarian Dance and Czardas
1st Theme — T214

4th Movement
2nd Theme — T215

Symphony No. 1,
Op. 13,
"Rêverie d'Hiver"

1st Movement
1st Theme,
A — T216

1st Movement
1st Theme,
B — T217

1st Movement
2nd Theme — T218

2nd Movement
1st Theme — T219

2nd Movement
2nd Theme,
A — T220

2nd Movement
2nd Theme,
B — T221

3rd Movement
1st Theme — T222

3rd Movement
2nd Theme — T223

4th Movement
1st Theme — T224

4th Movement
2nd Theme — T225

Symphony No. 2,
in C Minor, Op. 17,
"Little Russia"

1st Movement
1st Theme — T226

1st Movement
2nd Theme — T227

1st Movement
3rd Theme,
A — T228

1st Movement
3rd Theme,
B — T229

2nd Movement / 1st Theme — T230
2nd Movement / 2nd Theme — T231
3rd Movement / 1st Theme, A — T232
3rd Movement / 1st Theme, B — T233
3rd Movement / 1st Theme — T234
4th Movement / 1st Theme — T235
4th Movement / 2nd Theme — T236

Symphony No. 3, in D, Op. 29, "Polish"

1st Movement / Intro. — T237
1st Movement / 1st Theme — T238
1st Movement / 2nd Theme — T239
1st Movement / 3rd Theme — T240
2nd Movement / 1st Theme — T241
2nd Movement / 2nd Theme — T242
2nd Movement / 3rd Theme — T243
3rd Movement / 1st Theme — T244
3rd Movement / 2nd Theme — T245
3rd Movement / 3rd Theme — T246
4th Movement / 1st Theme — T247
4th Movement / 2nd Theme — T248
4th Movement / 3rd Theme — T249

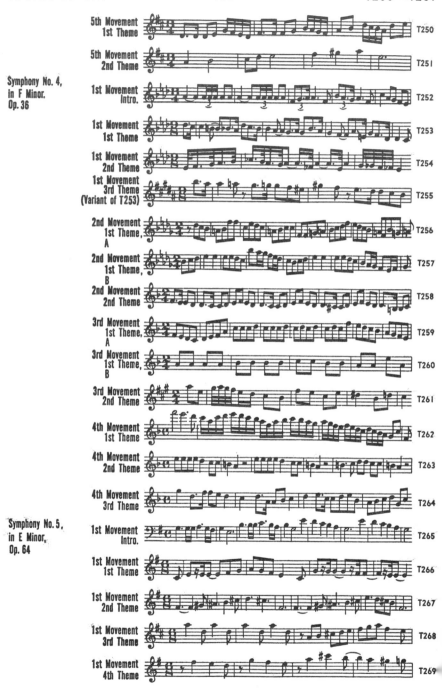

Symphony No. 4,
in F Minor.
Op. 36

Symphony No. 5,
in E Minor.
Op. 64

5th Movement
1st Theme — T250

5th Movement
2nd Theme — T251

1st Movement
Intro. — T252

1st Movement
1st Theme — T253

1st Movement
2nd Theme — T254

1st Movement
3rd Theme
(Variant of T253) — T255

2nd Movement
1st Theme,
A — T256

2nd Movement
1st Theme,
B — T257

2nd Movement
2nd Theme — T258

3rd Movement
1st Theme,
A — T259

3rd Movement
1st Theme,
B — T260

3rd Movement
2nd Theme — T261

4th Movement
1st Theme — T262

4th Movement
2nd Theme — T263

4th Movement
3rd Theme — T264

1st Movement
Intro. — T265

1st Movement
1st Theme — T266

1st Movement
2nd Theme — T267

1st Movement
3rd Theme — T268

1st Movement
4th Theme — T269

2nd Movement 1st Theme — T270
2nd Movement 2nd Theme — T271
2nd Movement 3rd Theme — T272
3rd Movement 1st Theme — T273
3rd Movement 2nd Theme — T274
4th Movement 1st Theme — T275
4th Movement 2nd Theme — T276
4th Movement 3rd Theme — T277
4th Movement 4th Theme — T278
4th Movement 5th Theme — T279

Symphony No. 6, in B Minor, Op. 74 "Pathétique"
By permission of Associated Music Publishers, Inc.

1st Movement Intro. — T280
1st Movement 1st Theme — T281
1st Movement 2nd Theme — T282
1st Movement 3rd Theme — T283
2nd Movement 1st Theme — T284
2nd Movement 2nd Theme — T285
3rd Movement 1st Theme — T286
3rd Movement 2nd Theme — T287
3rd Movement 3rd Theme — T288
4th Movement 1st Theme — T289

4th Movement
2nd Theme — T290

Theme & Variations,
Op. 19, No. 6, Pft. — T291

Trio in A Min., Op. 50,
Pft., Vn. & Vcl.

1st Movement
1st Theme — T292

1st Movement
2nd Theme — T293

2nd Movement
Theme & Variations — T294

TURINA, Joaquín (1882-1949)

Danzas Fantásticas,
Orch. or Pft.

Ensueño
1st Theme,
A — T295

1st Theme,
B — T296

2nd Theme — T297

3rd Theme — T298

Orgia
1st Theme — T299

2nd Theme — T300

Fandanguillo,
Guitar
By permission of Associated
Music Publishers, Inc.

1st Theme — T301

2nd Theme — T302

Femmes d'Espagne
(Mujeres Españolas)
Copyright by Editions Salabert
Editions Salabert, 22 Rue
Chaucat, Paris Salabert, Inc.,
1 East 57 St., N. Y.

L'Andalouse
Sentimentale
1st Theme — T303

2nd Theme — T304

3rd Theme — T305

La Oración del Torero
Quart., Str.

1st Theme — T306

2nd Theme — T307

3rd Theme — T308

3rd Movement
2nd Theme — V27

3rd Movement
3rd Theme — V28

4th Movement
1st Theme — V29

4th Movement
2nd Theme — V30

Symphony No. 4,
in F Minor
Copyright by the
Oxford University Press
Reproduced by permission.

1st Movement
1st Theme — V31

1st Movement
2nd Theme — V32

1st Movement
3rd Theme — V33

1st Movement
4th Theme — V34

2nd Movement — V35

3rd Movement
1st Theme — V36

3rd Movement
2nd Theme — V37

3rd Movement
3rd Theme — V38

4th Movement
1st Theme,
A — V39

4th Movement
1st Theme.
B — V40

4th Movement
2nd Theme — V41

The Wasps
(Aristophanes)
Orch.

1st Movement
Overture
1st Theme — V42

1st Movement
2nd Theme — V43

1st Movement
3rd Theme — V44

2nd Movement
Entr'acte — V45

3rd Movement
March Past of the Kitchen Utensils
1st Theme — V46

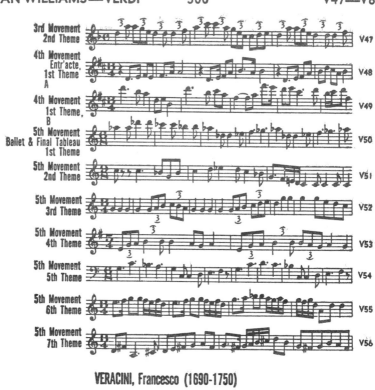

3rd Movement
2nd Theme   V47

4th Movement
Entr'acte,
1st Theme
A   V48

4th Movement
1st Theme,
B   V49

5th Movement
Ballet & Final Tableau
1st Theme   V50

5th Movement
2nd Theme   V51

5th Movement
3rd Theme   V52

5th Movement
4th Theme   V53

5th Movement
5th Theme   V54

5th Movement
6th Theme   V55

5th Movement
7th Theme   V56

VERACINI, Francesco (1690-1750)

Largo,
Vn. & Pft.   V57

Sonata in E Minor
Vn. & Pft.   1st Movement
Intro.   V58

1st Movement
Theme   V59

2nd Movement   V60

3rd Movement
Minuet   V61

4th Movement
Gavotte   V62

5th Movement
Gigue   V63

VERDI, Giuseppe (1813-1901)

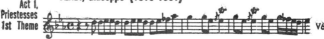

Aida,
Opera   Act I,
Dance of the Priestesses
1st Theme   V64

2nd Movement — V85

3rd Movement
1st Theme — V86

3rd Movement
2nd Theme — V87

4th Movement — V88

La Traviata, Opera

Act I,
Prelude
1st Theme — V89

2nd Theme — V90

I Vespri Siciliani,
Overture

1st Theme — V91

2nd Theme — V92

VIEUXTEMPS, Henri (1820-1881)

Ballade et Polonaise
Op. 38
Vn. & Pft.

1st Theme — V93

2nd Theme — V94

3rd Theme — V95

4th Theme — V96

5th Theme — V97

Concerto No. 4
in D Minor,
Vn. & Orch.

1st Movement
1st Theme,
A — V98

1st Movement
1st Theme,
B — V99

1st Movement
2nd Theme — V100

2nd Movement
1st Theme — V101

2nd Movement
2nd Theme — V102

3rd Movement
1st Theme — V103

VILLA-LOBOS, Heitor (1887-1959)

VINCI, Leonardo (1690-1730)

VIOTTI, Giovanni (1753-1824)

3rd Movement
2nd Theme — VI04

4th Movement
1st Theme — VI05

4th Movement
2nd Theme — VI06

Bachianas-Brasileiras,
No. 4, Pft.
1st Theme — VI07

2nd Theme — VI08

3rd Theme — VI09

Saudades das
Selvas Brasileiras, Pft.
By permission of Associated
Music Publishers, Inc.
No. 1 — VI10

No. 2 — VI11

Sonata in D.
Fl. & Harpsi.
1st Movement — VI12

2nd Movement — VI13

3rd Movement — VI14

4th Movement — VI15

5th Movement — VI16

Concerto No. 22,
in A Minor,
Vn. & Orch.
1st Movement
1st Theme — VI17

1st Movement
2nd Theme — VI18

1st Movement
3rd Theme — VI19

2nd Movement
1st Theme — VI20

2nd Movement 2nd Theme — VI2I

3rd Movement — VI22

VISÉE, Robert de (17th-18th Century)

Petite Suite in D Minor, Guitar   Prelude — VI23

Allemande — VI24

Sarabande — VI25

Gigue — VI26

VITALI, Tommaso Antonio (c. 1665-1711)

Ciaconna, Vn. & Pft. — VI27

VIVALDI, Antonio (c. 1675-1741)

Concerto in A, Vn. & Orch.   1st Movement 1st Theme — VI28

1st Movement 2nd Theme — VI29

2nd Movement — VI30

3rd Movement — VI3I

Concerto in A Minor, Viola d'Amore & Orch.   1st Movement — VI32

2nd Movement — VI33

3rd Movement — VI34

Concerto in C Vn. & Orch.   1st Movement Intro. — VI35

1st Movement Theme — VI36

2nd Movement — VI37

2nd Movement — VI58

3rd Movement — VI59

Concerto Grosso in B Minor, Op. 3, No. 10 Orch.
1st Movement — VI60

2nd Movement — VI61

3rd Movement — VI62

Concerto Grosso in D Minor, Op. 3, No. 11 Orch.
1st Movement — VI63

2nd Movement — VI64

3rd Movement — VI65

Largo from Sonata in C Min., Vn. & Pft. — VI65a

Il Pastor Fido Pastorale, Op. 13, No. 4 Vn. & Harpsi. — VI66

Sonata No. 5 in E Minor, Vcl. & Harpsi.
1st Movement — VI67

2nd Movement — VI68

3rd Movement — VI69

4th Movement — VI70

Sonata in D Minor, Op. 2, No. 3, Vn. & Pft.
1st Movement — VI71

2nd Movement — VI72

3rd Movement — VI73

4th Movement — VI74

Trio Sonata in G Minor, Op. 1, No. 1 2 Vns. & Pft.
1st Movement Prelude — VI75

2nd Movement Allemande — VI76

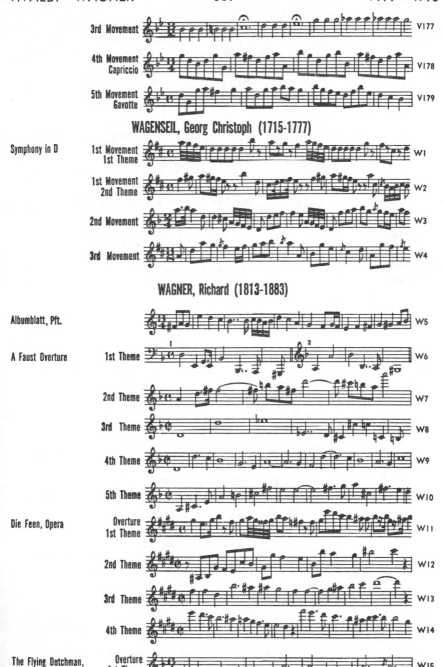

3rd Movement — V177

4th Movement
Capriccio — V178

5th Movement
Gavotte — V179

WAGENSEIL, Georg Christoph (1715-1777)

Symphony in D

1st Movement
1st Theme — W1

1st Movement
2nd Theme — W2

2nd Movement — W3

3rd Movement — W4

WAGNER, Richard (1813-1883)

Albumblatt, Pft. — W5

A Faust Overture

1st Theme — W6

2nd Theme — W7

3rd Theme — W8

4th Theme — W9

5th Theme — W10

Die Feen, Opera

Overture
1st Theme — W11

2nd Theme — W12

3rd Theme — W13

4th Theme — W14

The Flying Dutchman,
Opera

Overture
1st Theme — W15

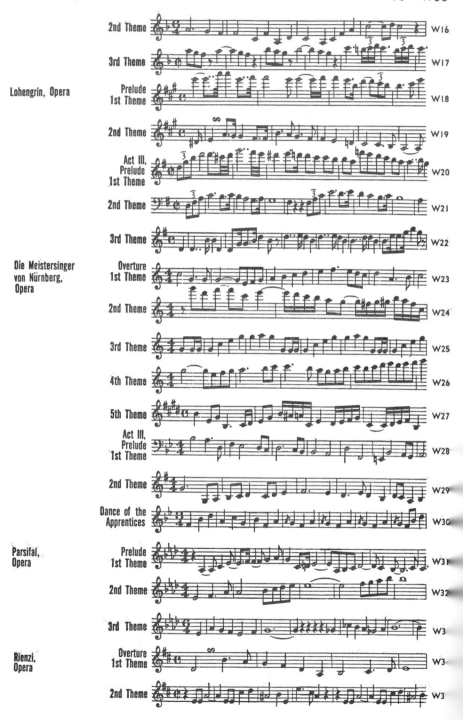

Lohengrin, Opera

2nd Theme — W16
3rd Theme — W17
Prelude 1st Theme — W18
2nd Theme — W19
Act III, Prelude 1st Theme — W20
2nd Theme — W21
3rd Theme — W22

Die Meistersinger von Nürnberg, Opera

Overture 1st Theme — W23
2nd Theme — W24
3rd Theme — W25
4th Theme — W26
5th Theme — W27
Act III, Prelude 1st Theme — W28
2nd Theme — W29
Dance of the Apprentices — W30

Parsifal, Opera

Prelude 1st Theme — W31
2nd Theme — W32
3rd Theme — W33

Rienzi, Opera

Overture 1st Theme — W34
2nd Theme — W35

7th Theme — W75

8th Theme — W76

Act II, March Intro. — W77

1st Theme — W78

2nd Theme — W79

3rd Theme — W80

Bacchanale (Venusberg Music) 1st Theme — W81

2nd Theme — W82

3rd Theme — W83

4th Theme — W84

Tristan und Isolde, Opera
Prelude 1st Theme — W85

2nd Theme — W86

Act III Prelude 1st Theme — W87

2nd Theme — W88

3rd Theme — W89

Love Death 1st Theme — W90

2nd Theme — W91

WALDTEUFEL, Emil (1837-1915)

Dolores Waltzes
Op. 170, Orch.
Courtesy Carl Fischer, Inc., N.Y.

No. 1 1st Theme — W92

2nd Theme — W93

Espaňa, Waltzes
Op. 286, Orch.
Courtesy Carl Fischer,
Inc., N. Y.

Estudiantina, Waltzes
Op. 191, Orch.
Courtesy Carl Fischer,
Inc., N. Y.

1. Same as C71. 2. Same as C72. 3. Same as C75.

Sirenenzauber (Sirens)
Waltzes, Op. 154
Orch.

No. 1 1st Theme — W134

2nd Theme — W135

No. 2 1st Theme — W136

2nd Theme — W137

No. 3 1st Theme — W138

2nd Theme — W139

No. 4 — W140

The Skaters, Waltzes
Op. 183, Orch.
Courtesy Carl Fischer,
Inc., N. Y.

No. 1 1st Theme — W141

2nd Theme — W142

No. 2 1st Theme — W143

2nd Theme — W144

No. 3 1st Theme — W145

2nd Theme — W146

No. 4 — W147

WALLACE, William Vincent (1812-1865)

Maritana,
Overture

1st Theme — W148

2nd Theme — W149

3rd Theme — W150

4th Theme — W151

5th Theme — W152

WALTON, William Turner (1902-)

Concerto
Viola & Orch.
Copyright by the Oxford
University Press.
Reproduced by permission.

1st Movement 1st Theme — W153

1st Movement 2nd Theme — W154

2nd Movement 1st Theme — W155

2nd Movement 2nd Theme — W156

2nd Movement 3rd Theme — W157

3rd Movement 1st Theme — W158

3rd Movement 2nd Theme — W159

Concerto
Vn. & Orch.
Copyright by the Oxford
University Press.
Reproduced by permission.

1st Movement 1st Theme — W160

1st Movement 2nd Theme — W161

2nd Movement 1st Theme, A — W162

2nd Movement 1st Theme, B — W163

2nd Movement 2nd Theme — W164

2nd Movement 3rd Theme — W165

3rd Movement 1st Theme — W166

3rd Movement 2nd Theme — W167

Crown Imperial,
Coronation March,
Orch.
Copyright by the Oxford
University Press.
Reproduced by permission.

1st Theme — W168

2nd Theme — W169

3rd Theme — W170

4th Theme — W171

Façade, Suite No. 1, Orch.
Copyright by the Oxford University Press.
Reproduced by permission.

Polka 1st Theme — W172

2nd Theme — W173

3rd Theme — W174

Valse 1st Theme — W175

2nd Theme — W176

A Swiss Yodeling Song 1st Theme — W177

2nd Theme (Parody on William Tell) — W178

3rd Theme — W179

Tango-Pasodoble 1st Theme — W180

2nd Theme — W181

Tarantella-Sevillana 1st Theme — W182

2nd Theme — W183

Façade, Suite No. 2, Orch.
Copyright by the Oxford University Press.
Reproduced by permission.

Fanfare — W184

Scotch Rhapsody 1st Theme — W185

2nd Theme — W186

Country Dance — W187

Noche Española 1st Theme — W188

2nd Theme — W189

Popular Song — W190

Old Sir Faulk   W191

Portsmouth Point, Overture
Copyright by the Oxford University Press.
Reproduced by permission.

1st Theme, A   W192

1st Theme, B   W193

2nd Theme   W194

WARLOCK, Peter (1894-1930)

Capriol, Suite for Orch.

1st Movement Basse Dance   W195

2nd Movement Pavane   W196

3rd Movement Tordion   W197

4th Movement Bransles   W198

5th Movement Pieds-en-l'air   W199

6th Movement Mattachins   W200

Serenade for Str. Orch.
Copyright by the Oxford University Press.
Reproduced by permission.

1st Theme   W201

2nd Theme   W202

WEBER, Carl Maria Von (1786-1826)

Abu Hassan, Overture

1st Theme   W203

2nd Theme   W204

Concertstück, Op. 79, Pft. & Orch.

1st Theme   W205

2nd Theme   W206

3rd Theme   W207

4th Theme   W208

Jubel-Ouvertüre

Oberon,
Overture

Peter Schmoll
und Seine Nachbarn,
Overture

Polacca Brillante,
Op. 72, Pft.

Preciosa,
Overture

3rd Theme   W229
4th Theme   W230
5th Theme   W231
Intro.
1st Theme   W232
2nd Theme   W233
1st Theme   W234
2nd Theme   W235
3rd Theme   W236
4th Theme
God Save the King   W237
Intro.   W238
1st Theme   W239
2nd Theme   W240
3rd Theme   W241
Intro.   W242
1st Theme   W243
2nd Theme   W244
1st Theme   W245
2nd Theme   W246
1st Theme   W247
2nd Theme   W248

4th Movement 3rd Theme — W269

WEINBERGER, Jaromir (1896-1967)

Schwanda, Opera
By permission of Associated Music Publishers, Inc.

Polka — W270

Fugue — W271

Under the Spreading Chestnut Tree, (Variations and Fugue on an old English tune), Orch.
By permission of Associated Music Publishers, Inc.

1st Theme Theme for Variations — W272

2nd Theme Theme for Fugue — W273

WIENIAWSKI, Henri (1835-1880)

Concerto No. 2 in D Minor, Op. 22, Vn. & Orch.

1st Movement 1st Theme — W274

1st Movement 2nd Theme — W275

2nd Movement Romance — W276

3rd Movement 1st Theme — W277

3rd Movement 2nd Theme — W278

Dudziarz (Mazurka), Op. 19, No. 2 Vn. & Pft.

1st Theme — W279

2nd Theme — W280

Kujawiak, Op. 3, Vn. & Pft.

Intro. — W281

1st Theme — W282

2nd Theme — W283

3rd Theme — W284

Legende, Op. 17 Vn. & Pft.

1st Theme — W285

2nd Theme — W286

Obertass
(Mazurka)
Op.19, No. 1,
Vn. & Pft.
    1st Theme   W287
    2nd Theme   W288

Polonaise Brillante,
Op. 4,
Vn. & Pft.
    1st Theme   W289
    2nd Theme   W290
    3rd Theme   W291

Polonaise Brillante,
No. 2, Op. 21,
Vn. & Pft.
    1st Theme   W292
    2nd Theme   W293
    3rd Theme   W294

Souvenir de Moscou,
Airs Russes, Op. 6
Vn. & Pft.
    1st Theme   W295
    2nd Theme, A   W296
    2nd Theme, B   W297

WOLF, Hugo (1860-1903)

Italian Serenade,
Str. Quart. or Str. Orch.
By permission of Associated
Music Publishers, Inc.
    1st Theme   W298
    2nd Theme, A   W299
    2nd Theme, B   W300

WOLF-FERRARI, Ermanno (1876-1948)

The Jewels of the Madonna,
Copyright renewal assigned
1939 to G. Schirmer, Inc.
    Act II Intermezzo   W301
    Act III Intermezzo, 1st Theme   W302
    2nd Theme   W303

Apache Dance
1st Theme   W304

2nd Theme — W305

The Secret of Suzanne, Overture
Copyright 1910 by
Josef Weinberger, Leipzig.

1st Theme — W306

2nd Theme — W307

3rd Theme — W308

YSAŸE, Théo (1865-1918)

Variations, Op. 10, 2 Pfts.
By permission of Associated
Music Publishers, Inc.

Theme — Y1

ZANDONAI, Riccardo (1883-1944)

Giulietta E Romeo Symphonic Episode, Orch.
Copyright 1928
by G. Ricordi & Co., Inc.

1st Theme — Z1

2nd Theme — Z2

3rd Theme — Z3

ZARZYCKI, Alexander (1834-1895)

Mazurka, Op. 26, Vn. & Pft.
Copyright 1899
by Carl Fischer, Inc., N. Y.

1st Theme — Z4

2nd Theme — Z5

3rd Theme — Z6

ZIMBALIST, Efrem (1889-   )

Quartet in E Minor, Str.
Copyright 1938
by G. Schirmer, Inc.

1st Movement — Z7

2nd Movement
1st Theme — Z8

2nd Movement
2nd Theme — Z9

3rd Movement
1st Theme — Z10

3rd Movement
2nd Theme — Z11

4th Theme — Z12

TRANSPOSITION KEY

C	D	E	F	G	A	B	C	
C♯	D♯	E♯	F♯	G♯	A♯	B♯	C♯	} enharmonic[x]
D♭	E♭	F	G♭	A♭	B♭	C	D♭	
D	E	F♯	G	A	B	C♯	D	
E♭	F	G	A♭	B♭	C	D	E♭	
E	F♯	G♯	A	B	C♯	D♯	E	
F	G	A	B♭	C	D	E	F	
F♯	G♯	A♯	B	C♯	D♯	E♯	F♯	} enharmonic[x]
G♭	A♭	B♭	C♭	D♭	E♭	F	G♭	
G	A	B	C	D	E	F♯	G	
A♭	B♭	C	D♭	E♭	F	G	A♭	
A	B	C♯	D	E	F♯	G♯	A	
B♭	C	D	E♭	F	G	A	B♭	
B	C♯	D♯	E	F♯	G♯	A♯	B	} enharmonic[x]
C♭	D♭	E♭	F♭	G♭	A♭	B♭	C♭	

[x] Sounding the same but written differently.

This chart, though not necessary to the use of the notation key, should be helpful to the reader in explaining key relationships. For example, the fifth note in the key of C is G, its equivalent in the key of A is E.

HOW TO USE
THE NOTATION INDEX*

To identify a given theme, play it in the key of C† and look it up under its note sequence using the following alphabet as a guide:

A Ab A♯ **B** Bb B♯ **C** Cb C♯ **D** Db D♯

E Eb E♯ **F** Fb F♯ **G** Gb G♯

Double flats follow flats; double sharps follow sharps.

The letter and number to the right of the definition indicate the place in the alphabetic section of the book where the theme may be found in its original key with the name of the composition and the composer.

Trills, turns, grace notes, and other embellishments are not taken into consideration here. However, it must be remembered that the appoggiatura is a regular note. In rare cases the grace note may be of such nature as to give the aural impression of being a regular note, in which case it is included in this section.

Keys are, in the main, determined by the harmonic structure of the opening bars, not by the cadence. The phrase that begins in C and goes to G is considered to be in C. Themes that may be analyzed in two keys are listed under both keys. There are themes that defy key definition. However, if the melodic line carries a key implication of its own, if only for the first few notes, that key is used. If the theme carries no such implication, then, for the sake of convenience, the first note is assumed to be C and the rest transposed accordingly.

Memory plays strange tricks and it is possible that the desired theme may be remembered inaccurately. We have occasionally listed a theme incorrectly as well as correctly if there is a popular misconception about it.

Each definition has been carried to six places except in the case of duplication. Duplicates are continued to a point of difference, but in no case to more than eleven places. When a note is repeated many times, for space conservation an exponent is used, *i.e.* $G\ G\ G\ G\ G\ G = G^6$.

H. B.

* Publisher's note: The Notation Index was conceived by Harold Barlow.
† C Major for major themes, C Minor for minor themes.

NOTATION INDEX

C B C D Eb D Db	S1089
C B C D Eb D F	V89
C B C D Eb D G F#	B923
C B C D Eb D G G	K89
C B C D Eb Eb D Eb F	M57
C B C D Eb Eb D Eb F	B340
C B C D Eb F D	B1826
C B C D Eb F Eb D C	B26
C B C D Eb F Eb D G	H519
C B C D Eb F G Ab	S1134
C B C D Eb F G G	B274
C B C D Eb G Ab Bb	B103
C B C D Eb G Ab G	C324
C B C D F E C	H440
C B C D F E D	H439
C B C D F Eb	H774
C B C D G A B C B	B959
C B C D G A B C D	B346
C B C D G C	H470
C B C D G E	S811
C B C D G G	S835
C B C E C A	B1615
C B C E C B	F82
C B C E C D	G163
C B C E C G E E	P319
C B C E C G E F G	W219
C B C E C G E F G	L279
C B C E C G G	H380
C B C E D B	B1508
C B C E D C B	B1734
C B C E D C D	M228
C B C E D E D	S548
C B C E D E F	S543
C B C E D E G	B231
C B C E D# E	B1604
C B C E E F	C548
C B C E F A	H594
C B C E F G	W273
C B C E F# G	S834
C B C E G A	B945
C B C E G C	B333
C B C E G F#	W259
C B C E G G E	S539
C B C E G G G	M875
C B C Eb B C	B725
C B C Eb C B	P128
C B C Eb C C	B697
C B C Eb C G	H460

C B C Eb D C B C A	C580
C B C Eb D C B C Eb	M177
C B C Eb D G	S218
C B C Eb F# B	P193
C B C Eb G B	C312
C B C Eb Gb Cb	P193
C B C F C Db	B469
C B C F D Eb	H68
C B C F E D D	S513
C B C F F Eb	B717
C B C F# G E	H855
C B C G A F	T64
C B C G A G A	B341
C B C G A G C	B875
C B C G Ab C B	B304
C B C G Ab C F	T7
C B C G Ab F G Eb F	B76
C B C G Ab F G Eb F	B91
C B C G Ab G C	B117
C B C G Ab G Eb	M284
C B C G Ab G F Eb F	C18
C B C G Ab G F Eb F	E20
C B C G C A	O24
C B C G C B	I 6
C B C G C D	H760
C B C G C G	L303
C B C G E C C	M726
C B C G E C F	H611
C B C G E C G	B48
C B C G E D E A	B371
C B C G E D E C	M618
C B C G E F	B1622
C B C G E G	B163
C B C G Eb D C	B120
C B C G Eb D Eb Bb	P324
C B C G Eb D Eb F	B1680
C B C G Eb D Eb G	C466
C B C G F F	T276
C B C G F G Ab	S170
C B C G F G C	B40
C B C G G A	S232
C B C G G F	C419
C B C G G G C B	B694
C B C G G G C D	B58
C B C G G G C D	B87
C B C G G G D	M122
C B C G G G G B	M475
C B C G G G G G	B1058

C G C C B F	M405
C G C C B G	G266
C G C C C B	H251
C G C C C E	S1629a
C G C C D Ab	G15
C G C C D E	M1014
C G C C E C	H18
C G C C Eb D	R344
C G C C G C	H283
C G C D C B	B191
C G C D C D	H260
C G C D C G C Bb	B478
C G C D C G C D	S519
C G C D E C	D159
C G C D E E	B618
C G C D E F E	D256
C G C D E F G A	M47
C G C D E F G C	G84
C G C D E F G F	S1186
C G C D Eb C	D381
C G C D Eb D C D	M28
C G C D Eb D C G	G31
C G C D Eb D Eb C B	B276
C G C D Eb D Eb C G	B1118
C G C D Eb D Eb F	P22
C G C D Eb Eb	D408
C G C D Eb F F#	H854
C G C D Eb F G	M64
C G C D F Eb	L85
C G C D G D E	G158
C G C D G D Eb	P365
C G C D G E	K75
C G C E C C	S1638
C G C E C E G E C	M745
C G C E C E G E G	M1002
C G C E C E G G E	B850
C G C E C E G G G	H306
C G C E C G C	C186
C G C E C G D	C183
C G C E D B	H194
C G C E D C	S126
C G C E D D	H703
C G C E D G	B1676
C G C E Eb C	S1365
C G C E F E	M480
C G C E G A	B1793
C G C E G C	B551
C G C E G E	S1431
C G C E G F D	B797
C G C E G F E	H531
C G C E G F#	A60
C G C Eb Ab G	W149
C G C Eb Ab G	B1469
C G C Eb C Eb	K85
C G C Eb D B	B617
C G C Eb D C	P77
C G C Eb D F	H222
C G C Eb D G Bb	B61
C G C Eb D G C Eb	B1419
C G C Eb D G C G	S198
C G C Eb Eb D C	M967
C G C Eb Eb D D	H115
C G C Eb F D	M882
C G C F C Eb C	B1169
C G C F C Eb D	B70
C G C F C Eb F	D168
C G C F Eb Ab	M17
C G C F G C	R184
C G C G A B	F216
C G C G A G	M120
C G C G B E A	R39
C G C G Bb C	T122a
C G C G C B A G A	B80
C G C G C B A G C	M976
C G C G C Bb	B477
C G C G C D E D C	M7
C G C G C D E D C	K86
C G C G C D Eb C	B1739
C G C G C D Eb D	M1
C G C G C E G E	S478
C G C G C E G F#	B1784
C G C G C Eb	P328
C G C G C G Ab	P227
C G C G C G C B	T310
C G C G C G C E	M754
C G C G C G C G C	K109
C G C G C G C G D	C576
C G C G C G D	C281
C G C G D G C	S209
C G C G D G D	C558
C G C G E C A	S1357
C G C G E C G	S864
C G C G F G	B1117k
C G C G G C	R30
C G C G G G C	L22
C G C G G G F	E41

E G G D G G	M37
E G G E C E	B834
E G G E D C	D437
E G G E E D C♯	O28
E G G E E D E	T168
E G G E E E	S1166
E G G F E D	G11
E G G F E G	S1263
E G G F F E	S1105
E G G F♯ A G	B719
E G G F♯ D F	W145
E G G F♯ F♯ A	T97
E G G G E B	S1281
E G G G E D	B822
E G G G F D	R86
E G G G F E	R321
E G G G F G	B1770
E G G G F♯ G	R325
E G G G G A	W308
E G G G G G E	S853
E G G G G G G	B1371
E G G♯ A E D	P86
E G G♯ A E D♯	S1670
E G G♯ E G♯ A	S1520
E G♯ E G♯ E F	B1797
E♭ A♭ A♭ D G G	B160
E♭ A♭ D E♭ A♭ D	W189
E♭ A♭ E A A♯ B	C69
E♭ A♭ G C D C B	C249
E♭ A♭ G C D C D	T244
E♭ A♭ G E♭ C E♭	T216
E♭ A♭ G F E♭ D	B1338
E♭ A♭ G G F♯ A♭	S723
E♭ B B E♭ E♭ D	L128
E♭ B C A♭ G E♭	B1694
E♭ B C B♭ A♭ G	W205
E♭ B C D E♭ E♭	T237
E♭ B C E♭ G B♭	S1486
E♭ B C G F E♭	H511
E♭ B E♭ B B C	C233
E♭ B E♭ D C G	I 120
E♭ B♭ A♭ G F A♭	S135
E♭ C A G E♭ C	B1799
E♭ C A♭ A♭ B♭ G	C513
E♭ C A♭ A♭ G F	G7
E♭ C A♭ C E♭ A♭	S925
E♭ C B B G C	G139
E♭ C B C D E♭	C461

E♭ C B♭♭ G E♭ C	B1799
E♭ C C A♭ G E♭	T249
E♭ C C B E♭ C	G236
E♭ C C B♭ C G	D197
E♭ C C E C C	H293
E♭ C D E♭ C D	I 15
E♭ C D E♭ C E♭	C327
E♭ C D E♭ F B	H13
E♭ C D E♭ G F	A42
E♭ C E♭ C A♭ G	B1040
E♭ C E♭ C B E	H813
E♭ C E♭ C E♭ C B♭	W159
E♭ C E♭ C E♭ C D E♭ F D	S1524
E♭ C E♭ C E♭ C D E♭ F E♭	D2
E♭ C E♭ C E♭ C E♭	B491
E♭ C E♭ C E♭ C G	J12
E♭ C E♭ C E♭ D	F175
E♭ C E♭ D B C	T193
E♭ C E♭ D B D	P1
E♭ C E♭ D C D	P79
E♭ C E♭ E♭ D B	C520
E♭ C E♭ F E♭ C	C92
E♭ C E♭ F♯ G A♭	B1731
E♭ C E♭ G C E♭	B402
E♭ C F C E♭ C	G85
E♭ C F D G E♭	E22
E♭ C G A♭ G F	W296
E♭ C G B♭ A F G E♭	M372f
E♭ C G B♭ A F G G	M372d
E♭ C G C D F	H53
E♭ C G C E C	S1353
E♭ C G C E♭ C	L88
E♭ C G E♭ B♭ G	T118α
E♭ C G E♭ C G	W216
E♭ C G E♭ D B	M1024
E♭ C G E♭ D♭♭ A♭♭	H734
E♭ C G F E♭ D C D E♭	F209
E♭ C G F E♭ D C D F	G98
E♭ C G G E♭ C	B840
E♭ C G G G G	C557
E♭ C G♭ F E♭ C	F64
E♭ C♯ E♭ D E♭ C♯	C135
E♭ D A♭ D D C	B1386
E♭ D B C D C	R20
E♭ D B C E♭ G	W274
E♭ D B C G F	B1436
E♭ D B G D E♭	M271
E♭ D B♭ C D E♭	R313

INDEX OF TITLES